MS-Access 97
one step at a time

BOOKS AVAILABLE

By both authors:

BP306 A Concise Introduction to Ami Pro 3
BP327 DOS one step at a time
BP337 A Concise User's Guide to Lotus 1-2-3 for Windows
BP341 MS-DOS explained
BP343 A concise introd'n to Microsoft Works for Windows
BP346 Programming in Visual Basic for Windows
BP351 WordPerfect 6 explained
BP352 Excel 5 explained
BP353 WordPerfect 6.0 for Windows explained
BP354 Word 6 for Windows explained
BP362 Access one step at a time
BP372 CA-SuperCalc for Windows explained
BP387 Windows one step at a time
BP388 Why not personalise your PC
BP399 Windows 95 one step at a time*
BP400 Windows 95 explained*
BP402 MS Office one step at a time
BP405 MS Works for Windows 95 explained
BP406 MS Word 95 explained
BP407 Excel 95 explained
BP408 Access 95 one step at a time
BP409 MS Office 95 one step at a time
BP415 Using Netscape on the Internet
BP419 Using Microsoft Explorer on the Internet
BP420 E-mail on the Internet
BP426 MS-Office 97 explained
BP428 MS-Word 97 explained
BP429 MS-Excel 97 explained
BP430 MS-Access 97 one step at a time

By Noel Kantaris:

BP232 A Concise Introduction to MS-DOS
BP258 Learning to Program in C
BP259 A Concise Introduction to UNIX*
BP261 A Concise Introduction to Lotus 1-2-3
BP264 A Concise Advanced User's Guide to MS-DOS
BP274 A Concise Introduction to SuperCalc 5
BP284 Programming in QuickBASIC
BP325 A Concise User's Guide to Windows 3.1

MS-Access 97 one step at a time

by

N. Kantaris
and
P.R.M. Oliver

BERNARD BABANI (publishing) LTD.
THE GRAMPIANS
SHEPHERDS BUSH ROAD
LONDON W6 7NF
ENGLAND

PLEASE NOTE

Although every care has been taken with the production of this book to ensure that any projects, designs, modifications and/or programs, etc., contained herewith, operate in a correct and safe manner and also that any components specified are normally available in Great Britain, the Publishers and Author(s) do not accept responsibility in any way for the failure (including fault in design) of any project, design, modification or program to work correctly or to cause damage to any equipment that it may be connected to or used in conjunction with, or in respect of any other damage or injury that may be so caused, nor do the Publishers accept responsibility in any way for the failure to obtain specified components.

Notice is also given that if equipment that is still under warranty is modified in any way or used or connected with home-built equipment then that warranty may be void.

First Published – August 1997
Reprinted – December 1998

British Library Cataloguing in Publication Data:

A catalogue record for this book is available from the British Library

ISBN 0 85934 430 4

Cover Design by Gregor Arthur
Cover illustration by Adam Willis
Printed and Bound in Great Britain by Cox & Wyman Ltd, Reading

ABOUT THIS BOOK

MS-Access 97 one step at a time has been written to help users to store and retrieve information using this latest Windows database from Microsoft. No previous knowledge of database design is assumed.

The book does not describe how to install Microsoft Windows 95, or how to set up your computer's hardware. If you need to know more about these topics, then may we suggest that you select an appropriate level book for your needs from the 'Books Available' list - the books are graduated in complexity with the less demanding *One step at a time* series, followed by the *Concise Introduction* series, to the more detailed *Explained* series. They are all published by BERNARD BABANI (publishing) Ltd.

In the first chapter, we give an overview of the database systems and we define the elements that make up an Access relational database management system. The hardware and software requirements of your system are also discussed, so that you know in advance the minimum system configuration for the successful installation and use of the package.

Below we list the major enhancements found in this latest version of Microsoft Access 97 for Windows 95 over the previous version. These are:

- Revamped online help system and extended IntelliSense technology.
- New and improved Wizards, making it easy to create and maintain a number of common business and personal databases. There are Wizards to create your tables, forms and reports.
- The ability to import data into Access quickly and easily from other databases.
- The ability to reorganise imported data into tables for maximum efficiency.

- The ability to share work with others across a network.
- The ability to find information in a database with just a few mouse clicks.
- The ability to quickly format forms and reports in a consistent style.
- The ability to automate repetitive tasks and create custom applications with the use of Visual Basic.
- The ability to use Access with Excel 97 to manage your data effectively.

Most features of the package (old and new) will be discussed using simple examples that the user is encouraged to type in, save, and modify as more advanced features are introduced. This provides the new user with an example that aims to help with the learning of the most commonly used features of the package, and should help to provide the confidence needed to tackle some of the more advanced features later.

This book was written with the busy person in mind. It is not necessary to learn all there is to know about a subject, when reading a few selected pages can usually do the same thing quite adequately!

With the help of this book, it is hoped that you will be able to come to terms with Microsoft Access and get the most out of your computer in terms of efficiency, productivity and enjoyment, and that you will be able to do it in the shortest, most effective and informative way.

If you would like to purchase a Companion Disc for any of the listed books by the same author(s), apart from the ones marked with an asterisk, containing the file/program listings which appear in them, then fill in the form at the back of the book and send it to Phil Oliver at the stipulated address.

ABOUT THE AUTHORS

Noel Kantaris graduated in Electrical Engineering at Bristol University and after spending three years in the Electronics Industry in London, took up a Tutorship in Physics at the University of Queensland. Research interests in Ionospheric Physics, led to the degrees of M.E. in Electronics and Ph.D. in Physics. On return to the UK, he took up a Post-Doctoral Research Fellowship in Radio Physics at the University of Leicester, and then in 1973 a lecturing position in Engineering at the Camborne School of Mines, Cornwall, (part of Exeter University), where since 1978 he has also assumed the responsibility for the Computing Department.

Phil Oliver graduated in Mining Engineering at Camborne School of Mines in 1967 and since then has specialised in most aspects of surface mining technology, with a particular emphasis on computer related techniques. He has worked in Guyana, Canada, several Middle Eastern countries, South Africa and the United Kingdom, on such diverse projects as: the planning and management of bauxite, iron, gold and coal mines; rock excavation contracting in the UK; international mining equipment sales and international mine consulting for a major mining house in South Africa. In 1988 he took up a lecturing position at Camborne School of Mines (part of Exeter University) in Surface Mining and Management.

ACKNOWLEDGEMENTS

We would like to thank the staff of Text 100 Limited for providing the software programs on which this work was based. We would also like to thank colleagues at the Camborne School of Mines for the helpful tips and suggestions which assisted us in the writing of this book.

CONTENTS

1. PACKAGE OVERVIEW

Microsoft Access is a database management system (DBMS) designed to allow users to store, manipulate and retrieve information easily and quickly. A database is a collection of data that exists and is organised around a specific theme or requirement. It can be of the 'flat-file' type, or it can have relational capabilities, as in the case of Access, which is known as a relational database management system (RDBMS).

The main difference between flat-file and relational database systems is that the latter can store and manipulate data in multiple 'tables', while the former systems can only manipulate a single table at any given time. To make accessing the data easier, each row (or **record**) of data within a database table is structured in the same fashion, i.e., each record will have the same number of columns (or **fields**).

We define a database and its various elements as:

Database	A collection of data organised for a specific theme in one or more tables.
Table	A two-dimensional structure in which data is stored, like in a spreadsheet
Record	A row of information in a table relating to a single entry and comprising one or more fields.
Field	A single column of information of the same type, such as people's names.

In Access 97 the maximum size of a database is 1 gigabyte and can include linked tables in other files. The number of objects in a database is limited to 32,768, while the maximum number of fields in a table is limited to 255.

A good example of a flat-file database is the invoicing details kept on clients by a company. These details could include name of client, description of work done, invoice number, and amount charged, as follows:

NAME	Consultancy	Invoice	Value
VORTEX Co. Ltd	Wind Tunnel Tests	9701	120.84
AVON Construction	Adhesive Tests	9702	103.52
BARROWS Associates	Tunnel Design Tests	9703	99.32
STONEAGE Ltd	Carbon Dating Tests	9704	55.98
PARKWAY Gravel	Material Size Tests	9705	180.22
WESTWOOD Ltd	Load Bearing Tests	9706	68.52

Such a flat-file DBMS is too limited for the type of information normally held by most companies. If the same client asks for work to be carried out regularly, then the details for that client (which could include address, telephone and fax numbers, contact name, date of invoice, etc.), will have to be entered several times. This can lead to errors, but above all to redundant information being kept on a client - each entry will have to have the name of the client, their address, telephone and fax numbers.

The relational facilities offered by Access, overcome the problems of entry errors and duplication of information. The ability to handle multiple tables at any one time allows for the grouping of data into sensible subsets. For example, one table, called client, could hold the names of the clients, their addresses, telephone and fax numbers, while another table, called invoice, could hold information on the work done, invoice number, date of issue, and amount charged. The two tables must have one unique common field, such as a client reference number. The advantage is that details of each client are entered and stored only once, thus reducing the time and effort wasted on entering duplicate information, and also reducing the space required for data storage.

Hardware and Software Requirements

If Microsoft Access 97 is already installed on your computer, you can safely skip this and the next section of this chapter.

To install and use Access 97, you need an IBM-compatible PC equipped with Intel's 80486 (or higher) processor. In addition, you need the following:

- Windows 95, Windows NT or Windows NT Advanced Server version.
- Random access memory (RAM): 8MB; 16MB recommended when running large databases.
- Hard disc space available for Access 97: 50 MB for Access and 10 MB for converters, filters, and data access tools.
- Video adapter: VGA or higher resolution. If you are embedding colour pictures, you will need a 256-colour video adapter.
- Pointing device: Microsoft Mouse or compatible.

Realistically, to run MS Access 97 with reasonable sized databases, you will need a Pentium PC with at least 16MB of RAM. To run Microsoft Access 97 from a network, you must also have a network compatible with your Windows operating environment, such as Microsoft's Windows 95, Windows NT, LAN Manager, or Novell's NetWare.

Although it is possible to operate Microsoft Access from the keyboard, the availability of a mouse is highly desirable. After all, pointing and clicking at an option on the screen to start an operation or command, is a lot easier than having to learn several different key combinations.

Installing Access

Installing Access on your computer's hard disc is made very easy with the use of the SETUP program, which even configures Access automatically to take advantage of the computer's hardware.

If you are installing from floppy discs, insert the first Setup disc (Disc 1) in the A: drive, or if you are installing from a CD-ROM, insert the CD in the CD-ROM drive. If you are installing from a network drive, make a note of the drive letter because you will need it later. Then do the following:

- Click the **Start** button on the Windows 95 Taskbar and select **Settings, Control Panel**.
- On the displayed Control Panel window, double-click the Add/Remove Programs icon, shown here.

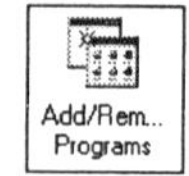

- On the Add/Remove Programs Properties dialogue box, click the Install/Uninstall tab and press the **Install** button.
- SETUP will scan your disc for already installed parts of Microsoft Office and will advise you as to the folder in which you should install Access. This will most likely be **Msoffice** - we suggest you accept all the default options.
- Follow the SETUP instructions, and when the Maintenance dialogue box appears on the screen, similar to the one shown on the next page, press the **Select All** button.
- Pressing **Continue** starts the installation of Microsoft Access.
- When a new disc is required (if you are installing from floppy discs), the installation program will inform you by displaying a similar dialogue box to the one shown on the next page.

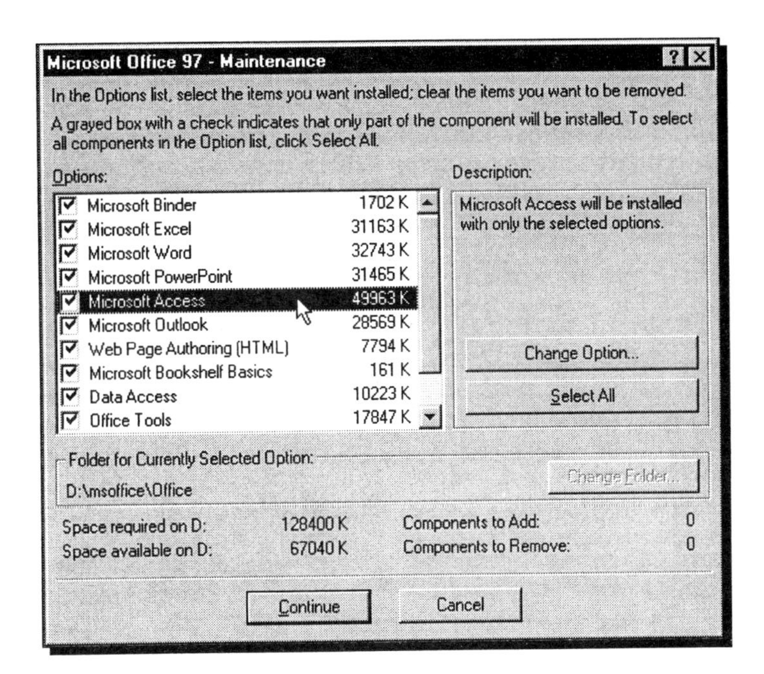

When all discs have been read, the SETUP program will modify your system files automatically so that you can start Access easily. It even detects your computer's processor and display, and configures Access to run smoothly with your system.

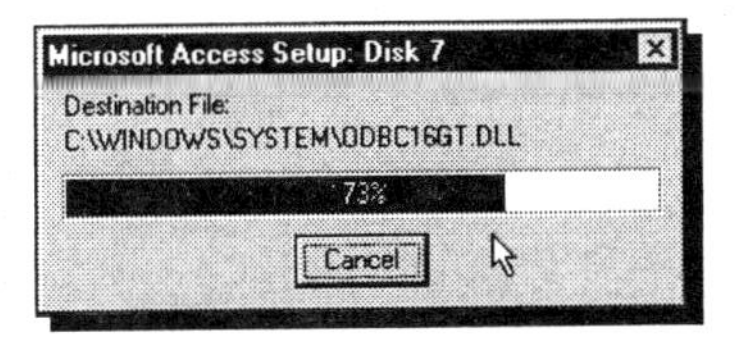

Finally, Access creates and displays a new entry in the **Start, Programs** cascade menu, with the icon shown here. Clicking this menu entry will start Microsoft Access. If you have MS-Office installed, SETUP also adds Access to the Microsoft Shortcut Bar facility (see overleaf).

The Office Shortcut Bar

During installation, the Office Shortcut Bar is collated and added to the Windows Start Up program so that it will be displayed automatically on your screen whenever you start your PC. The contents of a Microsoft Shortcut Bar used with a previous version of Office will be preserved. The Shortcut Bar will be displayed when you restart your computer.

The Microsoft Office Shortcut Bar, provides a convenient way to work with your documents and the Office applications by complementing the Windows **Start** menu.

The various icons on the Shortcut Bar, shown here, have the following function:

Getting Results Book

New Office Document

Open Office Document

Microsoft Bookshelf Basics

New Note

New Message

New Journal Entry

Microsoft Outlook

New Appointment

New Task

New Contact

The first icon of the above Office Toolbar (Getting Results Book) is only available to you if you are connected to a company's network or the Internet and have installed a browser, such as Microsoft's Explorer, or Netscape. This option allows you to use browser-style query techniques on both HTML and Office documents on an internal network or the Internet.

The function of other icons on the toolbar is as follows:

The New Office Document button: Allows you to select in the displayed dialogue box the tab containing the type of document you want to work with. Double-clicking the type of document or template you want, automatically loads the appropriate application.

The Open Office Document button: Allows you to work with an existing document. Opening a document, first starts the application originally used to create it.

The Microsoft Bookshelf Basics: Allows a preview of the world of information found in the complete version of the Bookshelf which provides access to three major reference books; *The American Heritage Dictionary*, *The Original Roget's Thesaurus*, and *The Columbia Dictionary of Quotations*. This facility requires you to have a CD-ROM.

The New buttons: Allow you to make a New Note, a New Message, or a New Journal Entry to schedule your time effectively.

The Microsoft Outlook button: Activates the Office 97 new desktop manager used to manage your e-mail, contact lists, tasks and documents.

The New Appointment button: Allows you to add a new appointment in your management system. This caters for all-day or multiple-day events and a meeting planner, including meeting request processing and attendance lists.

The New Task button: Allows you to add a new task in your management system, including automatic composition of an e-mail message summarising a task and automatic tracking of tasks sent to other users.

The New Contact button: Allows you to enter a new contact in Outlook's database, or to send an e-mail message direct from the contact manager and use hyperlinks for direct access to a contact's home page on the Internet.

The Mouse Pointers

In Microsoft Access, as with all other graphical based programs, the use of a mouse makes many operations both easier and more fun to carry out.

Access makes use of the mouse pointers available in Windows 95, some of the most common of which are illustrated below. When Access is initially started up the first you will see is the hourglass, which turns into an upward pointing hollow arrow once the application screen appears on your display. Other shapes depend on the type of work you are doing at the time.

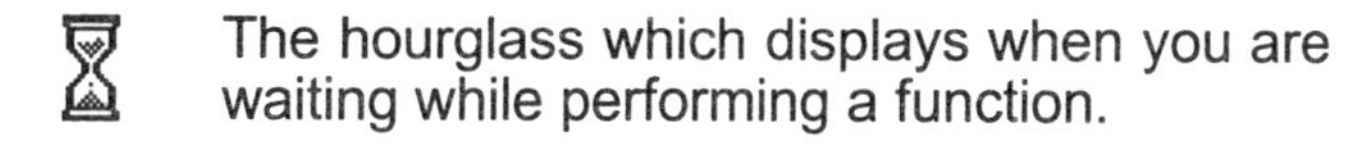

The hourglass which displays when you are waiting while performing a function.

The arrow which appears when the pointer is placed over menus, scrolling bars, buttons, and dialogue boxes.

The I-beam which appears in normal text areas of the screen.

The large 4-headed arrow which appears after choosing the **Control, Move/Size** command(s) for moving or sizing windows.

The double arrows which appear when over the border of a window, used to drag the side and alter the size of the window.

The Help hand which appears in the Help windows, and is used to access 'hypertext' type links.

Microsoft Access 97, like the rest of the Microsoft Office 97 applications and other Windows packages, have additional mouse pointers which facilitate the execution of selected commands. Some of these, shown on the next page, have the following functions:

⬇ The vertical pointer which appears when pointing over a column in a table and used to select the column.

➡ The horizontal pointer which appears when pointing at a row in a database table and used to select the row.

The slanted arrow which appears when the pointer is placed in the selection bar area of a database table.

The vertical split arrow which appears when pointing over the area separating two columns in a database table and used to size a column.

The horizontal split arrow which appears when pointing over the area separating two rows in a table and used to size a row.

\+ The frame cross which you drag to create a frame while designing a Form.

Access has a few additional mouse pointers to the ones above, but their shape is mostly self-evident.

Some Access operations display a '?' button, as shown here. Clicking this button changes the mouse pointer from its usual inclined arrow shape to the 'What's this?' shape. Pointing to an object in the dialogue box or window and clicking, gives additional information, as we shall see at the end of the next chapter, when we discuss context sensitive help.

2. STARTING ACCESS

Access is started in Windows either by clicking the **Start** button then selecting **Program** and clicking on the 'Microsoft Access' icon on the cascade menu, clicking the Access icon on the Old Office Shortcut Bar, or by clicking the 'Open a Document' icon on the Office Shortcut Bar and double-clicking on an Access database file. In the latter case the database will be loaded into Access at the same time.

When you start the Access program by double-clicking its icon, the following dialogue box is displayed on your screen:

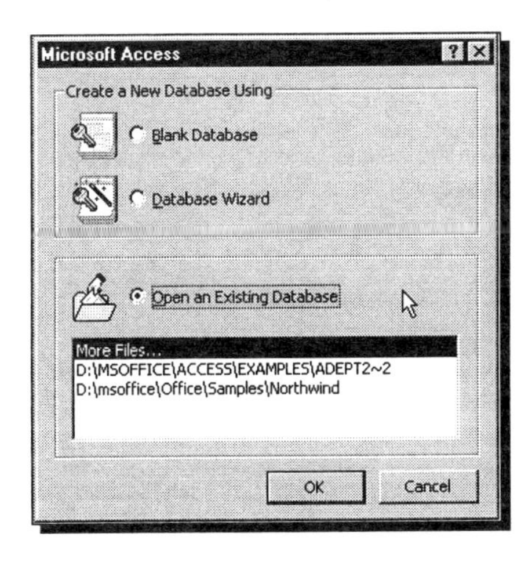

From this dialogue box, you can either create a new database, or **Open an Existing Database**. If you elect to create a new database, then you can select either to create a **Blank Database**, or use the **Database Wizard** to help you with the creation of the new database.

Access 97 makes extensive use of Wizards, which have been designed to help the new user to create databases more easily. In particular, the Database Wizard builds the necessary elements for 22 different databases for both home and business use. All you have to do is to answer a set of questions and the Wizard builds the database for you.

Parts of the Access Screen

Before we start designing a database, let us take a look at the Access opening screen. Below we also show the ***what's new*** help topic displaying its list.

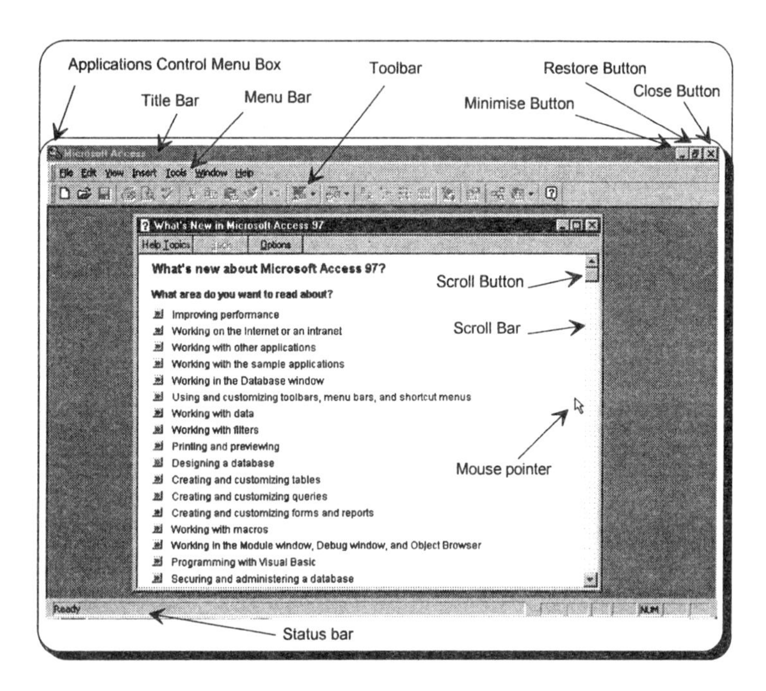

As you can see, these windows have common screen elements with those of other MS Office applications. As usual, depending on what you are doing with Access, the items on the menu bar can be different from those of the opening screen. For example, once a database table is opened the menu bar changes to the following:

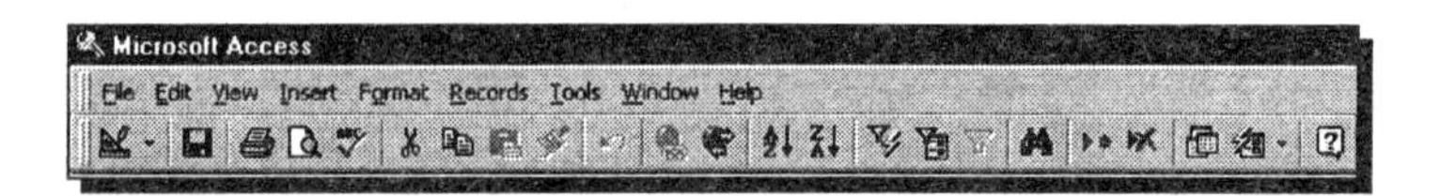

Although more than one window can be displayed simultaneously, only one is the active window (which normally displays on top of any other non-active windows. Title bars of non-active windows appear a lighter shade than those of the active one. In the above example, the Help Topics window is the active one. To activate another window, click with the left mouse button anywhere within it.

The various screen areas have the following functions:

Area	***Function***
Command button	Clicking on this button, (see upper-left corner of the Access window), displays a pull-down menu which can be used to control the program window. It includes commands for restoring, moving, sizing, maximising, minimising, and closing the window.
Title bar	The bar at the top of a window which displays the application name and the name of the current document.
Minimise box	When clicked on, this button minimises the application to the Windows Taskbar.
Restore button	Clicking on this button restores the active window to the position and size that was occupied before it was maximised. The Restore button is then replaced by a Maximise button, shown here, which is used to set the window to full screen size.

Close button	The extreme top right button that you click to close a window. 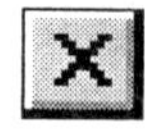
Menu bar	The bar below the Title bar which allows you to choose from several menu options. Clicking on a menu item displays the pull-down menu associated with that item. The options listed in the Menu bar depend on what you are doing at the time.
Toolbar	The bar below the Menu bar which contains buttons that give you mouse click access to the most often used functions in the program.
Scroll Buttons	The arrowheads at each end of each scroll bar which you click to scroll the screen up and down one line, or left and right 10% of the screen, at a time.
Scroll Bars	The areas on the screen (extreme right and bottom of each window) that contain scroll boxes in vertical and horizontal bars. Clicking on these bars allows you to reach the part of the window that might not be visible on the screen.
Status Bar	The bottom line of the window that displays status information, and in which a short help description appears when you point and click on a button.

The Menu Bar Options

Each window's menu bar option has associated with it a pull-down sub-menu. To activate the menu of a window, either press the <Alt> key, which causes the first option of the menu (in this case **File**) to be highlighted, then use the right and left arrow keys to highlight any of the options in the menu, or use the mouse to point to an option. Pressing either the <Enter> key, or the left mouse button, reveals the pull-down sub-menu of the highlighted menu option.

The sub-menu of the **File** option of the Access window, is shown below.

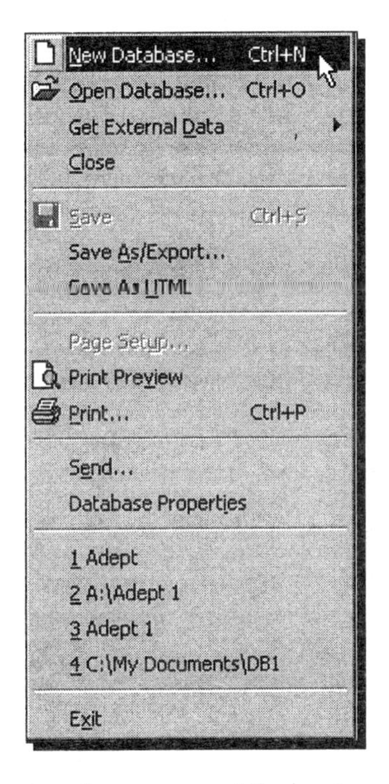

Menu options can also be activated directly by pressing the <Alt> key followed by the underlined letter of the required option. Thus pressing **Alt+F**, causes the pull-down sub-menu of **File** to be displayed.

You can use the up and down arrow keys to move the highlighted bar up and down a sub-menu, or the right and left arrow keys to move along the options in the menu bar. Pressing the <Enter> key selects the highlighted option or executes the highlighted command. Pressing the <Esc> key once, closes the pull-down sub-menu, while pressing the <Esc> key for a second time, closes the menu system.

Furthermore, depending on what you are doing with Access, different sub-menu options are available or become active. In general, menu options offer the following:

File	Produces a pull-down menu of mainly file related tasks, such as creating a **New** database, the ability to **Open**, or **Close** database files, and **Save** database files with the same name, or **Save As** a different name, or even **Save as HTML**. You can use **Page Setup** to set the margins and the size of your printed page, **Print Preview** a table or query on screen before committing it to paper, or **Print** it to paper and select your current printer. You can view a specific database's **Properties**, and export data in various formats using the **Send To** option. Finally, you can **Exit** the program. Above this last sub-menu option, Access also displays the last four databases you used so that you can open them easily.
Edit	Produces a pull-down menu which allows you to **Undo** changes made, **Cut**, **Copy** and **Paste** text, and **Delete** or **Rename** a database table or query. Once a table, or a query is opened, additional options become available, such as the ability to **Find** specific text in the opened item, **Find & Replace** text, jump to any record in a table, view and update **Links**.

View Gives you control on what you see on the screen. For example, you can choose to view several database elements, such as tables, queries, forms, etc., and view files as icons or lists. You can also select which toolbars you want to be displayed.

Insert Allows you to insert tables, queries, forms, reports, macros, or modules. You can even use the AutoForm and AutoReport to create forms and reports automatically.

Tools Allows you to spell-check your work, switch on the AutoCorrect facility, or use Office links. You can also add or change relationships between database tables, and specify the level of security required.

Window Allows you to display multiple windows on the screen in 'cascade' or 'tile' form, or arrange icons within an active window.

Help Activates the help menu which you can use to access the **Microsoft Access Help**, its **Contents and Index**, the **What's This** facility, or the **Microsoft on the Web** option (if you are connected to the Internet). The **About Microsoft Access** option gives you information on your system, or on Technical Support.

For a more detailed description of each sub-menu item, either highlight it and read the text on the status bar, or use the on-line **Help** system.

Shortcut Menus

To see a shortcut menu containing the most common commands applicable to an item, point with your mouse at the item and click the right mouse button. For example, left-clicking the adjacent Open Database icon, displays the Open dialogue box. Right-clicking within the file list area of this dialogue box, displays the short-cut menu shown below, with the following options:

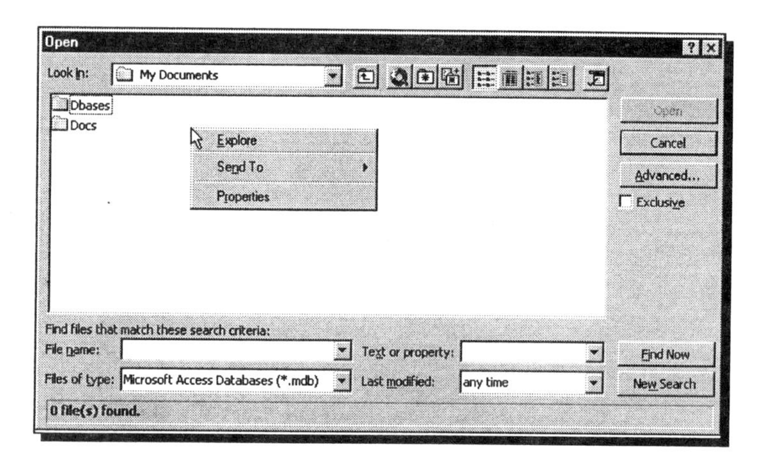

In this case we have the option to **Explore** the contents of the logged folder (My Documents), use the **Send To** option to send the contents of the folder to the 3½" Floppy, or the Briefcase, or send mail via Microsoft Outlook, or see the folder's **Properties**.

Having activated a shortcut menu, you can close it without taking any further action by simply pressing the <Esc> key.

Using Help in Access

The first time you start Access, it might be a good idea to look at the help available to you. To do this, cancel the opening dialogue box, then select the **Help, Contents and Index** command which causes the following Help screen to be displayed.

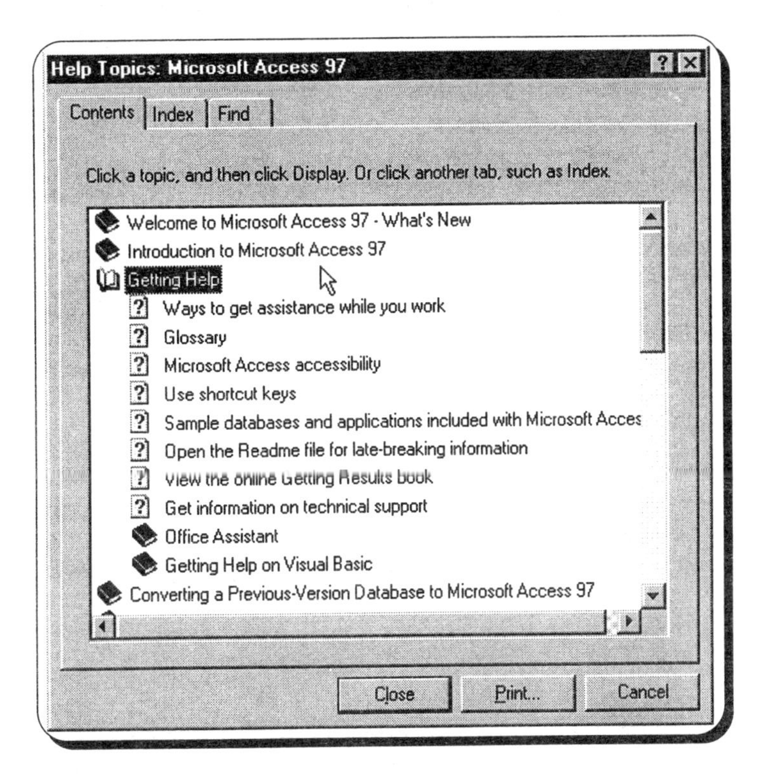

We suggest you spend a little time here browsing through the various help screens, particularly the first three; 'Welcome', 'Introduction', and 'Getting Help'. After doing so, click the Index tab of the Help Topics dialogue box, and type the text *database*. The following screen is then displayed.

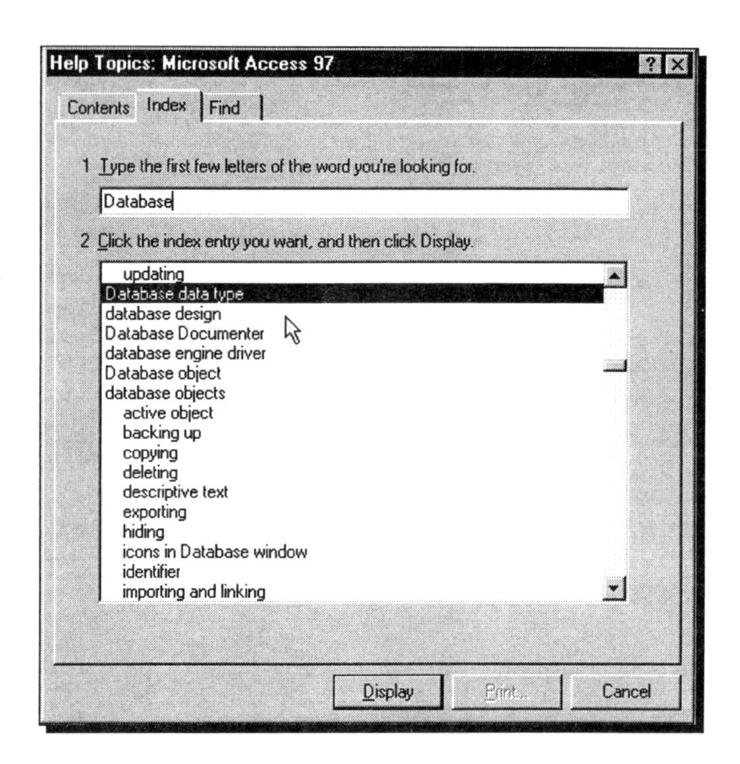

Have a look at the 'database design' topic. On selecting it and clicking the **Display** button, an additional screen opens up, as follows:

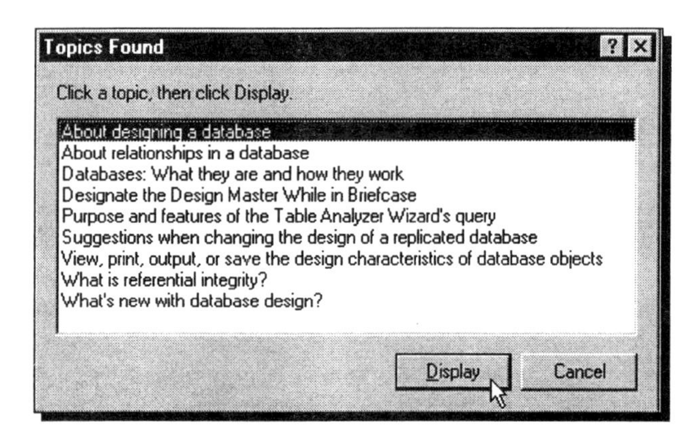

Using the Office Assistant

The Office Assistant is a central source of application information. No matter which Office 97 application you are using the Assistant is there to help you.

To find out how it works, click the Office Assistant button, shown here, with the left mouse button, type the word ***help*** in the displayed 'What would you like to do?' box, shown to the left, and left-click the **Search** button.

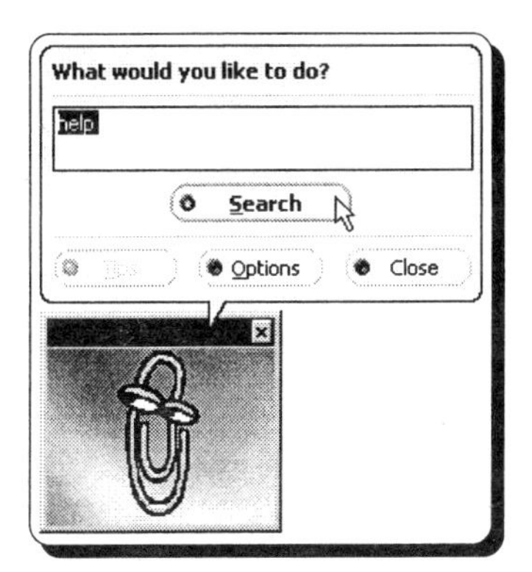

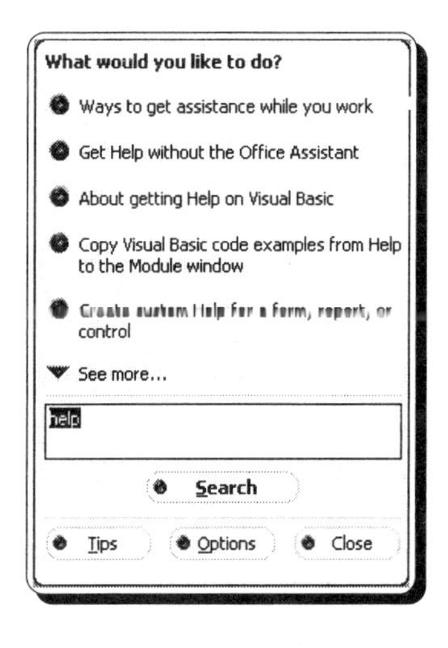

A list of help topics is then displayed, as shown to the right. To see more topics, left-click the small triangle at the bottom of the list. To find out how you can use the Office Assistant, click the 'Ways to get assistance while you work' option which causes the display of the screen shown on the next page. From this latter screen you can find out all there is to know about the Office Assistant.

The very same screen can be displayed from all Office applications, with only the title of the window changing to reflect the application in use.

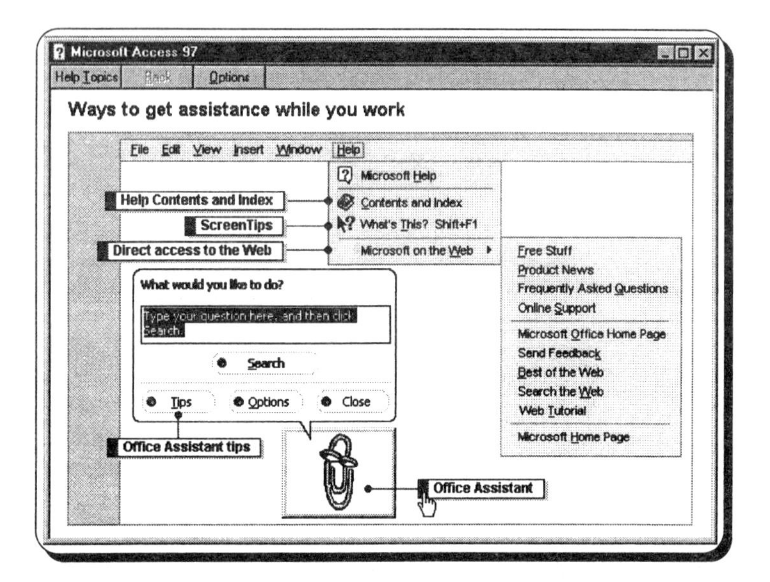

Clicking the left mouse button on areas of the screen that cause the mouse pointer to change to a pointing hand (there are five such areas), displays additional information on the selected topic. The changed pointer is shown at the bottom of the above screen dump.

Customising the Office Assistant:

You can customise the Office Assistant to a great degree. Not only can you change the way it responds to your enquiries, but you can even switch it off once you have mastered a particular Office application.

To see the default options settings of the Office Assistant, activate it, left-click on it, and left-click the **Options** button on the displayed box, shown here.

Doing this, causes the following dialogue box to be displayed on your screen:

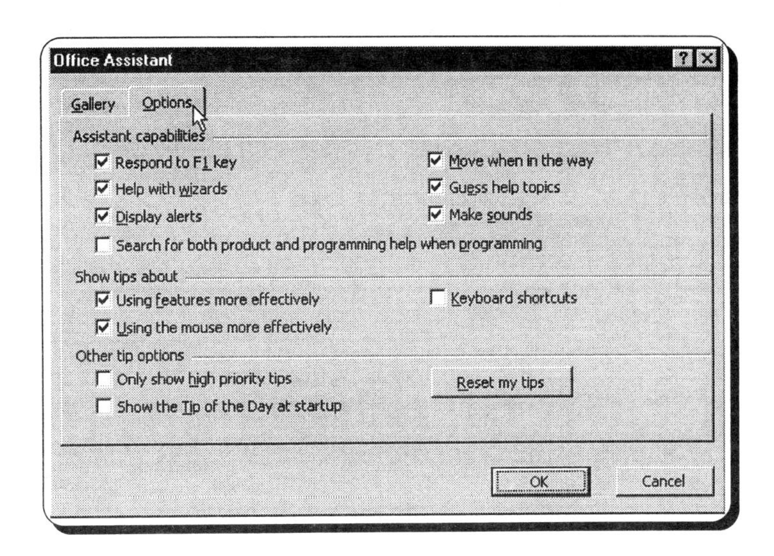

As you can see, it is possible to choose from several options. Should you want to change the shape of your Office Assistant (there are nine shapes to choose from - see next page), either left-click the Gallery tab of the above dialogue box, or right-click the Office Assistant and select the **Choose Assistant** option from the displayed menu, as shown below.

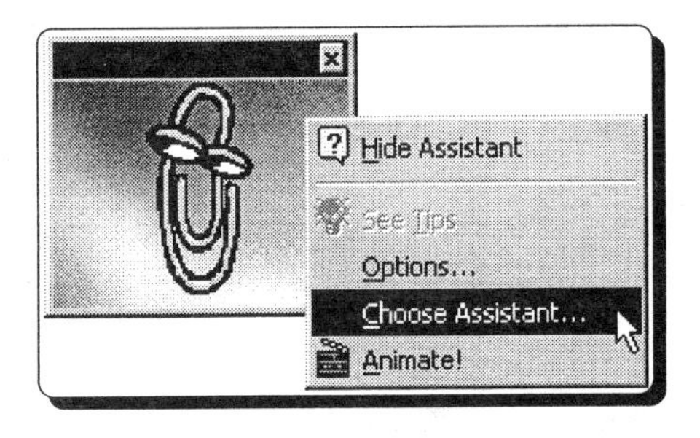

Either action displays the following dialogue box in which you can select your preferred Assistant shape by left-clicking the **Next** button.

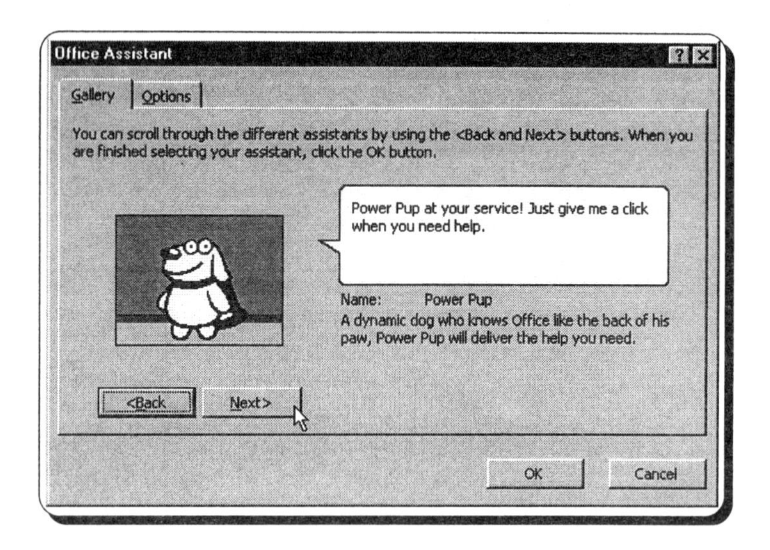

The shapes of the available Assistants are as follows:

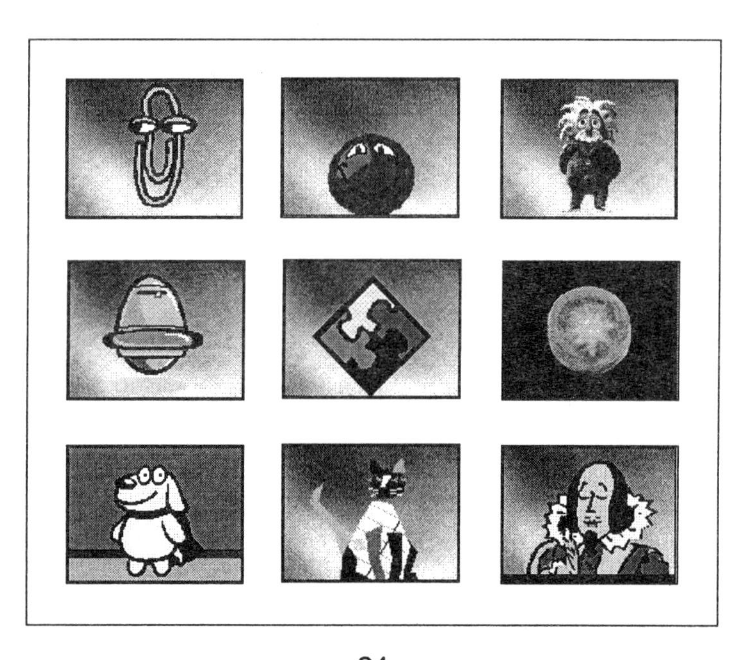

3. DATABASE BASICS

Database Elements

Before we start designing a database using Microsoft Access, it will be a good idea if we looked at the various elements that make up a database. To do so, start Access, which opens the Microsoft Access dialogue box.

Next, and if this is being done immediately after starting Access, select the **Database Wizard** option and click **OK**. Otherwise, either click the New Database icon, shown to the left, or use the **File, New Database** command. Any one of these three methods will cause the New Database dialogue box to be displayed, as shown below, provided the General tab is the active dialogue box tab at the time.

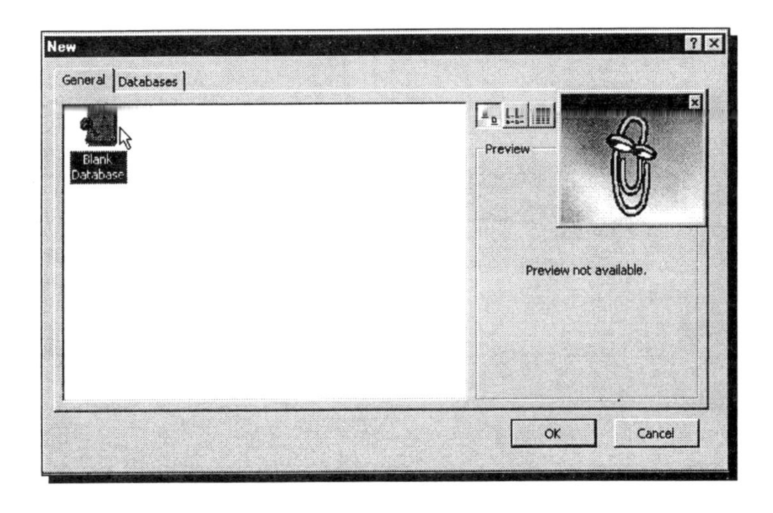

To create a new database, press the **OK** button. This opens the File New Database dialogue box shown on the next page.

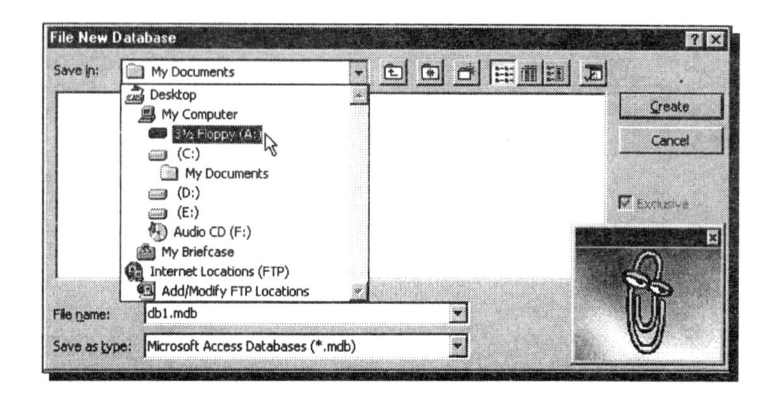

In the **File name** box, type the database name, say **Adept 1**, which replaces the default name **db1**. Access adds the extension **.mdb** which, however, you don't normally see. We also decided to save this example on floppy disc, therefore we clicked the down arrow against the **Save in** box and selected the **3½" Floppy (A:)** drive. Finally, pressing the **Create** button displays the Database dialogue box as follows:

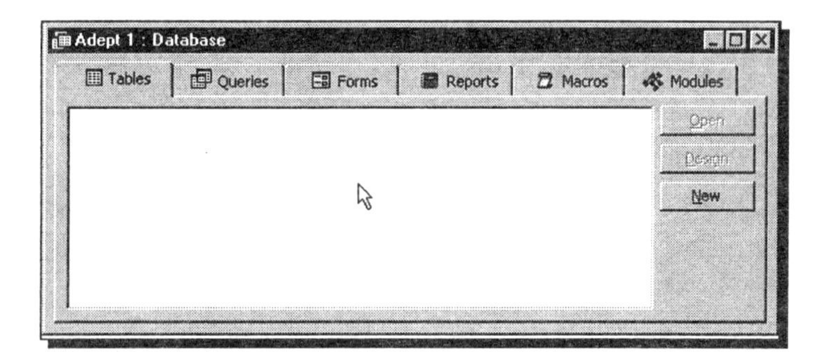

It is from here that you can design the various elements that make up a database, such as Tables, Queries, Forms, and Reports, all of which we will examine in some detail in this and the next three chapters.

Creating a Table

To design a database table, select the Tables tab and click the **New** button on the Database dialogue box, which displays the New Table, shown below immediately below the Database window. The first two options on the list, allow you to start designing a table from scratch, while the third option allows you to automatically select from a list of pre-defined table applications. The penultimate option allows you to import tables and objects from an external file into the current database, while the last option allows you to link a table in the current database to external tables.

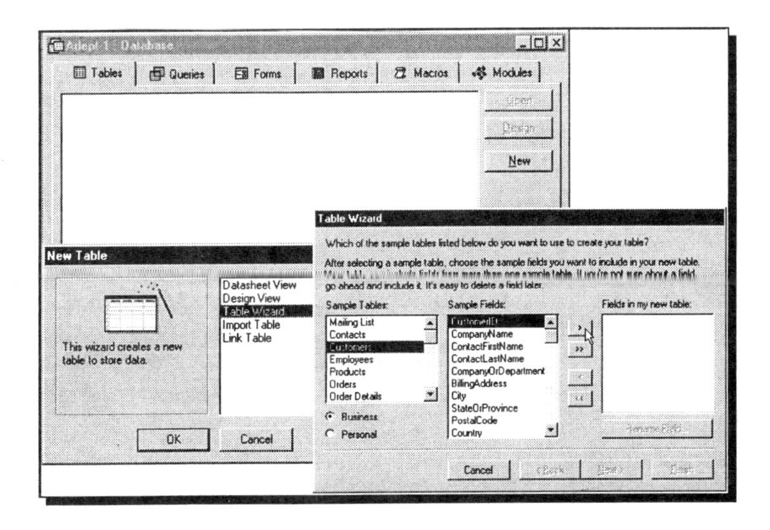

Selecting the third option and pressing **OK**, opens the Table Wizard dialogue box, shown at the lower right corner of the composite screen dump above.

The database we are going to create holds the invoicing details which the firm Adept Consultants keep on their clients. One table will hold the details of the clients, while another will hold the actual invoice details.

Choose 'Customers' from the **Sample Tables** list of the Table Wizard dialogue box, to reveal a list of appropriate fields for that table.

You can either select all the fields or you can select a few. For our example, we selected the following fields: CustomerID, CompanyName, BillingAddress, City, StateOrProvince, PostalCode, ContactTitle, PhoneNumber, FaxNumber and Notes, by highlighting each in turn and pressing the > button.

Don't worry if these field names are not exactly what you want, as they can be easily changed. To change field names, highlight them in turn in the 'Fields in my new table' list and click the **Rename Field** button to reveal the Rename field dialogue box shown here.

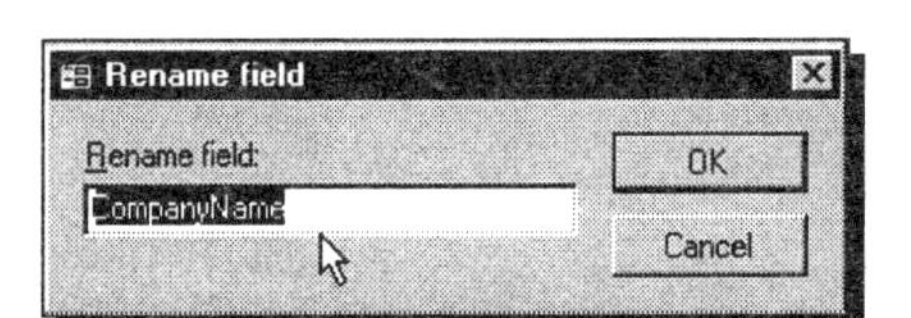

We suggest you change the selected field names to those listed below.

CompanyName	Name
BillingAddress	Address
City	Town
CustomerID	CustomerID
StateOrProvince	County
PostalCode	PostCode
ContactTitle	Contact
PhoneNumber	Phone
FaxNumber	Fax
Notes	Order

When you have completed renaming the field names, press the **Finish** button, which displays the Customers Table ready for you to enter information.

To redesign the table, including changing its field names, click the Design View icon shown here, or use the **View, Table Design** command. The following Table is displayed.

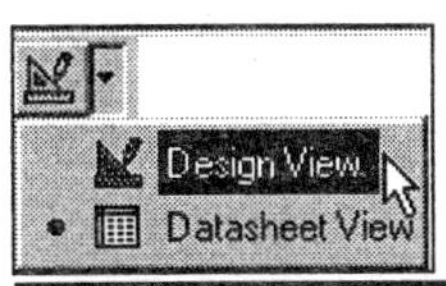

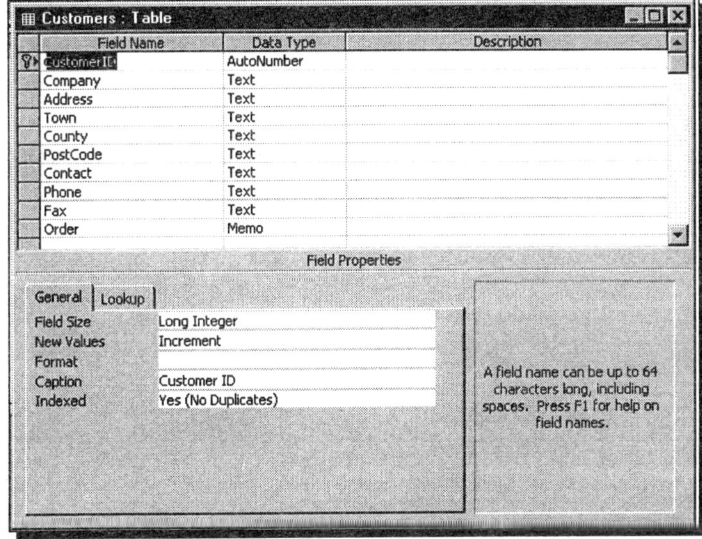

As each field name is highlighted, a Field Properties box appears at the bottom of the screen. If you were using this Table View to rename fields, then you should also edit the name appearing against the Caption property, or remove it altogether.

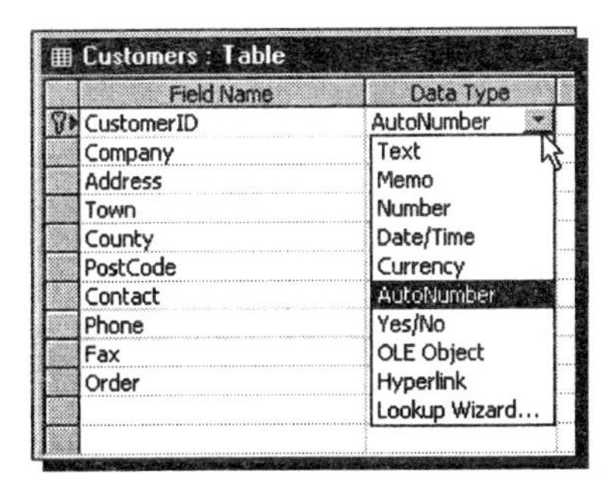

Next, place the cursor at the end of the Data Type descriptor of the CustomerID field which causes a down-arrow button to be displayed. Clicking this button, displays a drop-down list of data types, as shown here.

As we intend to use the first four letters of a company's name as the CustomerID field, change the current data type from Counter to Text. Similarly, change the data type of the last field (Order) from Memo to AutoNumber. Finally, place the cursor against the Phone and Fax fields and delete the entry against the Input Mask in the Field Properties box. The type of input mask displayed here is ideal for USA Phone and Fax numbers, but it does not correspond to the entry form usually adopted in the UK, so it is best removed.

Finally, first click the Save icon (or use the **File, Save** command) to save your design changes, then click the Datasheet View icon (or use the **View, Datasheet** command) to revert to the Customers table so that you can start entering information, as shown below.

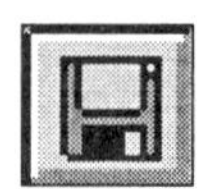

Customer ID	Name	Address	Town	County	Post Code	Contact
VORT	VORTEX Co. Ltd	Windy House	St. Austell	Cornwall	TR18 1FX	Brian Storm
AVON	AVON Construction	Riverside House	Stratford-on-Avon	Warwickshire	AV15 2QW	John Waters
BARR	BARROWS Associates	Barrows House	Bodmin	Cornwall	PL22 1XE	Mandy Brown
STON	STONEAGE Ltd	Data House	Salisbury	Wiltshire	SB44 1BN	Mike Irons
PARK	PARKWAY Gravel	Aggregate House	Bristol	Avon	BS55 2ZX	James Stone
WEST	WESTWOOD Ltd	Weight House	Plymouth	Devon	PL22 1AA	Mary Slim
GLOW	GLOWORM Ltd	Light House	Brighton	Sussex	BR87 4DD	Peter Summers
SILV	SILVERSMITH Co	Radiation House	Exeter	Devon	EX28 1PL	Adam Smith
WORM	WORMGLAZE Ltd	Glass House	Winchester	Hampshire	WN23 5TR	Richard Glazer
EALI	EALING Engines Design	Engine House	Taunton	Somerset	TN17 3RT	Trevor Miles
HIRE	HIRE Service Equipment	Network House	Bath	Avon	BA76 3WE	Nicole Webb
EURO	EUROBASE Co. Ltd	Control House	Penzance	Cornwall	TR15 8LK	Sarah Star

The widths of the above fields were changed so that all fields could be visible on the screen at the same time. To change the width of a field, place the cursor on the column separator until the cursor changes to the vertical split arrow, then drag the column separator to the right or left, to increase or decrease the width of the field.

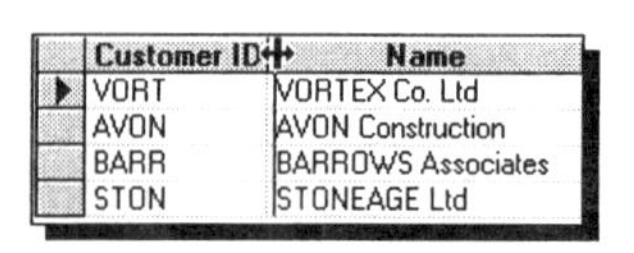

Customer ID	Name
VORT	VORTEX Co. Ltd
AVON	AVON Construction
BARR	BARROWS Associates
STON	STONEAGE Ltd

Sorting a Database Table

As you enter information into a database table, you might elect to change the field headings by clicking the Design Table icon and editing a field name, say from Name to CompanyName. If you do this, on return to the Customers table you will find that the records have sorted automatically in ascending order of the entries of the field in which you left the cursor while in the Design Table.

Contact	Phone	Fax	Order
Brian Storm	01776-223344	01776-224466	1
John Waters	01657-113355	01657-221133	2
Mandy Brown	01554-664422	01554-663311	3
Mike Irons	01765-234567	01765-232332	4
James Stone	01534-987654	01534-984567	5
Mary Slim	01234-667755	01234-669988	6
Peter Summers	01432-746523	01432-742266	7
Adam Smith	01336-997755	01336-996644	8
Richard Glazer	01123-654321	01123-651234	9
Trevor Miles	01336-010107	01336-010109	10
Nicole Webb	01875-558822	01875-552288	11
Sarah Star	01736-098765	01736-098567	12
			(AutoNumber)

If you want to preserve the order in which you entered your data, then sort by the last field (Order) with its type as AutoNumber. This can be done at any time, even after you finished entering all other information in your table.

Sorting a database table in ascending order of an AutoNumber type field, results in the database table displaying in the order in which the data was originally entered in that table. Above, we show the Contact field, so that you can cross-check the original order of your Customer table, as well as the rest of the information in that table not shown in the screen dump of the previous page.

To sort a database table in ascending or descending order of the entries of any field, place the cursor in the required field and click the Sort Ascending or Sort Descending icon, shown here.

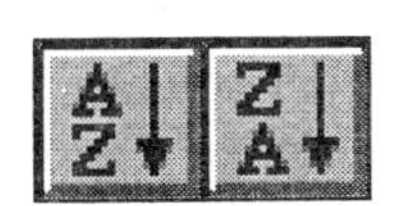

With the keyboard, select the **Records, Sort** command, then choose either the **Sort Ascending** or the **Sort Descending** option.

Applying a Filter to a Sort:

If you would like to sort and display only records that fit selected criteria, use the **Records, Filter, Advanced Filter/Sort** command, which opens the Filter dialogue box, shown below.

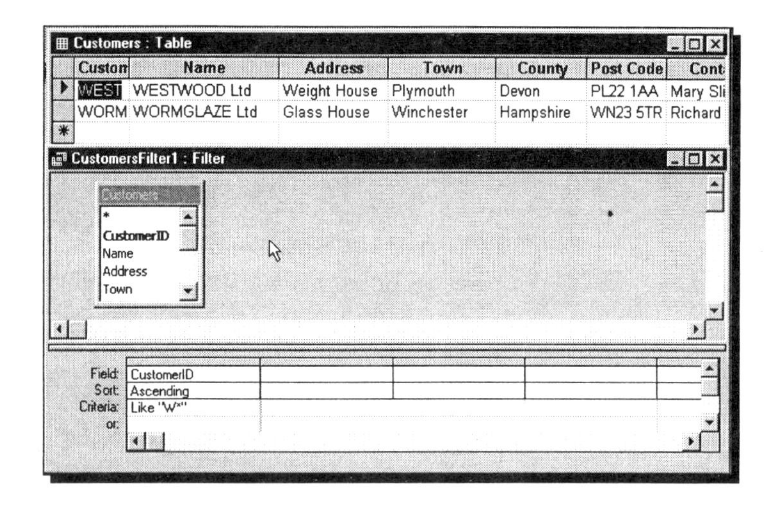

The upper portion of the dialogue box displays all the fields in the Customers table, while the lower portion is where you enter your filter restrictions. In the above example, we chose to view, in ascending order, the records within the CustomersID field that start with W - we typed W* and Access displayed *Like "W*"*.

On pressing the Apply Filter icon, the Customers table displays with only two entries, as seen in the above composite screen dump. To revert to the display of all the records, click the same icon again, which now appears on the Toolbar depressed, and bears the name Remove Filter.

Using a Database Form

Once a table has been selected from the Database window, clicking the down-arrow against the New Object button and selecting **AutoForm**, automatically displays each record of that table in form view. The created form for the Customers table is shown below.

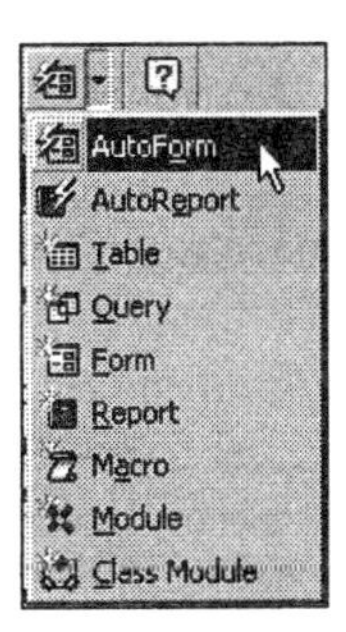

Forms can be used to enter, change or view data. They are mainly used to improve the way in which data is displayed on the screen.

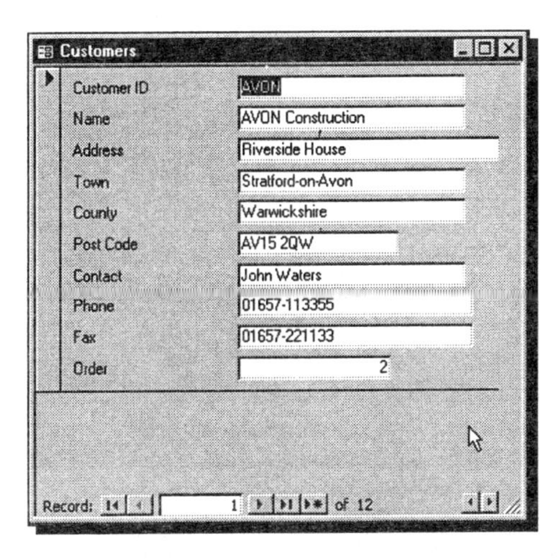

Forms can also be used to sort records in a database table in descending or ascending order of a selected field.

When you attempt to close a new **Form** window, you will be asked if you would like to save it. An Access database can have lots of different forms, each designed with a different purpose in mind. Saved forms are displayed in the Database window when you click the Forms tab. In the above example, we chose the default name suggested by Access, which was Customers.

In a later chapter we will discuss Form design in some detail, including their customisation.

Working with Data

Adding Records in a Table: Whether you are in Table view or Form view, to add a record, click the New Record icon, shown here.

When in Table view, the cursor jumps to the first empty record in the table (the one with the asterisk in the box to the left of the first field). When in Form view, Access displays an empty form which can be used to add a new record.

Finding Records in a Table: Whether you are in Table or Form view, to find a record click the Find icon, or use **Edit, Find**. This opens the following dialogue box:

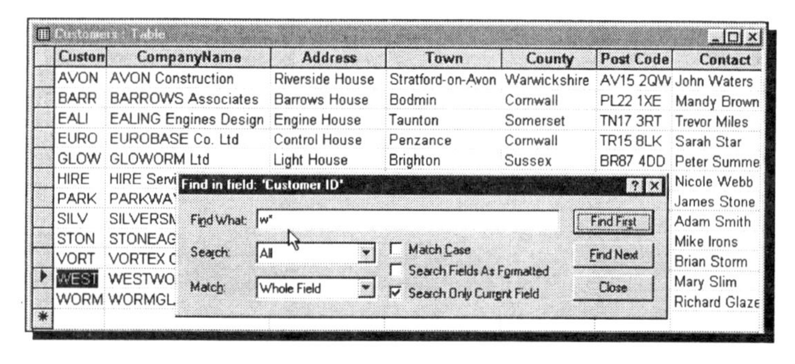

Note the field name on the Title bar, which is CustomerID, indicating that the cursor was in the CustomerID field before we clicked the Find icon or selected the **Find** command.

To find all the records starting with **w**, we type **w*** in the **Find What** box of the dialogue box. If the **Search Only Current Field** box is ticked, the search is carried out in that field. Pressing the **Find First** button, highlights the first record with the CustomerID 'WEST'. Pressing the **Find Next** button, highlights the next record that matches our selected criteria.

Deleting Records from a Table: To delete a record when in Table view, point to the box to the left of the record to highlight the entire record, as shown below, then press the <Del> key.

WEST	WESTWOOD Ltd	Weight House	Plymouth	Devon	PL22 1AA
WORM	WORMGLAZE Ltd	Glass House	Winchester	Hampshire	WN23 5TR

To delete a record when in Form view, first display the record you want to delete, then use the **Edit, Select Record** command to select the whole record, and press the <Del> key.

In both cases you will be given a warning and you will be asked to confirm your decision.

Delete, Insert, and Move Fields in a Table: To delete a field from a table, close any forms that might be open, then load the table from the Database window, then press the Design View icon, click the row selector to highlight the field you want to remove, as shown below, and press the Delete Row icon, shown here, or use the **Edit, Delete Rows** command.

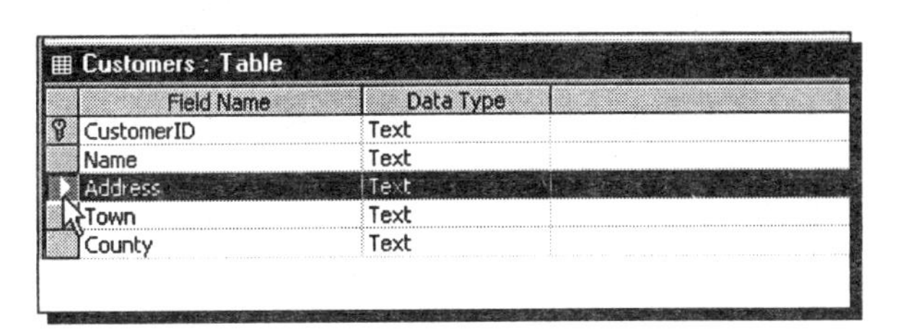

To insert a field in a table, display the table in Design View, and highlight the field above which you want to insert the new field, and press the Insert Row icon, shown here, or use the **Insert, Rows** command.

To move a field from its current to a new position in a table, select the field you want to move, then point to the row selector so that the mouse pointer is inclined as shown below, and drag the row to its new position.

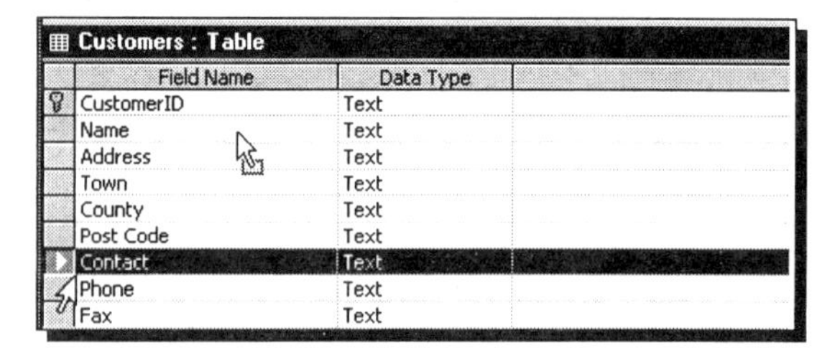

Note that while you are dragging the field, the mouse pointer changes to the one pointing at the Name field in the above composite. Releasing the mouse button, moves the Contact field to where the Name field is now and pushes all other fields one row down.

Printing a Table View:

You can print a database table by clicking the Print icon, or by using the **File, Print** command to display the Print dialogue box shown below. Alternatively, you can preview a database on screen by clicking the Preview icon.

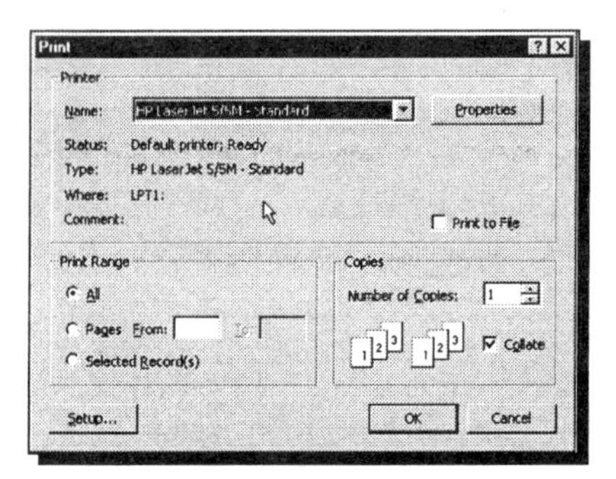

However, printing directly from here, produces a pre-defined print-out, the format of which you cannot control, apart from the margins and print orientation. To control these, click the **Setup** or **Properties** button.

For a better method of producing a printed output, see the Report Design section.

4. RELATIONAL DATABASE DESIGN

In order to be able to discuss relational databases, we will add to the database of the previous chapter an Orders table. To do this go through the following steps.

- Open the **Adept 1** database and use the **New** button on the Database window to add an Orders table to it.
- Use the Table Wizard and select Orders from the displayed **Sample Tables** list. Next, select the five fields displayed below under **Fields in my new table** from the **Sample Fields** list, and press the **Next** button.

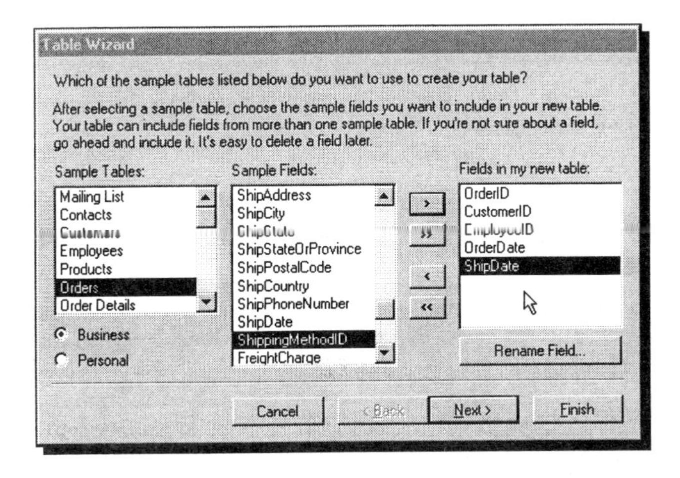

This displays the top dialogue box on the next page, in which you can, if you want to, change the name of the table. We elected to accept the default name, but we clicked the 'No, I'll set the primary key' radio button before pressing the **Next** key.

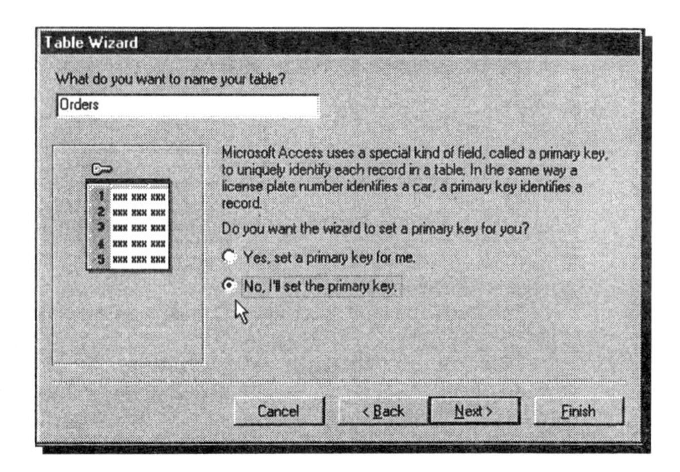

- On the next dialogue box you can select which field will hold data that is unique for each record. The key field must be unique in a table, and the OrderID field satisfies this requirement. This field is used by Access for fast searches.

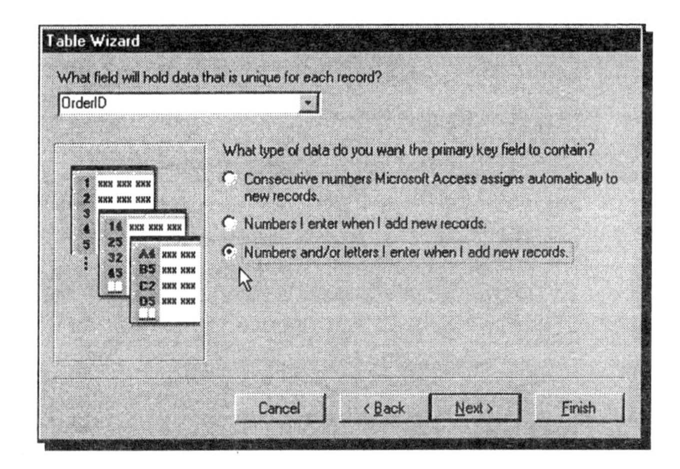

- Click the **Numbers and/or letters I enter when I add new records** radio button, before you press the **Next** button.

On the next dialogue box you specify whether the new table is related to any other tables in the database. The default is that it is not related.

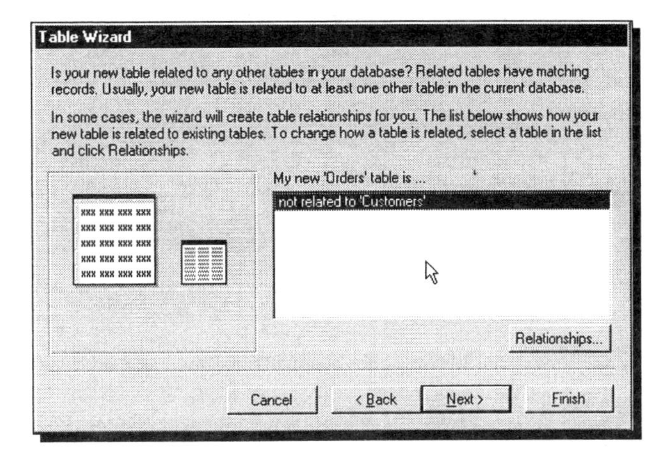

- Accept the default option, and press the **Next** button to reveal the final dialogue box.

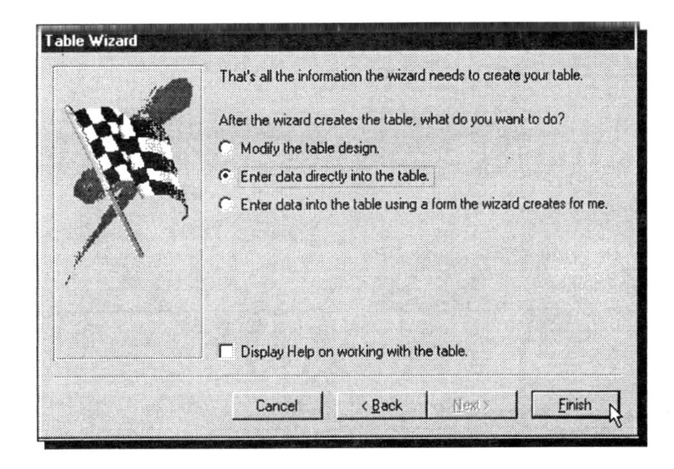

- Select the second option and press the **Finish** button, to let the Wizard create your table.

Although the two tables are actually related, we chose at this stage to tell the Wizard that they are not. This might appear to you as odd, but the Wizard makes certain assumptions about unique fields (for example, that ID fields are numbers), which is not what we want them to be. We choose to remain in control of the design of our database and, therefore, we will define the relationship between the two tables later.

The Wizard displays the newly created table ready for you to enter your data. However, before doing so, use the Design Table facility, as discussed previously, to change the Data Types of the selected Field Names to those displayed below.

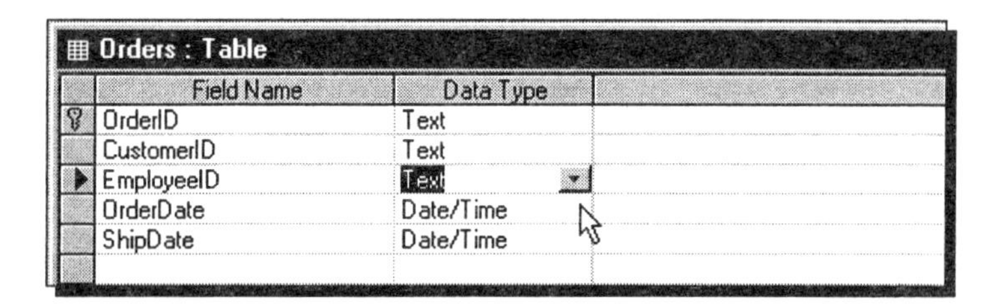

Orders : Table

Field Name	Data Type
OrderID	Text
CustomerID	Text
EmployeeID	Text
OrderDate	Date/Time
ShipDate	Date/Time

The information you need to enter in the Orders table is shown below.

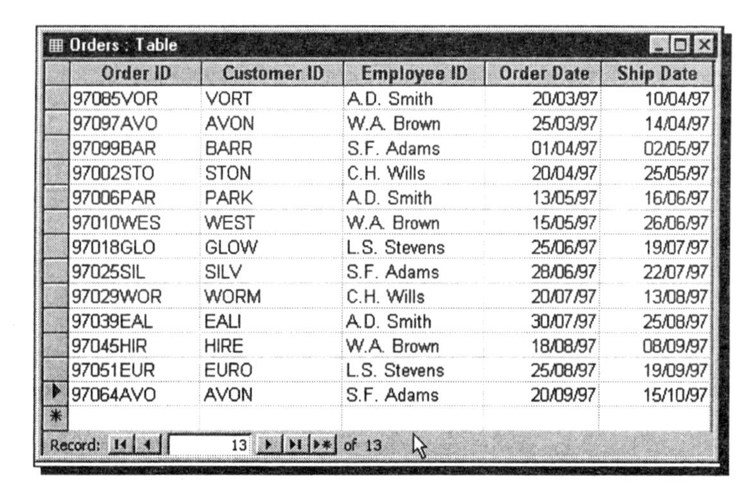

Orders : Table

Order ID	Customer ID	Employee ID	Order Date	Ship Date
97085VOR	VORT	A.D. Smith	20/03/97	10/04/97
97097AVO	AVON	W.A. Brown	25/03/97	14/04/97
97099BAR	BARR	S.F. Adams	01/04/97	02/05/97
97002STO	STON	C.H. Wills	20/04/97	25/05/97
97006PAR	PARK	A.D. Smith	13/05/97	16/06/97
97010WES	WEST	W.A. Brown	15/05/97	26/06/97
97018GLO	GLOW	L.S. Stevens	25/06/97	19/07/97
97025SIL	SILV	S.F. Adams	28/06/97	22/07/97
97029WOR	WORM	C.H. Wills	20/07/97	13/08/97
97039EAL	EALI	A.D. Smith	30/07/97	25/08/97
97045HIR	HIRE	W.A. Brown	18/08/97	08/09/97
97051EUR	EURO	L.S. Stevens	25/08/97	19/09/97
97064AVO	AVON	S.F. Adams	20/09/97	15/10/97

Record: 13 of 13

Relationships

Information held in two or more tables of a database is normally related in some way. In our case, the two tables, Customers and Orders, are related by the CustomerID field.

To build up relationships between tables, return to the Database window and press the Relationships icon

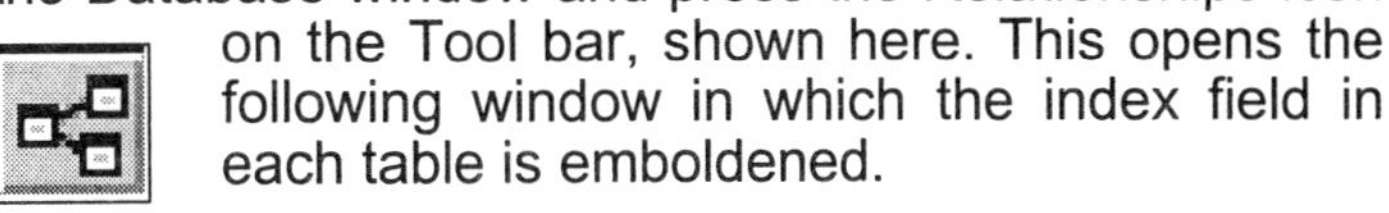

on the Tool bar, shown here. This opens the following window in which the index field in each table is emboldened.

You can build relationships between tables by dragging a field name from one table into another. In our example below, we have dragged CustomerID from the Customers table (by pointing to it, pressing the left

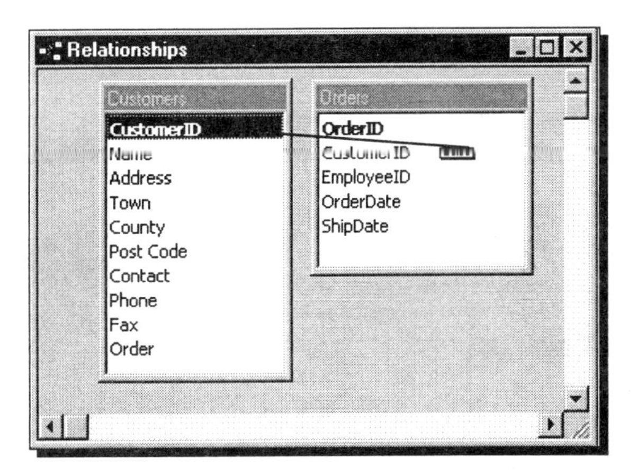

mouse button, and while keeping the mouse button pressed, dragging the pointer) to the required field in the other table, in this case CustomerID in the Orders table. Releasing the mouse button opens the dialogue boxes shown at the top of the next page (the second one by pressing the **Join Type** button on the first one).

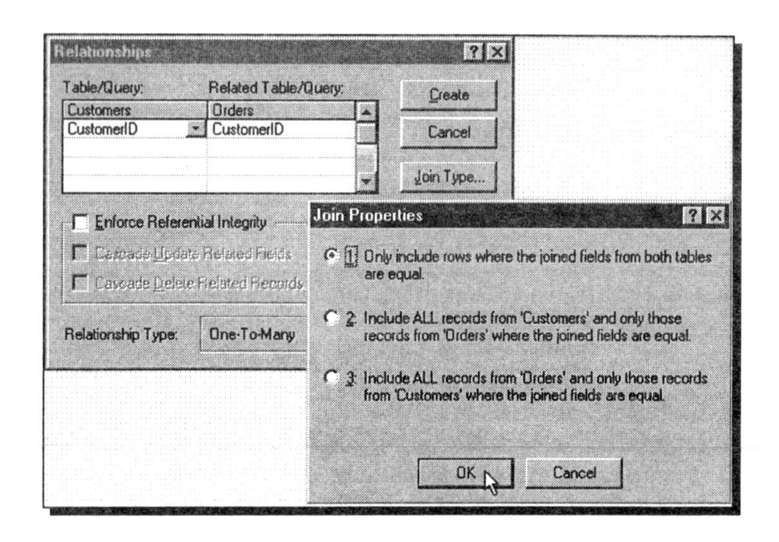

In the Join Properties dialogue box you can specify the type of join Access should create in new queries - more about this later. For the present, press the **OK** button on the Join Properties dialogue box, to close it, then check the **Enforce Referential Integrity** box in the Relationships dialogue box, and press the **Create** button.

Access creates and displays graphically the chosen type of relationship in the Relationships window shown here. Note the relationship '1 customer to many (∞) orders' symbolism in the Relationships window.

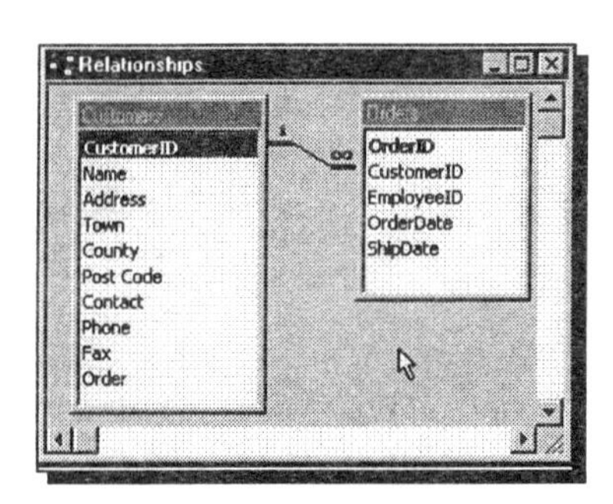

Because Access is a relational database, data can be used in queries from more than one table at a time. As we have seen, if the database contains tables with related data, the relationships can be defined easily.

Usually, the matching fields have the same name, as in our example of Customers and Orders tables. In the Customers table, the CustomerID field is the primary field and relates to the CustomerID field in the Orders table - there can be several orders in the Orders table from one customer in the Customers table.

The various types of relationships are as follows:

- Inherited - for attaching tables from another Access database. The original relationships of the attached database can be used in the current database.
- Referential - for enforcing relationships between records according to certain rules, when you add or delete records in related tables belonging to the same database. For example, you can only add records to a related table, if a matching record already exists in the primary table, and you cannot delete a record from the primary table if matching records exist in a related table.

Viewing and Editing Relationships:

To view the current relationships between tables, activate the Database window and press the Relationships icon. This displays the following:

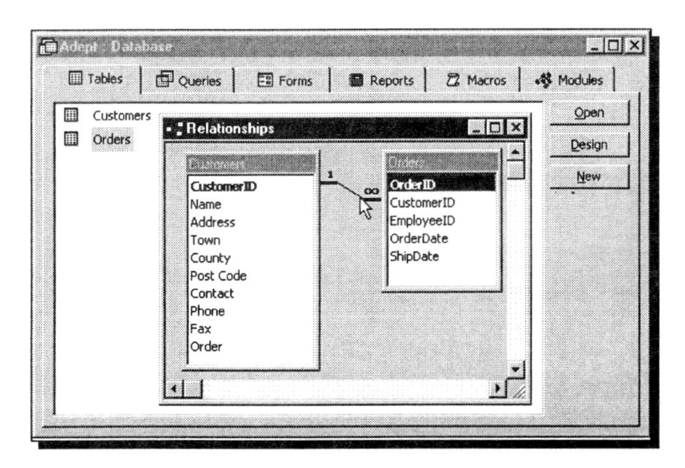

To edit a relationship, double-click the left mouse button at the pointer position shown on the previous screen dump. The tip of the mouse pointer must be on the inclined line joining the two tables in the Relationships window, as shown, before Access will respond. If you have difficulty with this action, first point to the relationship line and click once to embolden it, then use the **Relationships, Edit Relationship** command. Either of these two actions will open the Relationships dialogue box in which you can change the various options already discussed.

A given relationship can easily be removed altogether, by first activating it (pointing and clicking to embolden it), then pressing the <Del> key. A confirmation dialogue box will be displayed. To delete a table, you must first detach it from other tables, then select it in the Database Window and press the <Del> key. Think before you do this!

Creating an Additional Table

As an exercise, create a third table using the **Table Wizards** and select Invoices from the displayed **Sample Tables** list. Next, select the five fields displayed below - the names and their data types have been changed using the Design Table facility.

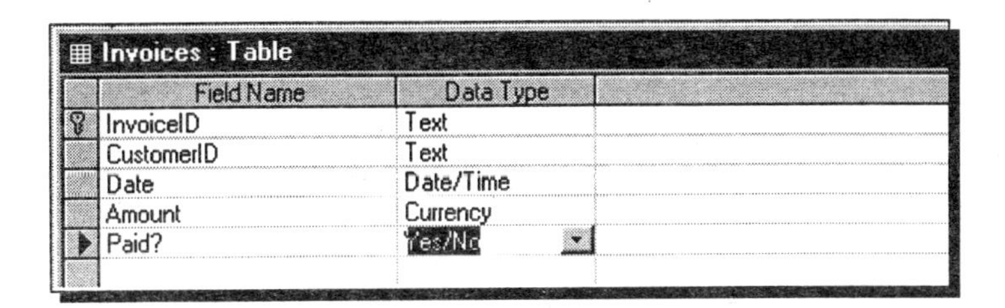

Invoices : Table

	Field Name	Data Type
🔑	InvoiceID	Text
	CustomerID	Text
	Date	Date/Time
	Amount	Currency
▶	Paid?	Yes/No

Next, enter the data given below and build up appropriate relationships between the Invoices table, the Customers table and the Orders table, as shown on the next page.

AD9701	VORT	10/04/97	£120.84	No
AD9702	AVON	14/04/97	£103.52	Yes
AD9703	BARR	02/05/97	£99.32	No
AD9704	STON	25/05/97	£55.98	No
AD9705	PARK	16/06/97	£180.22	No
AD9706	WEST	26/06/97	£68.52	No
AD9707	GLOW	19/07/97	£111.56	No
AD9708	SILV	22/07/97	£123.45	Yes
AD9709	WORM	13/08/97	£35.87	No
AD9710	EALI	25/08/97	£58.95	No
AD9711	HIRE	08/09/97	£290.00	No
AD9712	EURO	19/09/97	£150.00	No
AD9713	AVON	15/10/97	£135.00	No
				No

The relationships between the three tables should be arranged as follows:

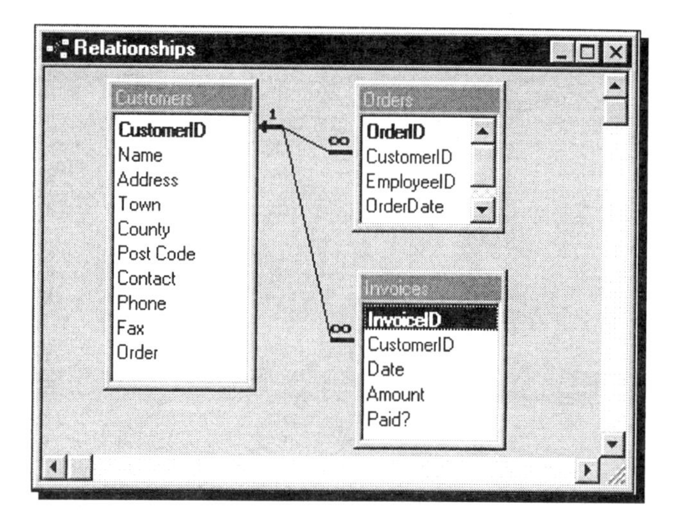

It is important that you should complete this exercise, as it consolidates what we have done so far and, in any case, we will be using all three tables in what comes next. So go ahead and try it.

5. CREATING A QUERY

You create a query so that you can ask questions about the data in your database tables. For example, we could find out whether we have more than one order from the same customer in our Adept database.

To do this, start Access, load **Adept 1**, and in the Database window click the Queries tab, followed by the **New** button which opens the New Query dialogue box. Selecting the **Find Duplicates Query Wizard**, displays the following:

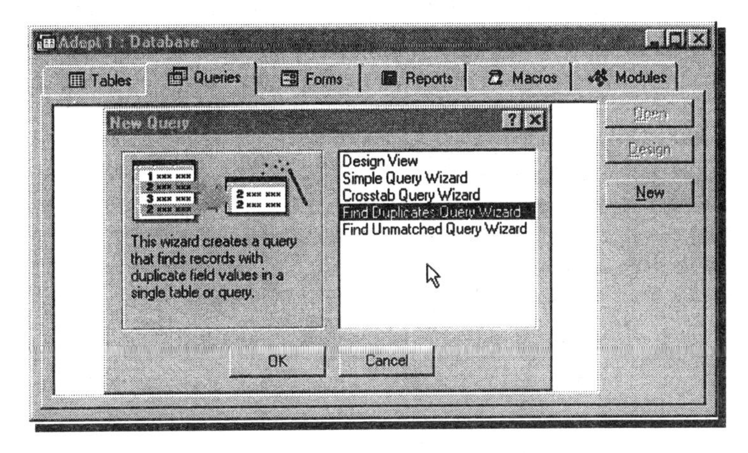

On clicking **OK**, the Find Duplicates Query Wizard dialogue box is displayed, as shown below.

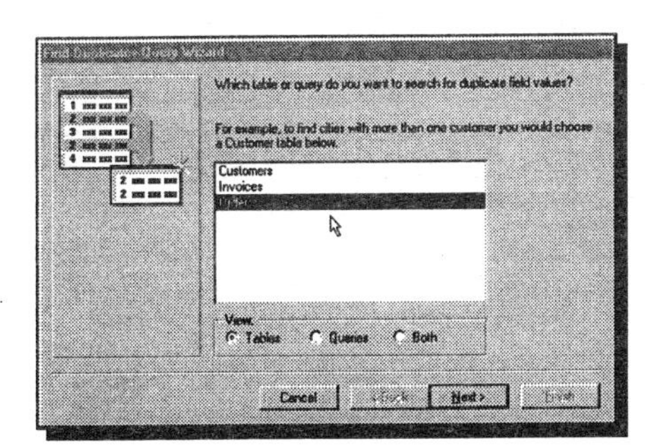

Next, select the Orders table from the displayed database tables in this dialogue box, and press the **Next** button.

On the following dialogue box select **CustomerID** as the field you want to check for duplicate values, then press the [>] button, followed by the **Next** button.

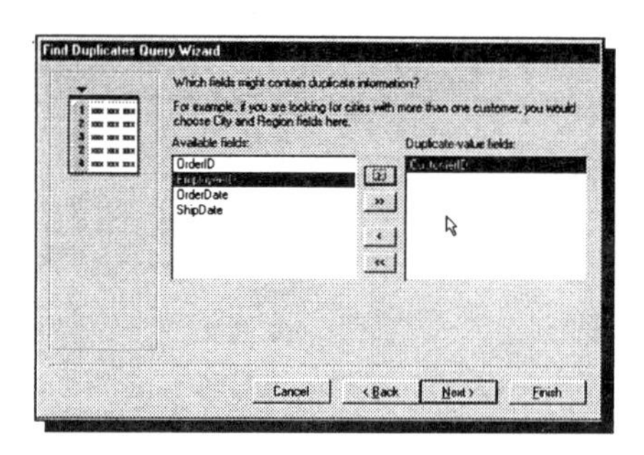

Finally, select the additional fields you would like to see along with the duplicate values, by selecting those you want from the next dialogue box, either one at a time or, if you decide to select all of them, as shown here, by clicking the [»] button. Clicking the **Finish** button displays the Select Query screen shown below.

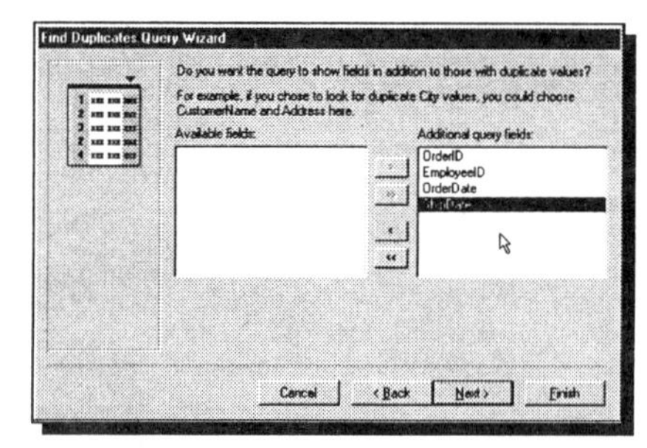

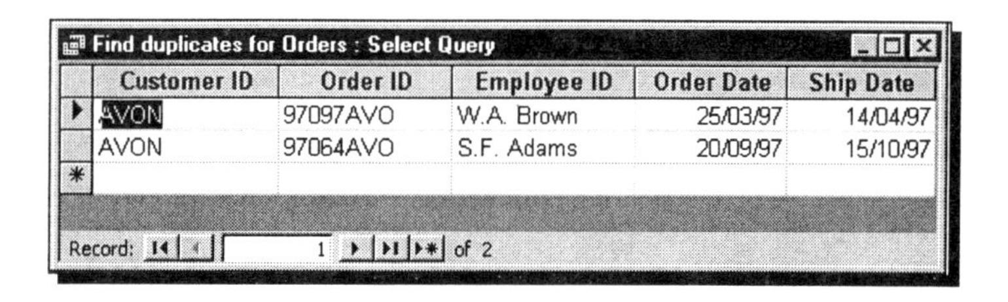

Find duplicates for Orders : Select Query

Customer ID	Order ID	Employee ID	Order Date	Ship Date
AVON	97097AVO	W.A. Brown	25/03/97	14/04/97
AVON	97064AVO	S.F. Adams	20/09/97	15/10/97

Record: 1 of 2

If you examine the original Orders table, you will indeed find that it contains two orders from AVON.

Types of Queries

The query we have created so far, is known as the *Select Query*, which is the most common type of query. However, with Access you can also create and use other types of queries, as follows:

- **Crosstab query** - used to present data with row and column headings, just like a spreadsheet. It can be used to summarise large amounts of data in a more readable form.
- **Action query** - used to make changes to many records in one operation. For example, you might like to remove from a given table all records that meet certain criteria. Obviously, this type of query has to be treated with care!
- **Union query** - used to match fields from two or more tables.
- **Pass-through query** - used to pass commands to a SQL (pronounced 'sequal') database (see below).
- **Data-definition query** - used to create, change, or delete tables in an Access database using SQL statements.

SQL stands for Structured Query Language, often used to query, update, and manage relational databases. Each query created by Access has an associated SQL statement that defines the action of that query. Thus, if you are familiar with SQL, you can use such statements to view and modify queries, or set form and report properties. However, these actions can be done more easily with the QBE (query-by-example) grid, to be discussed next. If you design union queries, pass-through queries, or data-definition queries, then you must use SQL statements, as these types of queries can not be designed with the QBE grid. Finally, to create a sub-query, you use the QBE grid, but you enter an SQL SELECT statement for criteria, as we shall see in the next QBE grid example.

The Query Window

The Query window is a graphical query-by-example (QBE) tool. Because of Access' graphical features, you can use the mouse to select, drag, and manipulate objects in the query window to define how you would like to see your data.

An example of a ready made Query window can be seen by selecting the Find duplicates for Orders query and clicking the **Design** button on the Database window. This action opens the Select Query dialogue box shown below.

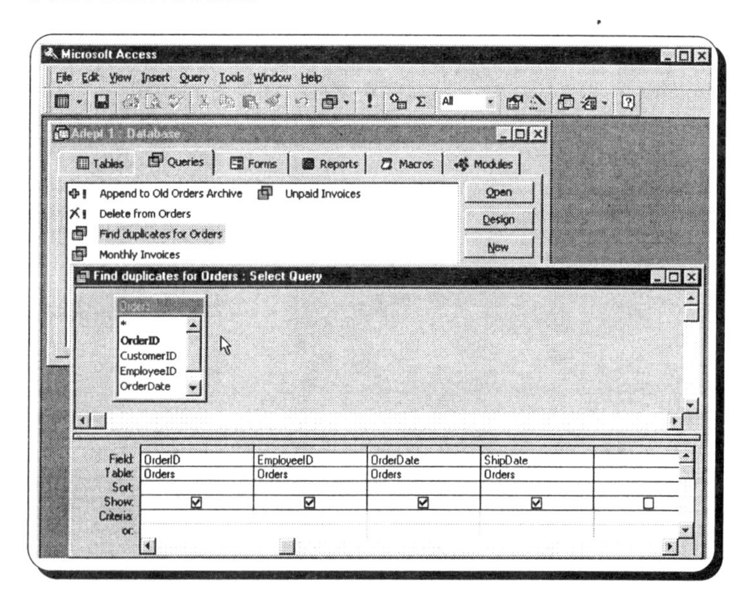

You can add a table to the top half of the Query window by simply dragging the table from the Database window. Similarly, you can add fields to the bottom half of the Query window (the QBE grid) by dragging fields from the tables on the top half of the Query window. In addition, the QBE grid is used to select the sort order of the data, or insert criteria, such as SQL statements.

To see the full SQL SELECT statement written by Access as the criteria selection when we first defined the query, use the **View, SQL View** command.

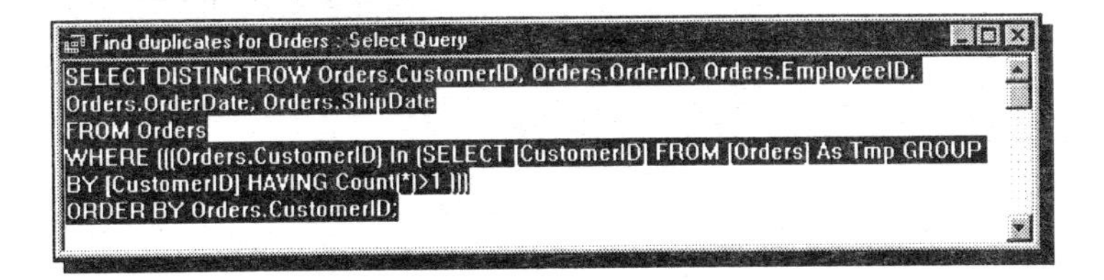

Note the part of the statement which states 'As Tmp GROUP'. Access collects the data you want as a temporary group, called a *dynaset*. This special set of data behaves like a table, but it is not a table; it is a dynamic view of the data from one or more tables, selected and sorted by the particular query.

Creating a New Query:

Below, we show a screen dump created by first clicking the Queries tab, then pressing the **New** button on the Database window. In the displayed New Query dialogue box, select Design View and press the **OK** button. This opens both the Select Query and the Show Table dialogue boxes shown overleaf.

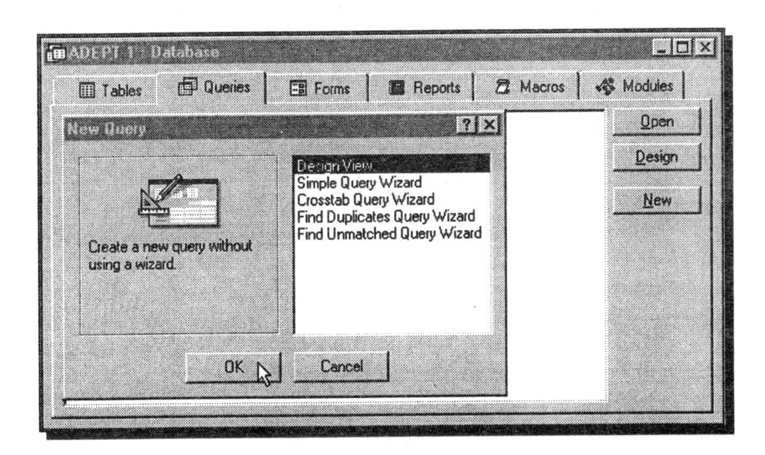

The Invoices and Customers tables were then added to the Select Query window, as shown below.

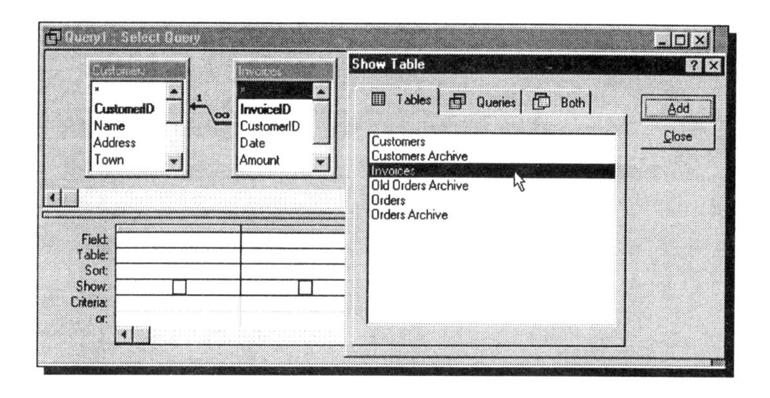

Adding Fields to a Query Window:

Below we show a screen in which the Paid? and InvoiceID fields have been dragged from the Invoices table and added to the Query window. In addition, the Name and Contact fields have been dragged from the Customers table and placed on the Query window, while the Phone field from the Customers table is about to be added to the Query window.

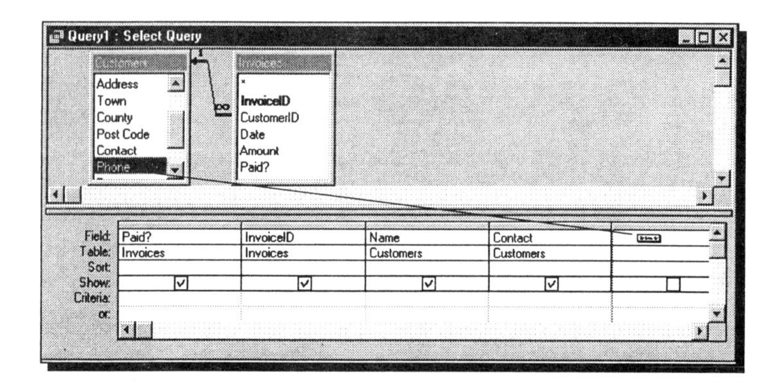

Having dragged all five fields from the two tables onto the QBE grid, we have added the word No as the criteria on the Paid? field and selected Ascending as the Sort for the InvoiceID field.

Note that the Invoices and Customers tables are joined by a line that connects the two CustomerID fields. The join line was created when we designed the tables and their relationships in the previous chapter. Even if you have not created these relationships, Access will join the tables in a query automatically when the tables are added to a query, provided each table has a field with the same name and a compatible data type and one of those fields is a primary key. A primary field is displayed in bold in the Query window.

If you have not created relationships between your tables yourself, or Access has not joined your tables automatically, you can still use related data in your query by joining the tables in the Query window.

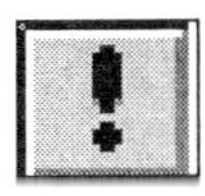

Clicking the Run icon on the Toolbar, shown here, instantly displays all the unpaid invoices with the details you have asked for, as follows:

Unpaid Invoices : Select Query

Paid?	Order ID	Amount	Invoice No	Name	Contact	Phone
No	97085VOR	£120.84	AD9701	VORTEX Co. Ltd	Brian Storm	01776-223344
No	97099BAR	£99.32	AD9703	BARROWS Associat	Mandy Brown	01554-664422
No	97002STO	£55.98	AD9704	STONEAGE Ltd	Mike Irons	01765-234567
No	97006PAR	£180.22	AD9705	PARKWAY Gravel	James Stone	01534-987654
No	97010WES	£68.52	AD9706	WESTWOOD Ltd	Mary Slim	01234-667755
No	97018GLO	£111.56	AD9707	GLOWORM Ltd	Peter Summe	01432-746523
No	97029WOR	£35.87	AD9709	WORMGLAZE Ltd	Richard Glaze	01123-654321
No	97039EAL	£58.95	AD9710	EALING Engines Des	Trevor Miles	01336-010107
No	97045HIR	£290.00	AD9711	HIRE Service Equipm	Nicole Webb	01875-558822
No	97051EUR	£150.00	AD9712	EUROBASE Co. Ltd	Sarah Star	01736-098765
No	97097AVO	£135.00	AD9713	AVON Construction	John Waters	01657-113355
No	97064AVO	£135.00	AD9713	AVON Construction	John Waters	01657-113355

Record: 1 of 12

To save your newly created query, use the **File, Save As/Export** command, and give it a name such as 'Unpaid Invoices' in the Save As dialogue box.

Types of Criteria

Access accepts the following expressions as criteria:

Arithmetic Operators		***Comparison Operators***		***Logical Operators***	
*	Multiply	<	Less than	And	And
/	Divide	<=	Less than or equal	Or	Inclusive or
+	Add	>	Greater than	Xor	Exclusive or
-	Subtract	>=	Greater than or equal	Not	Not equivalent
		=	Equal	Eqv	Equivalent
		<>	Not equal	Imp	Implication

Other operators		
Between	Between 50 And 150	All values between 50 and 150
In	In("Bath","Bristol")	All records with Bath and Bristol
Is	Is Null	All records with no value in that field
Like	Like "Brian *"	All records with Brian something in field
&	[Name]&" "&[Surname]	Concatenates strings

Using Wildcard Characters in Criteria:

In the previous example we used the criteria A* to mean any company whose name starts with the letter A. The asterisk in this criteria is known as a wildcard character.

To search for a pattern, you can use the asterisk (*) and the question mark (?) as wildcard characters when specifying criteria in expressions. An asterisk stands for any number of characters, while a question mark stands for any single character in the same position as the question mark.

The following examples show the use of wildcard characters in various types of expressions:

Entered Expression	Meaning	Examples
a?	Any two-letter word beginning with A	am, an, as, at
???d	Any four-letter word ending with d	find, hand, land yard
Sm?th	Any five-letter word beginning with Sm and ending with th	Smith Smyth
fie*	Any word starting with the letters fie	field, fiend, fierce, fiery
*ght	Any word ending with ght	alight, eight, fight, light, might, sight
*/5/97	All dates in May '97	1/5/97
a	Any word with the letter a in it	Brian, Mary, star, yard

Combining Criteria

By specifying additional criteria in a Query window you can create powerful queries for viewing your data. In the examples below we have added the field Amount to our Unpaid Invoices query.

The AND Criteria with Different Fields: When you insert criteria in several fields, but in the same row, Access assumes that you are searching for records that meet all of the criteria. For example, the criteria below list the records shown on the next page.

Field:	Paid?	Amount	InvoiceID	Name	Contact
Table:	Invoices	Invoices	Invoices	Customers	Customers
Sort:					
Show:	☑	☑	☑	☑	☑
Criteria:	No	Between 50 And 150			Like "M*"
or:					

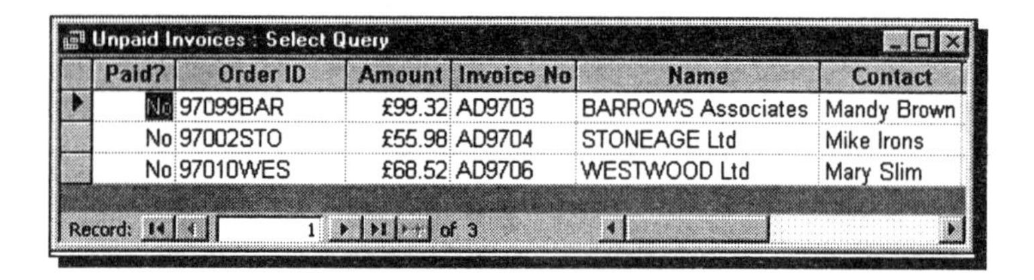

Unpaid Invoices : Select Query

Paid?	Order ID	Amount	Invoice No	Name	Contact
No	97099BAR	£99.32	AD9703	BARROWS Associates	Mandy Brown
No	97002STO	£55.98	AD9704	STONEAGE Ltd	Mike Irons
No	97010WES	£68.52	AD9706	WESTWOOD Ltd	Mary Slim

Record: 1 of 3

The OR Criteria with the Same Field: If you include multiple criteria in one field only, then Access assumes that you are searching for records that meet any one of the specified criteria. For example, the criteria <50 or >100 in the field Amount, shown below, list the required records, only if the No in the Paid? field is inserted in both rows.

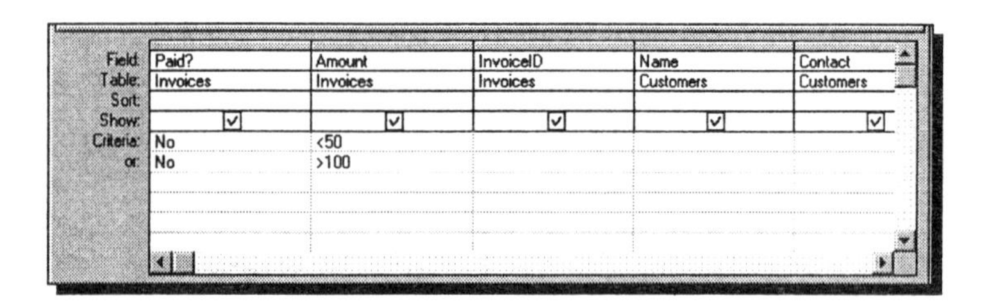

Field:	Paid?	Amount	InvoiceID	Name	Contact
Table:	Invoices	Invoices	Invoices	Customers	Customers
Sort:					
Show:	☑	☑	☑	☑	☑
Criteria:	No	<50			
or:	No	>100			

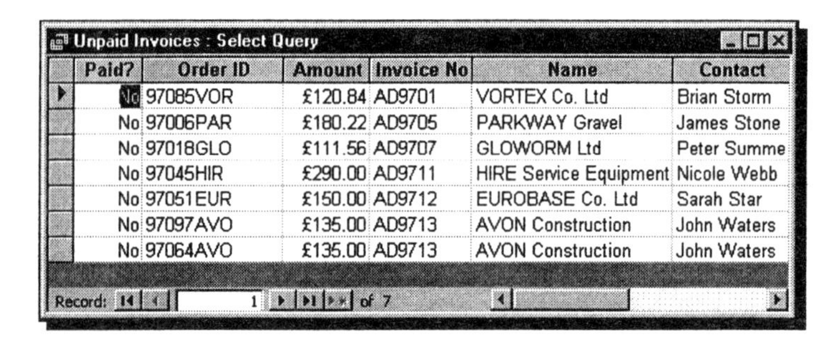

Unpaid Invoices : Select Query

Paid?	Order ID	Amount	Invoice No	Name	Contact
No	97085VOR	£120.84	AD9701	VORTEX Co. Ltd	Brian Storm
No	97006PAR	£180.22	AD9705	PARKWAY Gravel	James Stone
No	97018GLO	£111.56	AD9707	GLOWORM Ltd	Peter Summe
No	97045HIR	£290.00	AD9711	HIRE Service Equipment	Nicole Webb
No	97051EUR	£150.00	AD9712	EUROBASE Co. Ltd	Sarah Star
No	97097AVO	£135.00	AD9713	AVON Construction	John Waters
No	97064AVO	£135.00	AD9713	AVON Construction	John Waters

Record: 1 of 7

The OR Criteria with Different Fields: If you include multiple criteria in different fields, but in different rows, then Access assumes that you are searching for records that meet either one or the other of the specified criteria. For example, the criteria Yes in the Paid? field and the criteria <50 in the Amount field, but in different rows, list the following records.

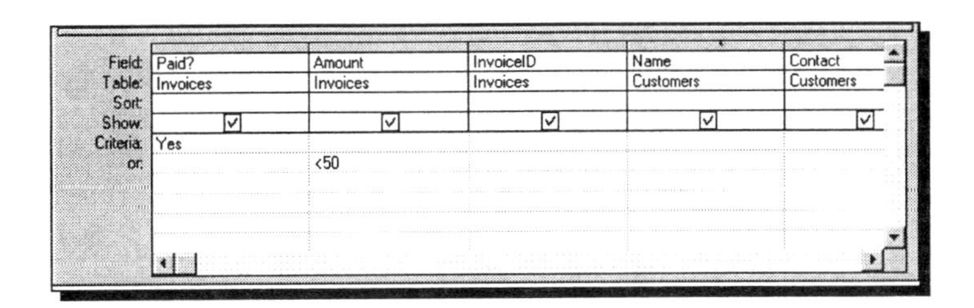

Field:	Paid?	Amount	InvoiceID	Name	Contact
Table:	Invoices	Invoices	Invoices	Customers	Customers
Sort:					
Show:	☑	☑	☑	☑	☑
Criteria:	Yes				
or:		<50			

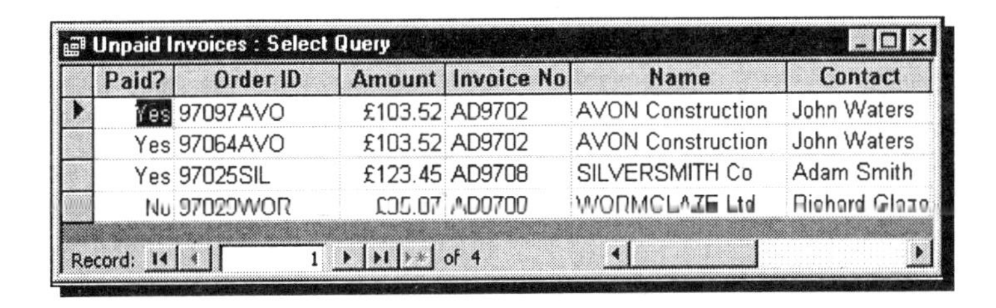

Unpaid Invoices : Select Query

Paid?	Order ID	Amount	Invoice No	Name	Contact
Yes	97097AVO	£103.52	AD9702	AVON Construction	John Waters
Yes	97064AVO	£103.52	AD9702	AVON Construction	John Waters
Yes	97025SIL	£123.45	AD9708	SILVERSMITH Co	Adam Smith
No	97020WOR	£35.07	AD9700	WORMGLAZE Ltd	Richard Glaze

Record: 1 of 4

The AND and OR Criteria Together: The following choice of criteria will cause Access to retrieve either records that have Yes in the Paid? field and the company's name starts with the letter A, or records that the invoice amount is less than £50.

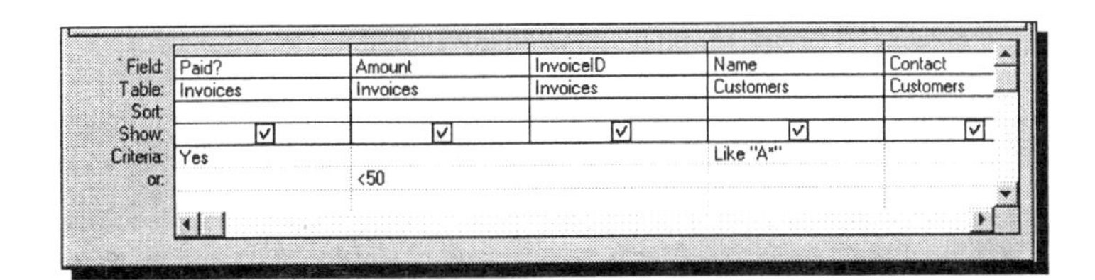

Field:	Paid?	Amount	InvoiceID	Name	Contact
Table:	Invoices	Invoices	Invoices	Customers	Customers
Sort:					
Show:	☑	☑	☑	☑	☑
Criteria:	Yes			Like "A*"	
or:		<50			

The retrieved records from such a query are shown below.

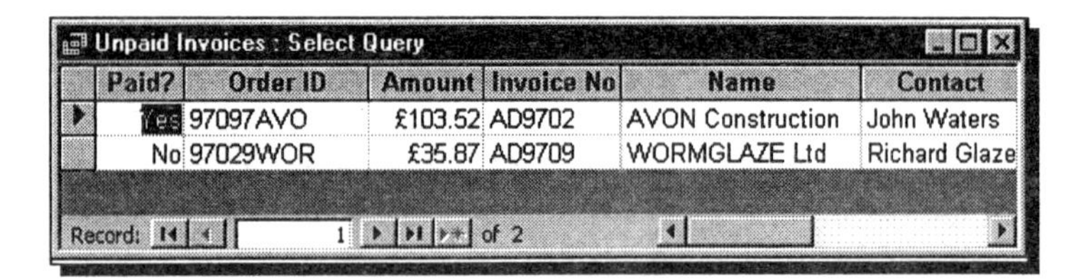

Unpaid Invoices : Select Query

Paid?	Order ID	Amount	Invoice No	Name	Contact
Yes	97097AVO	£103.52	AD9702	AVON Construction	John Waters
No	97029WOR	£35.87	AD9709	WORMGLAZE Ltd	Richard Glaze

Record: 1 of 2

Creating Calculated Fields

Let us assume that we would like to increase the amounts payable on all invoices overdue by more than 30 days from today by 0.5%, as a penalty for not settling an account on time. We can achieve this by creating a calculated field in our database.

To create a calculated field, open **Adept 1**, click the Query tab on the Database window, double-click the Unpaid Invoices query, and click the Design View button on the Toolbar. Next, insert a field after the Amount field by highlighting the column after it and using the **Insert Columns** command. Now type in the Field row of the newly inserted empty column, the following information:

```
New Amount:[Amount]*1.005
```

where *New Amount:* is our chosen name for the calculated field - the colon is essential. If you do not supply a name for the calculated field, Access uses the default name *Expr1:*, which you can rename later. The square brackets enclosing the word Amount in the above expression indicate a field name.

Next, click the Properties button, shown here, or use the **View, Properties** command, to set the Format property to Currency.

Finally, add the Date field from the Invoices table to our query and type the expression <#01/05/97# in its Criteria field - the hash marks and leading zeros are supplied by Access if you do not type them yourself.

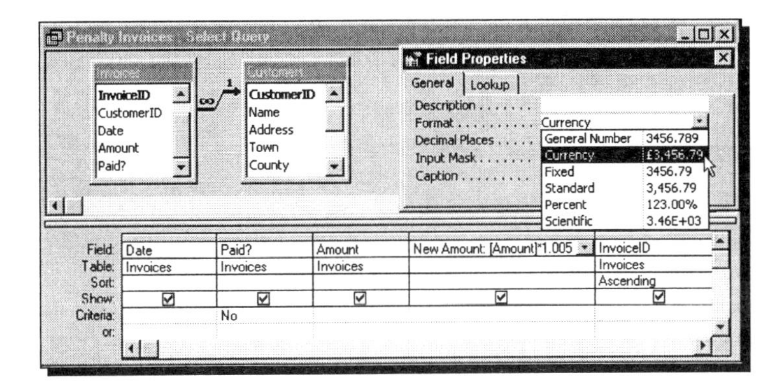

Clicking the Datasheet View button on the Toolbar, displays the following screen:

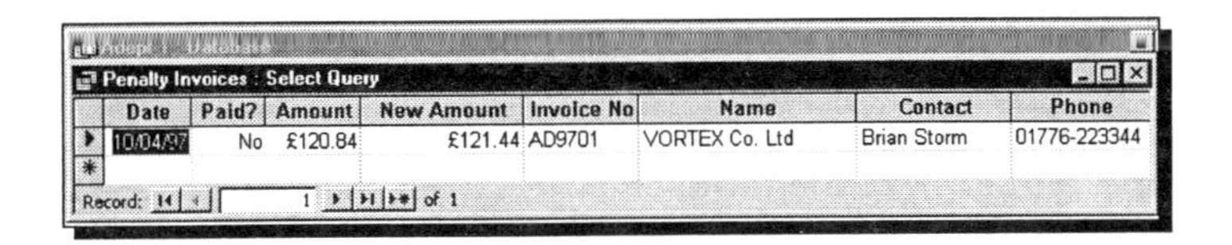

We suggest you save this query under the name Penalty Invoices.

Using Functions in Criteria

There are several functions that you can use in a calculated field of an Access query which can either be applied to extract information from a text field or date fields, or be used to calculate totals of entries.

Finding Part of a Text Field:

Let us assume that you want to find information that is part of a text field, like the area code (first 5 numbers) in the Phone field of our Customers table. To help you search a table for only part of a text field, Access provides three string functions. The syntax of these functions is as follows:

```
Left(stringexpr,n)
Right(stringexpr,n)
Mid(stringexpr,start,n)
```

The *stringexpr* argument can be either a field name or a text expression, while *n* is the number of characters you are searching for, and *start* is the position of the first character you want to start from.

Thus, to extract the area code of the text field Phone in our Customers table, open the Unpaid Invoices query, click the Design View button on the toolbar, and type in the Field row of an empty field, either

```
Area Codes:Left([Phone],5)
```

or

```
Area Codes:Mid([Phone],1,5)
```

Note that to distinguish between the name of a field and a text expression, the name of the field is enclosed in square brackets.

Next, click the Datasheet View button on the toolbar. The result of such a query is displayed below.

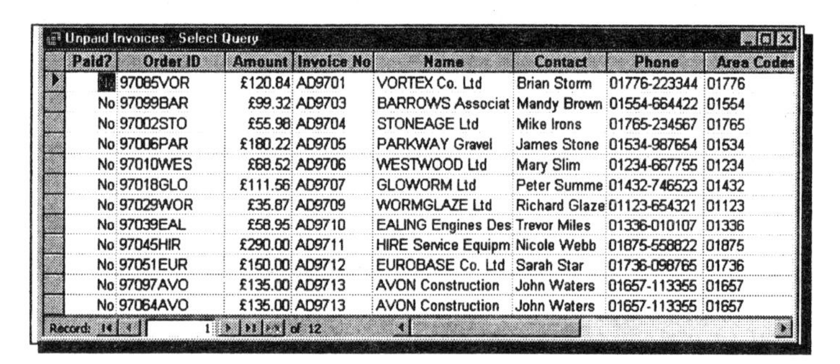

Unpaid Invoices : Select Query

Paid?	Order ID	Amount	Invoice No	Name	Contact	Phone	Area Codes
No	97085VOR	£120.84	AD9701	VORTEX Co. Ltd	Brian Storm	01776-223344	01776
No	97099BAR	£99.32	AD9703	BARROWS Associat	Mandy Brown	01554-664422	01554
No	97002STO	£55.98	AD9704	STONEAGE Ltd	Mike Irons	01765-234567	01765
No	97006PAR	£180.22	AD9705	PARKWAY Gravel	James Stone	01534-987654	01534
No	97010WES	£68.52	AD9706	WESTWOOD Ltd	Mary Slim	01234-667755	01234
No	97018GLO	£111.56	AD9707	GLOWORM Ltd	Peter Summe	01432-746523	01432
No	97029WOR	£35.87	AD9709	WORMGLAZE Ltd	Richard Glaze	01123-654321	01123
No	97039EAL	£58.95	AD9710	EALING Engines Des	Trevor Miles	01336-010107	01336
No	97045HIR	£290.00	AD9711	HIRE Service Equipm	Nicole Webb	01875-558822	01875
No	97051EUR	£150.00	AD9712	EUROBASE Co. Ltd	Sarah Star	01736-098765	01736
No	97097AVO	£135.00	AD9713	AVON Construction	John Waters	01657-113355	01657
No	97064AVO	£135.00	AD9713	AVON Construction	John Waters	01657-113355	01657

Record: 1 of 12

Finding Part of a Date Field:

To extract part of a date field, such as the month in which unpaid invoices were issued, type

```
Month:DatePart("m",[Date])
```

in the Field row of an empty field.

To extract the year in which unpaid invoices were issued, type

```
Year:DatePart("yyyy",[Date])
```

in the Field row of an empty field. This function returns the year in four digits, such as 1997.

The result of such a query is shown below.

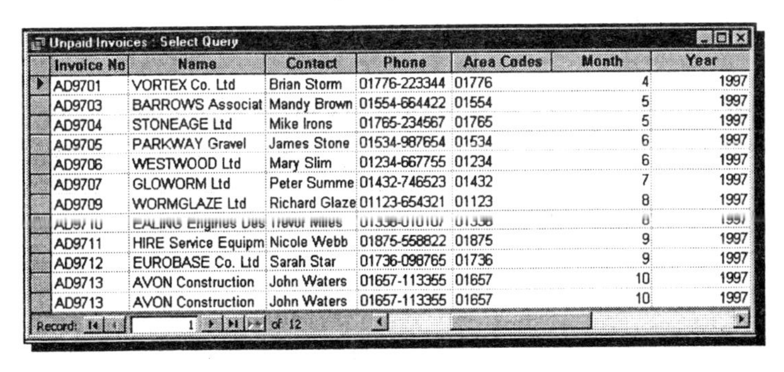

Unpaid Invoices : Select Query

Invoice No	Name	Contact	Phone	Area Codes	Month	Year
AD9701	VORTEX Co. Ltd	Brian Storm	01776-223344	01776	4	1997
AD9703	BARROWS Associat	Mandy Brown	01554-664422	01554	5	1997
AD9704	STONEAGE Ltd	Mike Irons	01765-234567	01765	5	1997
AD9705	PARKWAY Gravel	James Stone	01534-987654	01534	6	1997
AD9706	WESTWOOD Ltd	Mary Slim	01234-667755	01234	6	1997
AD9707	GLOWORM Ltd	Peter Summe	01432-746523	01432	7	1997
AD9709	WORMGLAZE Ltd	Richard Glaze	01123-654321	01123	8	1997
AD9710	EALING Engines Des	Trevor Miles	01336-010107	01336	8	1997
AD9711	HIRE Service Equipm	Nicole Webb	01875-558822	01875	9	1997
AD9712	EUROBASE Co. Ltd	Sarah Star	01736-098765	01736	9	1997
AD9713	AVON Construction	John Waters	01657-113355	01657	10	1997
AD9713	AVON Construction	John Waters	01657-113355	01657	10	1997

Record: 1 of 12

Calculating Totals in Queries:

It is possible that you might want to know the total value of outstanding invoices grouped by month. Access allows you to perform calculations on groups of records using *totals* queries, also known as *aggregate* queries.

The table overleaf lists the functions that can be used in queries to display totals. These functions are entered in the Totals row of a query which can be displayed by clicking the Totals button, shown here, while in Design View.

Function	Used to Find
Avg	The average of values in a field
Count	The number of values in a field
First	The field value from the first record in a table or query
Last	The field value from the last record in a table or query
Max	The highest value in a field
Min	The lowest value in a field
StDev	The standard deviation of values in a field
Sum	The total of values in a field
Var	The variance of values in a field

Below we show the one-table query to find the total of values of unpaid invoices grouped by month.

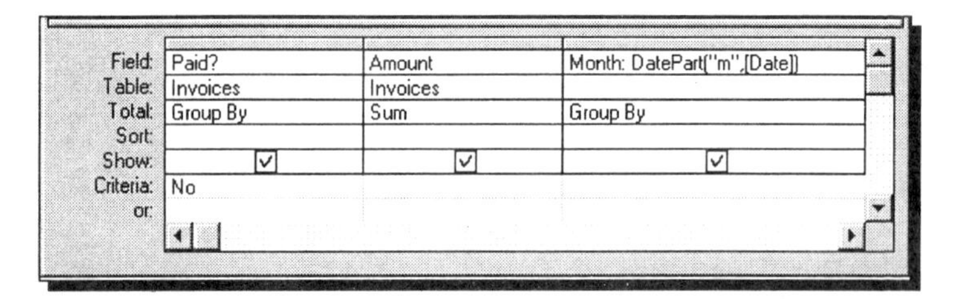

The retrieved records from such a query are shown below. We have named the query 'Monthly Invoices'.

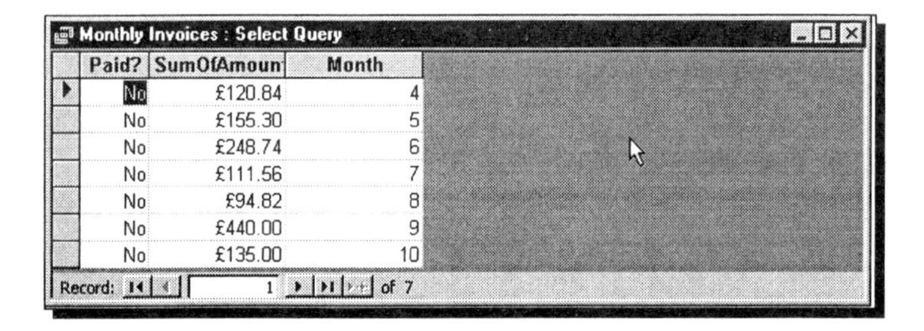

6. ADVANCED QUERIES

We have seen in the last chapter how to create a query with fields taken from two tables. The query in question was the Unpaid Invoices, shown below in Design View.

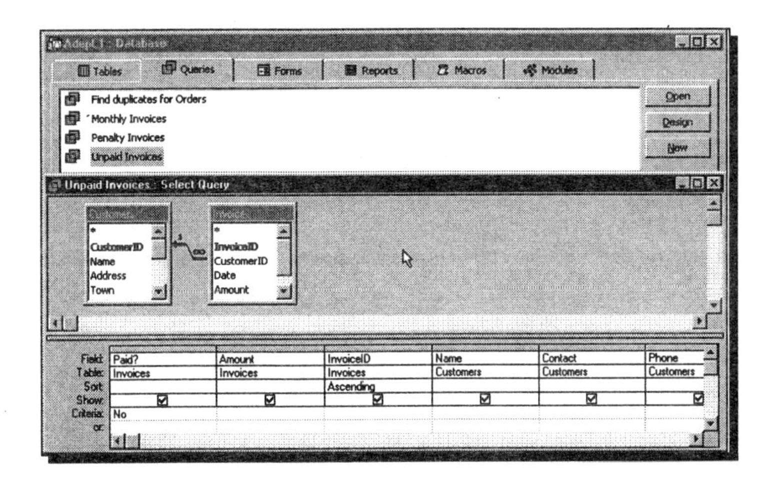

In order to make it easy for us to know which field in the above query comes from which table, Access displays the name of the table by default. This option is controlled from the **View, Table Names** command when in design View. When this menu option is ticked, Access adds the Table row in the QBE grid.

Now, suppose we would like to add the Orders table so that we can see the OrdersID field in extracted records of our query. To do this, click the Add Table button, shown here, which opens the Add Table dialogue box. Select Orders and click the **Add** button, then drag the OrdersID field onto the QBE grid, as shown overleaf.

From this point on, we found it convenient to make a copy of **Adept 1.mdb** database and name it **Adept 2.mdb**. We did this for management purposes only. You, of course, can continue using **Adept 1.mdb**.

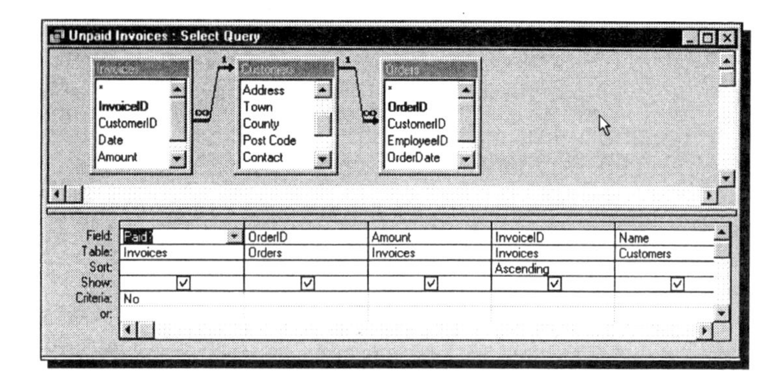

However, when you now click the Datasheet View button on the Tool bar to see the extracted records, Access displays the following message:

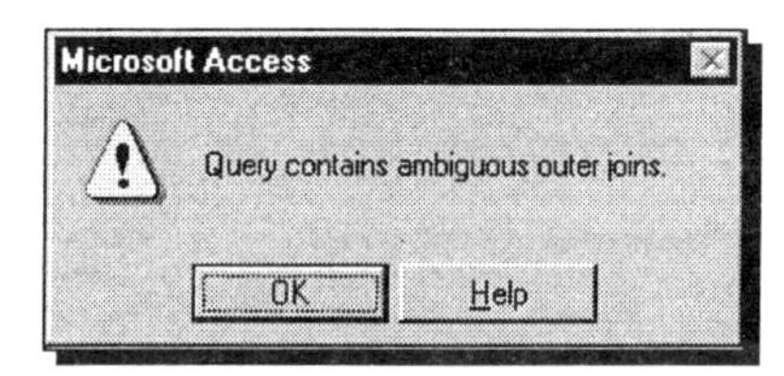

To correct this error, double-click the offending join to find out what type it is, which reveals the following dialogue box:

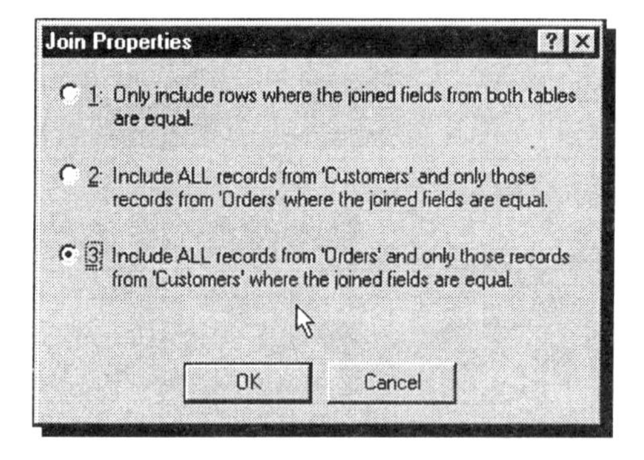

Obviously, option 3 is the wrong join. What we really need, is option 2. Select it to extract the correct records.

Types of Joins

Microsoft Access supports the following types of joins:

Types of joins	***Effect***
Equi-joins or Inner joins	A join in which records from two tables are combined and added to a dynaset only when there are equal values in the joined fields. For example, you can find records that show orders placed by each customer, with the dynaset containing only records for customers who have placed orders.
Outer joins	A join in which all the records from one table are added to the dynaset, and only those records from the other table for which values in the joined fields are equal. For example, you can find records that show all customers together with any orders they have placed.
Self-joins	A join in which records from one table are combined with other records from the same table when there are matching values in the joined fields. A self-join can be an equi-join or an outer join.

For an inner join, select option 1 from the Join Properties dialogue box. For an outer join, select option 2 or 3, depending on which records you want to include.

For example, choosing option 2 (also called a *left outer join*), in the case of our previous example, displays all the required records from the Customers table and only those records from Orders where the joined fields are equal. Option 3 (also called a *right outer join*), on the other hand, attempts to display all records in Orders and only those records from Customers where the joined fields are equal, resulting in some confusion in our particular example.

Creating a Parameter Query

A *Parameter Query* is a variation of the *Select Query* - the type we have been using so far. A Parameter Query is used when you frequently run the same query, but change the criteria each time you run it. Instead of having to make changes to the QBE grid, the design of a Parameter Query causes Access to prompt you for criteria. This type of query is particularly useful when used as a filter with forms.

To design a Parameter Query, design a **New** query in the normal way (do not use the Query Wizards), or change an existing Select Query. We have chosen the latter route and selected to change the Penalty Invoices query. In Design View, this now looks as follows:

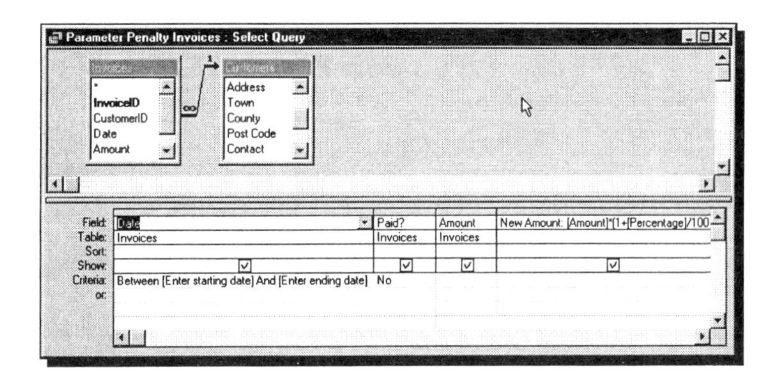

Note the two changes made to the above query. In the Date field we have entered two prompts (in square brackets) in the Criteria row, namely

```
[Enter starting date]
[Enter ending date]
```

and in the calculated field we have replaced the *1.005 by

```
*(1+[Percentage]/100)
```

Running this query, causes Access to ask for input values on three successive Enter Parameter Value boxes, as shown in the composite screen dump below:

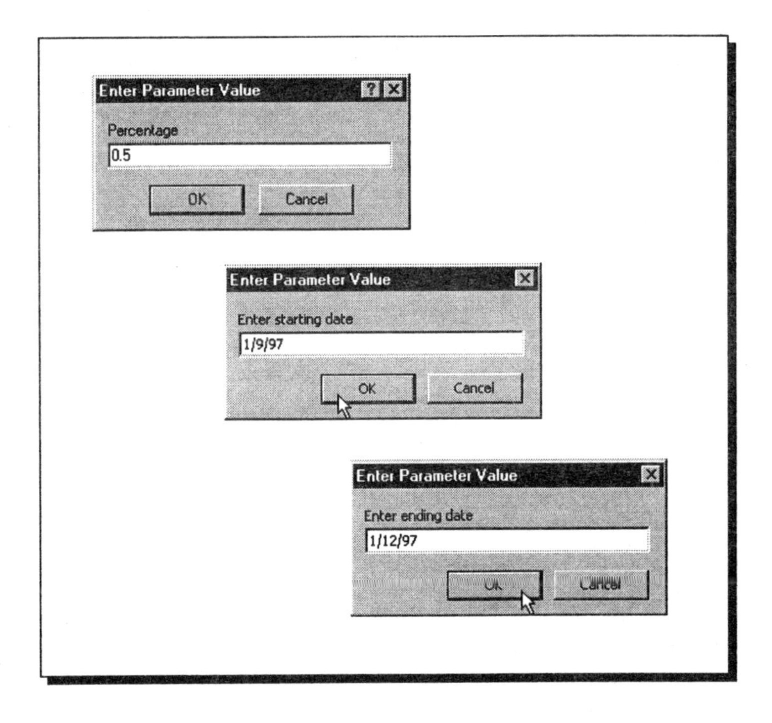

Providing the appropriate input information, displays the result of the search, as follows:

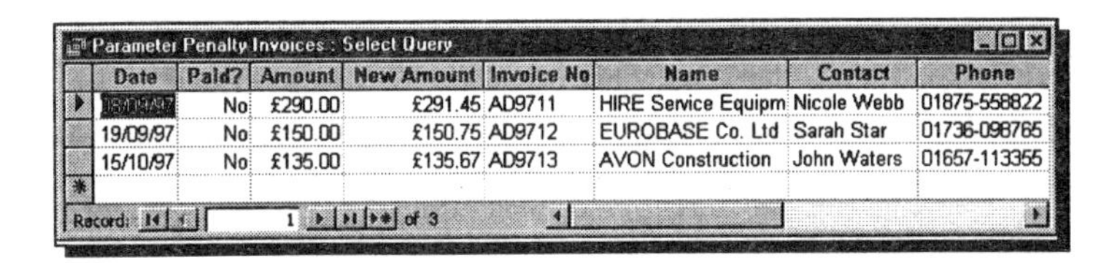

Parameter Penalty Invoices : Select Query

Date	Paid?	Amount	New Amount	Invoice No	Name	Contact	Phone
18/09/97	No	£290.00	£291.45	AD9711	HIRE Service Equipm	Nicole Webb	01875-558822
19/09/97	No	£150.00	£150.75	AD9712	EUROBASE Co. Ltd	Sarah Star	01736-098765
15/10/97	No	£135.00	£135.67	AD9713	AVON Construction	John Waters	01657-113355

Record: 1 of 3

We have saved this query under the name Parameter Penalty Invoices.

Creating a Crosstab Query

You create a *Crosstab Query* to display totals in a compact, spreadsheet format. A Crosstab query can present a large amount of summary data in a more readable form. The layout of the extracted data from such a query is ideal as the basis for a report.

For example, suppose we wanted to examine which of our employees was responsible for our customers' orders in each month. The information is contained in the Orders table of our database as follows:

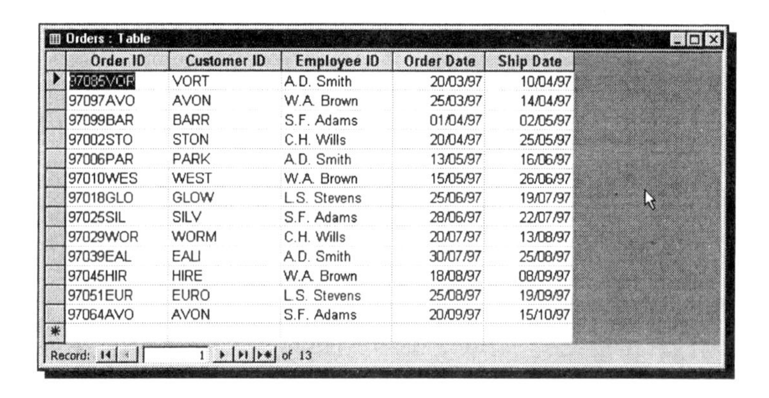

Orders : Table

Order ID	Customer ID	Employee ID	Order Date	Ship Date
97085VOR	VORT	A.D. Smith	20/03/97	10/04/97
97097AVO	AVON	W.A. Brown	25/03/97	14/04/97
97099BAR	BARR	S.F. Adams	01/04/97	02/05/97
97002STO	STON	C.H. Wills	20/04/97	25/05/97
97006PAR	PARK	A.D. Smith	13/05/97	16/06/97
97010WES	WEST	W.A. Brown	15/05/97	26/06/97
97018GLO	GLOW	L.S. Stevens	25/06/97	19/07/97
97025SIL	SILV	S.F. Adams	28/06/97	22/07/97
97029WOR	WORM	C.H. Wills	20/07/97	13/08/97
97039EAL	EALI	A.D. Smith	30/07/97	25/08/97
97045HIR	HIRE	W.A. Brown	18/08/97	08/09/97
97051EUR	EURO	L.S. Stevens	25/08/97	19/09/97
97064AVO	AVON	S.F. Adams	20/09/97	15/10/97

Record: 1 of 13

From the way this information is presented it is very difficult to work out who was responsible for which order in a given month. However, a Crosstab query that lists the names of the employees in rows and each month as a column heading, would be an ideal way to present this type of information.

To create a Crosstab query, open the **Adept 1** database and click first the Queries button, then the **New** button on the Database window. Next, select the **Crosstab Query Wizard** option from the list on the New Query dialogue box, as shown on the next page.

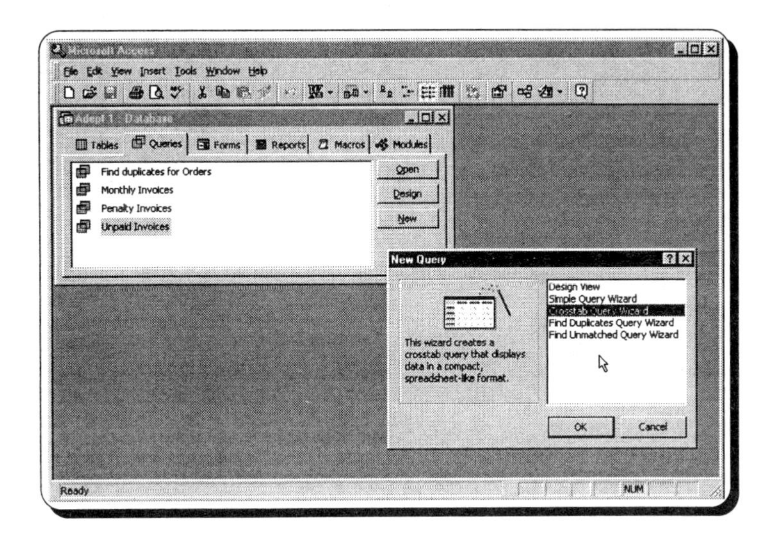

Pressing the **OK** button, causes the Crosstab Query Wizard dialogue box to appear on the screen. Select Orders from the displayed list of tables and press the **Next** button.

From the next dialogue box, select a maximum of three fields from the displayed list, which will become the row headings of the crosstab form. Choose OrderID, CustomerID, and EmployeeID, in that order, as shown here. The order you select these fields is important as Access will list the results of the query in alphabetical order of the first selected field.

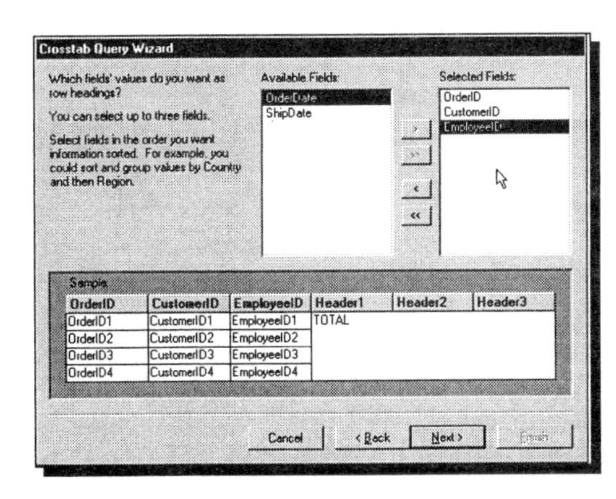

Having selected the three fields, click the **Next** button, and choose the OrderDate as the field whose value you want to be the column headings. Press **Next**, select Month as the time interval by which you want to group your columns and press **Next**. On the following dialogue box choose Count from the Function list and press **Next**. Finally, accept the default name for the query, and press **Finish**.

The results of this Crosstab query are shown below with reduced widths of the monthly columns so that you can see the whole year at a glance.

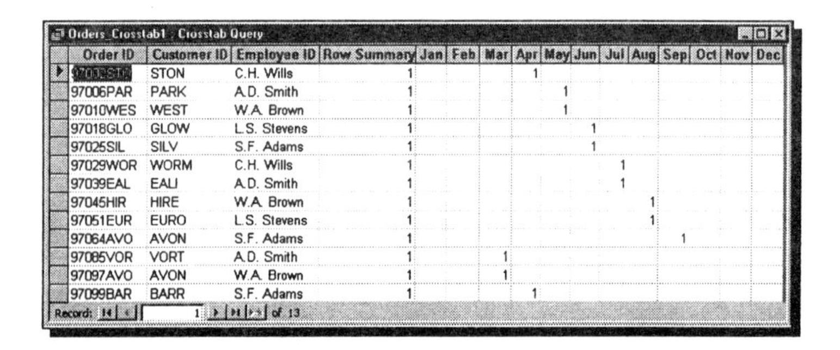

Orders_Crosstab1 : Crosstab Query

Order ID	Customer ID	Employee ID	Row Summary	Jan	Feb	Mar	Apr	May	Jun	Jul	Aug	Sep	Oct	Nov	Dec
[illegible]	STON	C.H. Wills	1				1								
97006PAR	PARK	A.D. Smith	1					1							
97010WES	WEST	W.A. Brown	1					1							
97018GLO	GLOW	L.S. Stevens	1						1						
97025SIL	SILV	S.F. Adams	1						1						
97029WOR	WORM	C.H. Wills	1							1					
97039EAL	EALI	A.D. Smith	1							1					
97045HIR	HIRE	W.A. Brown	1								1				
97051EUR	EURO	L.S. Stevens	1								1				
97064AVO	AVON	S.F. Adams	1									1			
97085VOR	VORT	A.D. Smith	1			1									
97097AVO	AVON	W.A. Brown	1			1									
97099BAR	BARR	S.F. Adams	1				1								

Record: 1 of 13

As you can see from the above screen, the required information is tabulated and is extremely easy to read. However, the displayed recordset is not updatable.

To see the underlying structure of the query, click the Design View button to display the QBE grid, as follows:

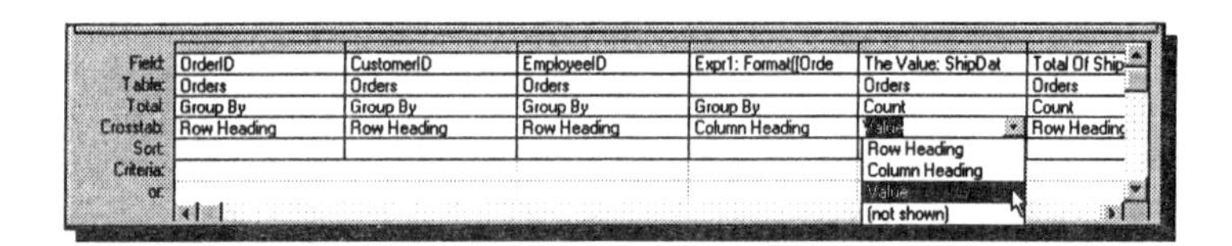

If you want to use a field for grouping, sorting, or setting criteria, but to exclude the field from the recordset, click the arrow in that field's Crosstab cell, and select **(not shown)** from the displayed list.

Creating Queries for Updating Records

When a query is based on either a single table or on two tables with a one-to-one relationship, all the fields in the query are updatable.

Queries which include more than one table, when some of the tables have a one-to-many relationship, are more difficult to design so that they are updatable. Usually, such a query could be designed to be updatable, which is also true of a query that includes an attached table, unless the attached table is a SQL database table with no unique index.

The easiest way of finding out whether you can update records, is to design the query, run it and try to change values in its various fields and also add data. If you can not change values in a field or add data, then you will be warned with an appropriate message on the Status bar.

All other types of queries, such as a Crosstab query, a query with totals, a query with Unique Values property set to Yes, a Union Query, a Pass-through query, a calculated or read-only field, can not be used to update data.

For example, if you try to change the second name under Employee ID from Smith to Smyth, you get the message "This Recordset is not updatable" on the Status bar at the bottom of the screen, as shown below.

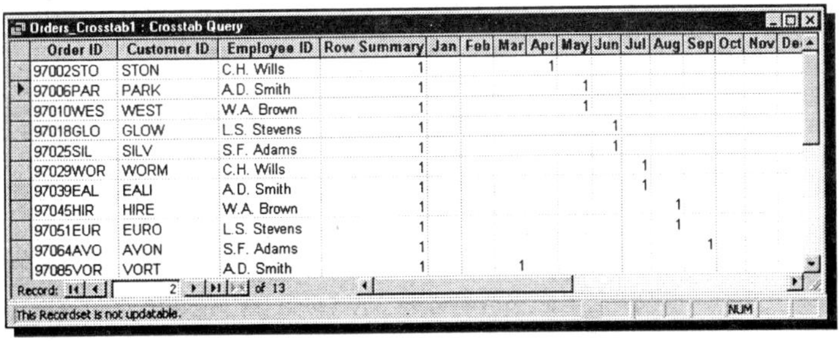

Orders_Crosstab1 : Crosstab Query

Order ID	Customer ID	Employee ID	Row Summary	Jan	Feb	Mar	Apr	May	Jun	Jul	Aug	Sep	Oct	Nov	De
97002STO	STON	C.H. Wills	1				1								
97006PAR	PARK	A.D. Smith	1					1							
97010WES	WEST	W.A. Brown	1					1							
97018GLO	GLOW	L.S. Stevens	1						1						
97025SIL	SILV	S.F. Adams	1						1						
97029WOR	WORM	C.H. Wills	1							1					
97039EAL	EALI	A.D. Smith	1							1					
97045HIR	HIRE	W.A. Brown	1								1				
97051EUR	EURO	L.S. Stevens	1								1				
97064AVO	AVON	S.F. Adams	1									1			
97085VOR	VORT	A.D. Smith	1			1									

Record: 2 of 13

This Recordset is not updatable. NUM

Creating Action Queries

You can create *Action Queries* in the same way as Select Queries. Action Queries are used to make bulk changes to data rather than simply displaying data. For this reason, Action Queries can be dangerous for the novice, simply because they change your database.

There are four different types of Action Queries, with the following functions:

Type of Query	***Function***
Append query	Adds records from one or more tables to another table or tables.
Delete query	Deletes records from a table or tables.
Make-table query	Creates a new table from all or part of another table or tables.
Update query	Changes the data in a group of records

In the previous version of Access, you could quickly create an Action query which moved old orders to an Old Orders Archive table, by using the Archive Query Wizard. A query created by this Wizard will still run quite happily in the new version of Access, but if you want to design such a query from scratch, then you will have to go through the following steps:

- Use the Make-table query to copy selected records from an existing table into a new named, say, Old Orders Archive table.
- Change the design of the Make-table query so that on subsequent execution of the query it Appends selected records from your original table to the Old Orders Archive table.
- Use the Delete query to delete the archived records from the original table.

In what follows, we will go through the steps necessary to create an Old Orders Archive query.

- Open the database **Adept 1** and click first the Queries tab, then the **New** button on the Database window.

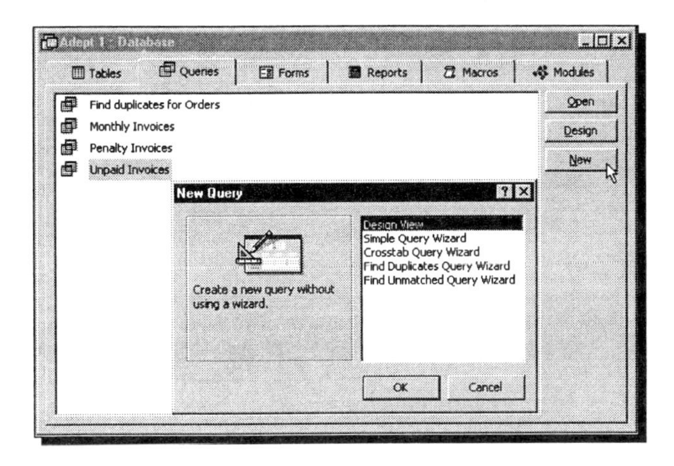

- Select Design View from the displayed list in the New Query dialogue box, shown above, and press **OK**.

- In the Show Table dialogue box that opens next, select Orders, as shown here, then press the **Add** button, followed by the **Close** button. This adds the Orders table to the Select Query window which also contains the QBE grid, so that you can design an appropriate query.

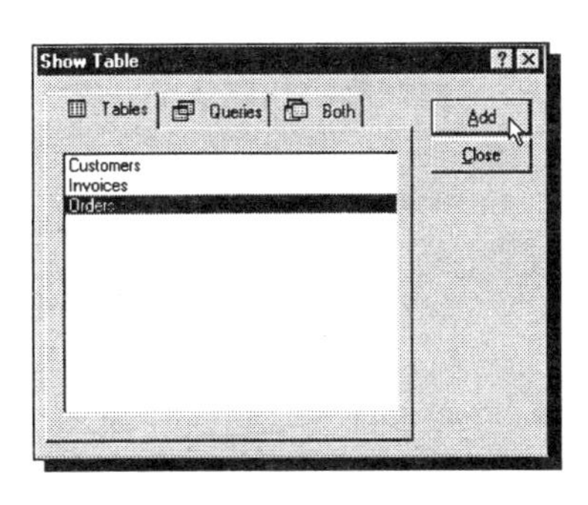

- Drag all the fields from the Orders table onto the QBE grid, and add in the OrderDate field the criteria <=4/4/97, as shown below.

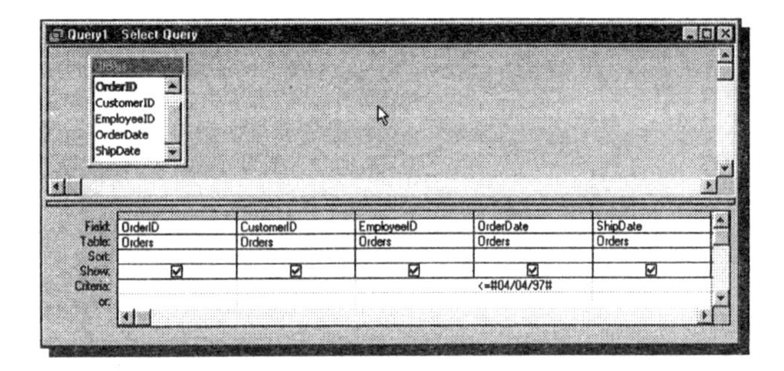

- Click the Query Type button on the Toolbar, shown here, which displays below it the adjacent menu-list of available query types. Select the **Make-Table** option and click the left mouse button which causes the Make Table dialogue box to appear on the screen. Type the name of the new table, say, Old Orders Archive, and press **OK**.

- Press the Run button on the Toolbar, shown here, which causes a warning dialogue box to be displayed. In our example, we are told that three records are about to be appended onto our new table. Pressing **Yes**, copies the selected records from the Orders table to the newly created Old Orders Archive table.

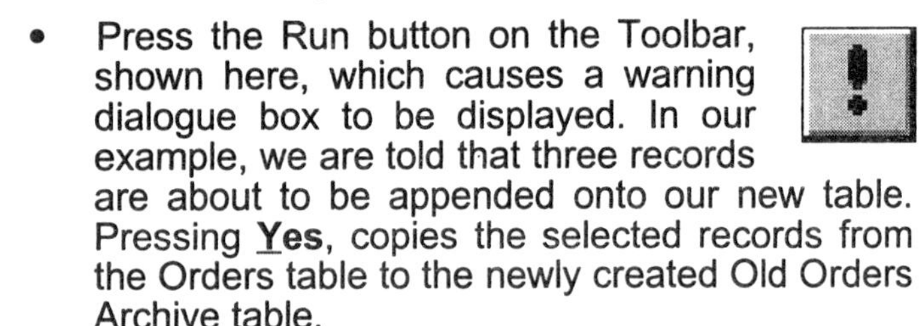

- Next, click the Query Type button on the Toolbar, but this time select the Append option. The Append dialogue box is displayed with the Old Orders Archive name appearing as default. Press **OK** and close the Append Query window.

* On clicking the 'X' button to close the Append Query window, you will be asked whether you would like your design to be saved. Select **Yes**.
* In the displayed Save As dialogue box, type the new name for the query. We chose to call it Append to Old Orders Archive.

As an exercise, go through the steps of designing the Make Table query, but select the Delete option of the Query Type menu. If you choose to do this, Access places two new queries in the Query list, as shown below. These have an exclamation point attached to their icon so that you don't run them inadvertently.

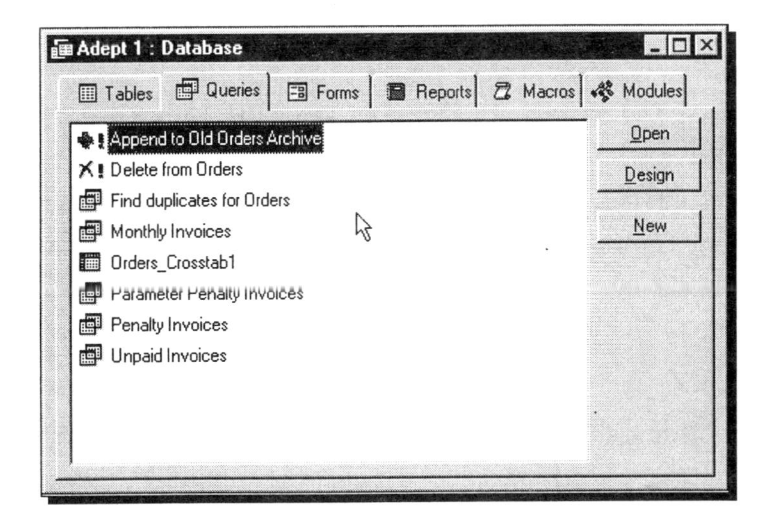

In all, there are four Action queries available in Access. Below we list these, together with their function.

1 The Make-Table query; used to create a table by retrieving the records that meet certain criteria and using them to create a new table.

2 The Append query; used to append (add) records from one table to another existing table.

3. The Update query; used to change data in existing tables, such as the cost per hour charged to your customers.
4. The Delete query; used to delete (remove) records that meet certain pre-defined criteria from a table.

7. USING FORMS & REPORTS

We saw towards the end of Chapter 3 how easy it was to create a single column form to view our Customers table. To see this again, open **Adept 1** and in the Database window click the Form tab, then double-click on Form1, which should display the following:

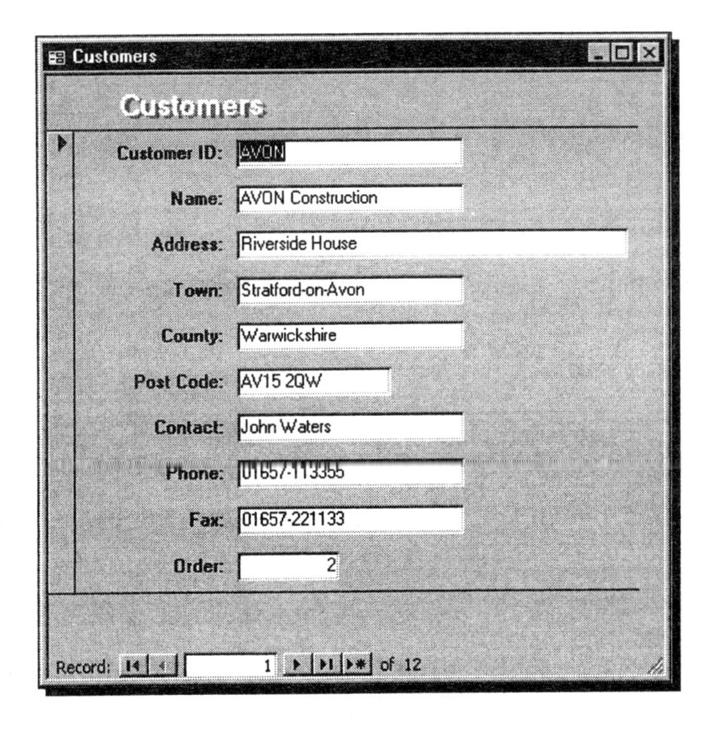

You can use forms to find, edit, and add data in a convenient manner. Access provides you with an easy way of designing various types of forms, some of which are discussed here. Forms look good on screen, but do not produce very good output on paper, whereas reports are designed to look good on paper, but do not necessarily look good on screen.

Using the Form Wizard

Using the Form Wizard, you can easily display data from either a table or a query in form view.

In the Database window, first click the Forms tab, then the **New** button which opens the New Form dialogue box in which you must choose either a table or a query on which to base the new form. In the screen dump below, we have chosen the Invoices table.

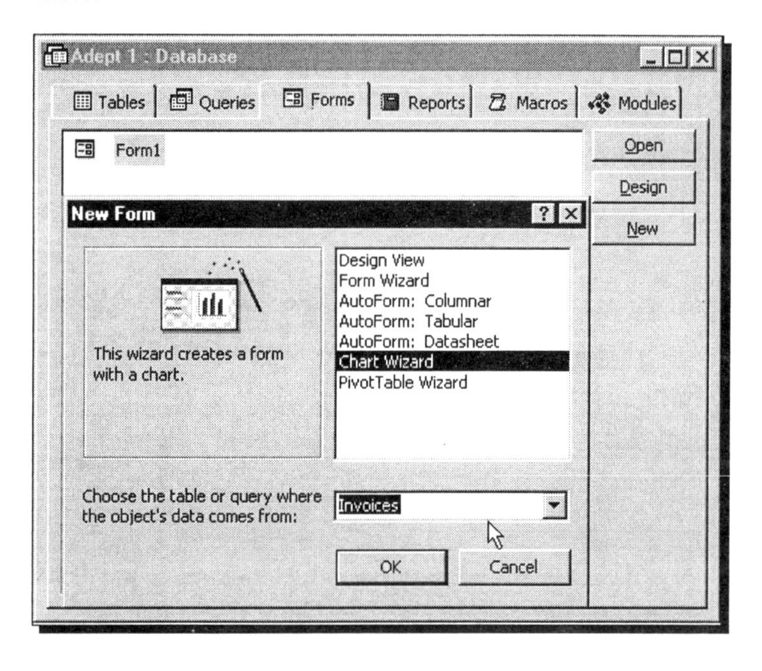

Next, select the **Chart Wizard** option which causes the Form Wizard to display a number of dialogue boxes. As usual, after making appropriate selections, click the **Next** button to progress through the automatic design of the particular form. As you can see from the above screen dump, there are 7 different types of forms available for you to choose from. Their function will be discussed shortly.

To continue with our example, the Wizard displays the following dialogue box in which you are asked to specify the fields that contain the data you want to chart. We chose InvoiceID and Amount.

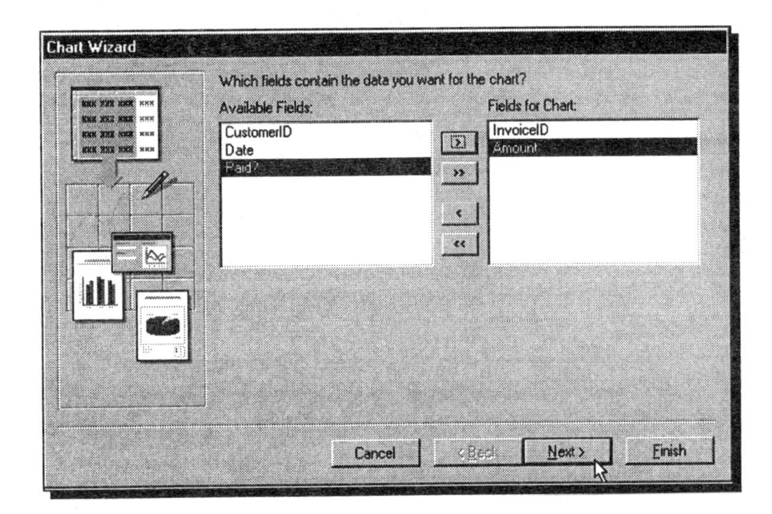

This opens another dialogue box in which you are asked what type of chart you would like. We chose the first one on the second row before pressing **Next**.

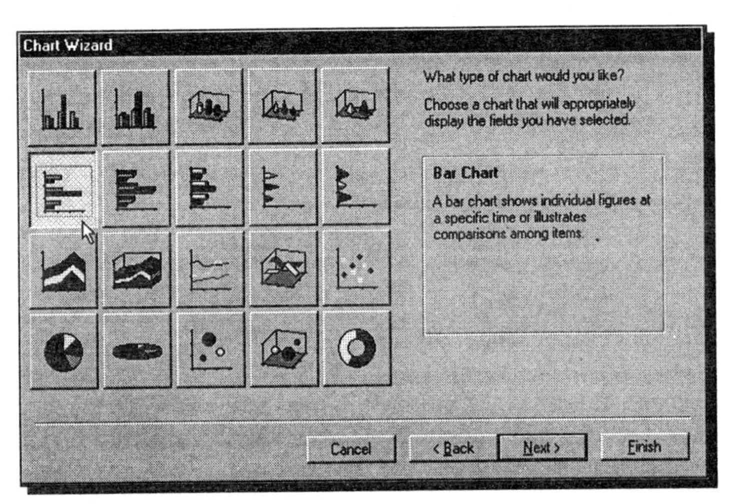

In the following dialogue box, double-click the x-axis button (the one with the caption 'SumOfAmount') and select 'None' from the list in the displayed Summarize dialogue box, shown below, and press **OK**.

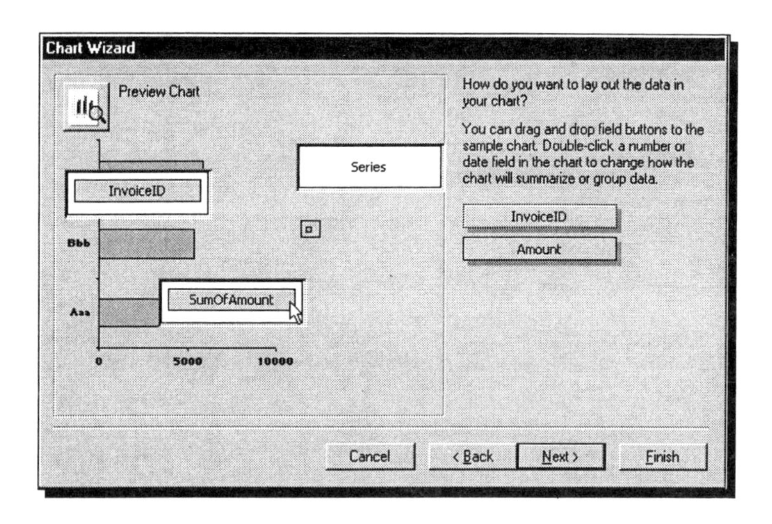

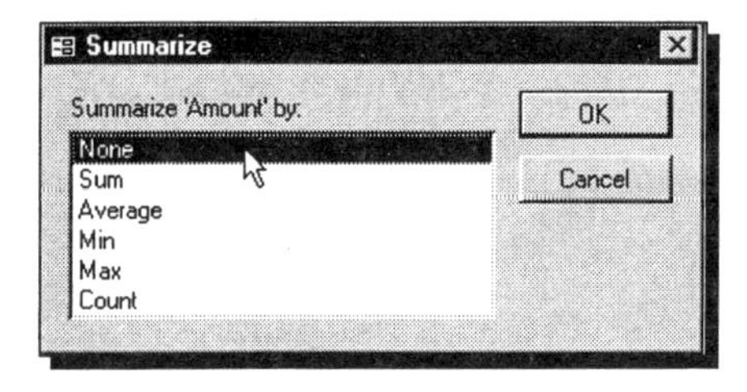

The Wizard then asks you what title and name to give to this form - we chose 'Invoice Amounts' and 'Invoice Chart'.

Pressing the **Finish** button, allows the Wizard to display the final result, shown here to the left. It is as easy as that to get a graphical view of the amounts involved in each of your invoices.

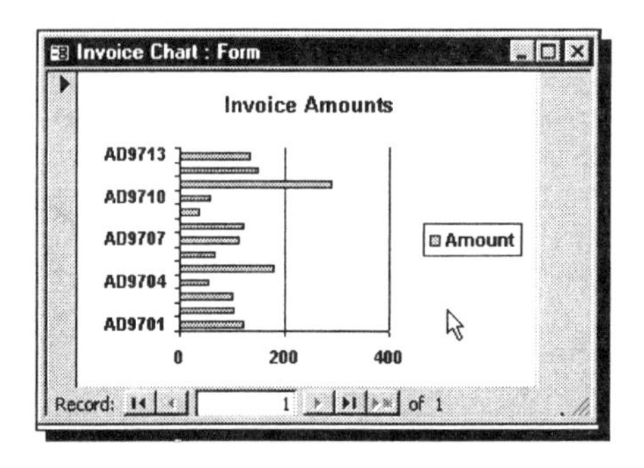

The available choice of Form Wizards have the following function:

Type of Form	*Function*
Design View	Designs a form from scratch.
Form Wizard	Automatically creates a form based on the fields you select.
AutoForm: Columnar	Creates a columnar form with all the field labels appearing in the first column and the data in the second. The form displays one record at a time.
AutoForm: Tabular	Tabulates a screen full of records in tabular form with the field labels appearing at the head of each column.
AutoForm: Datasheet	Similar to the Tabular form, but in worksheet display format.
Chart Wizard	Displays data graphically.
PivotTable Wizard	Creates a form with an Excel PivotTable - an interactive table that can summarise a large number of data using the format and calculation methods specified by the user.

Access also allows you to design a form that contains another form. This type of form, called main/subform, allows data from related tables to be viewed at the same time.

Customising a Form

You can customise a form by changing the appearance of text, data, and any other attributes. To have a look at some of these options, double click on Form1 to display the Customers form, then click the Design View button on the Toolbar.

What appears on your screen is shown below:

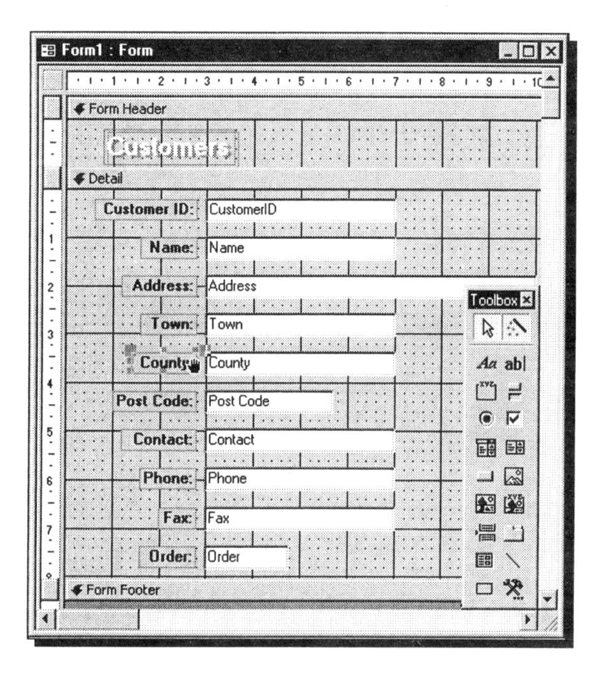

As you can see, a form in Design View is made up of boxes attached to a grid. Clicking at the County box, for example, causes markers to appear around it as shown above. When the mouse pointer is then placed within either the label box or data box, it changes to a hand which indicates that you can drag the box to a new position, as we have done above. This method moves both label and data boxes together.

If you look more closely at the markers around the label and data boxes, you will see that they are of different size, as shown below.

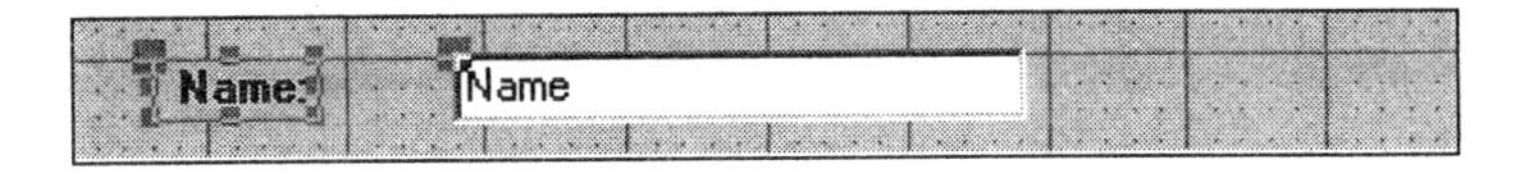

The larger ones are 'move' handles, while the smaller ones are 'size' handles. In the above example you can use the 'move' handles of either the label or the data box to move one independently of the other. The label box can also be sized. To size the data box, click on it so that the markers appear around it.

Boxes on a form can be made larger by simply pointing to the sizing handles and dragging them in the appropriate direction.

In addition to moving and enlarging label and data boxes, you can further customise a form using the various new buttons that appear on the Tool bar when in Design View, shown below in two tiers.

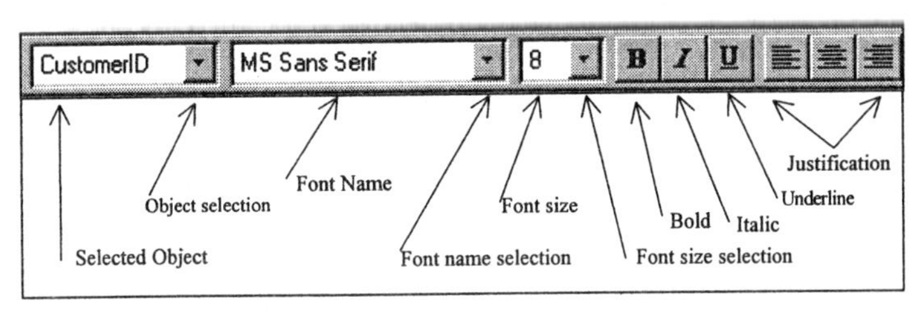

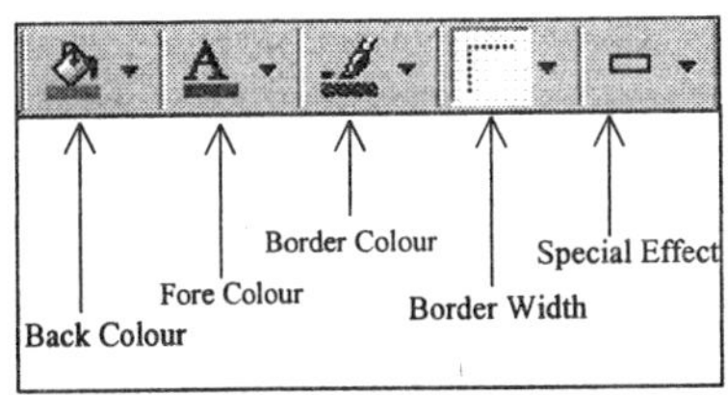

Do try and experiment with moving and sizing label and data boxes and also increasing their font size. If you don't like the result, simply don't save it. Skills gained here will be used in the Report design section later on.

The Toolbox

The Toolbox can be used either to design a Form or Report from scratch (a task beyond the scope of this book), or to add controls to them, such as a Combo (drop-down) box. The function of each tool on the Toolbox is listed below.

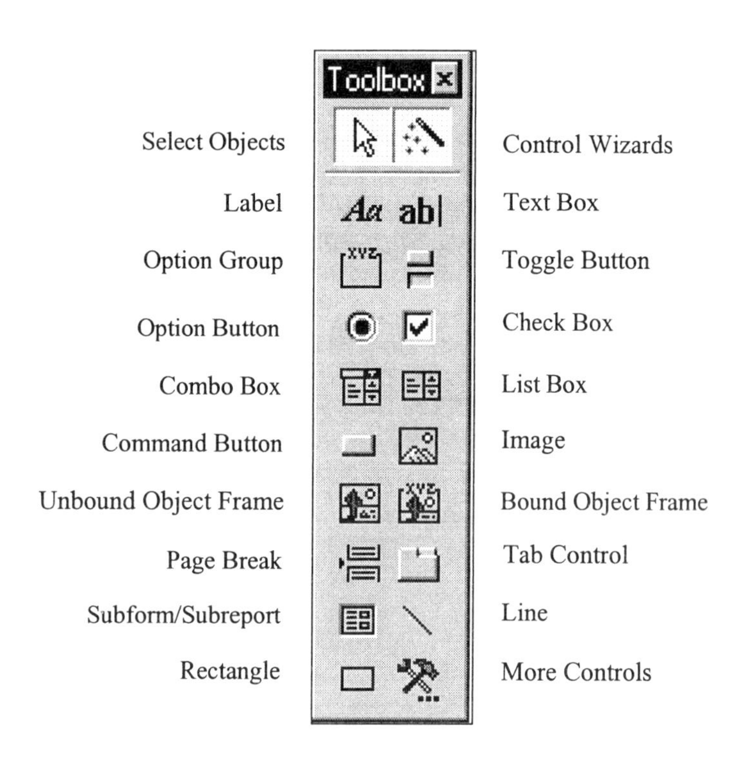

As an example of using the Toolbox, let us assume that we would like to use a form to enter new data into our Invoices table, but with the ability of selecting the CustomerID field from a drop-down menu - a Combo box.

To achieve the above, execute the following steps:

- In the Database window first click the Forms tab followed by the **New** button.
- In the New Form dialogue box select the **Form Wizard** option, choose Invoices as the table on which to base the new Form, and press the **OK** button.
- In the second dialogue box, select all the fields from the Invoices table, and click the **Next** button.
- In the third dialogue box, select **Columnar** as the preferred form layout, and press **Next**.
- In the fourth dialogue box, select **Standard** as the preferred style for your form and press **Next**.
- In the fifth dialogue box, name your form 'Add Invoices', and press **Finish**. The following form is created and displayed on your screen.

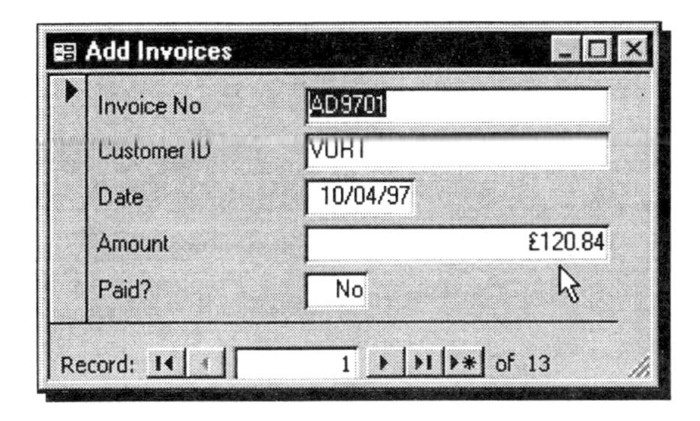

- When the above form appears on the screen, click the Design View button on the Toolbar, and enlarge the Add Invoices form so that both the Header and Footer sections are visible on the form.
- Click the CustomerID field on the form, and delete both its Label and Data boxes by clicking each individually and pressing the <Del> key.

- Click the Combo Box on the Toolbox, and point and click at the area where the CustomerID field used to be on the form.
- In the subsequent dialogue boxes, select options which will cause the Combo Box to look up the values from the Customers table, and from the CustomerID field and store a selected value in the CustomerID field. Specify that the Combo Box should have the label Customer ID:.
- Move and size both the Label and Data boxes of the Combo box into the position shown below.

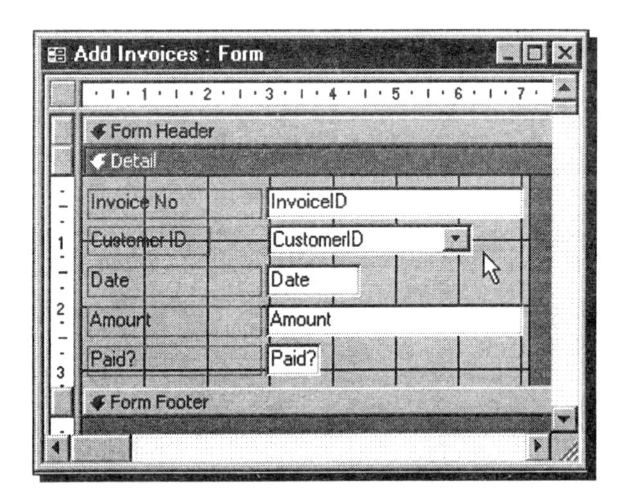

- Click the Form View button on the Toolbar, followed by the New Record button at the bottom of the Add Invoices form, both of which are shown below.

- The entry form should now look as follows:

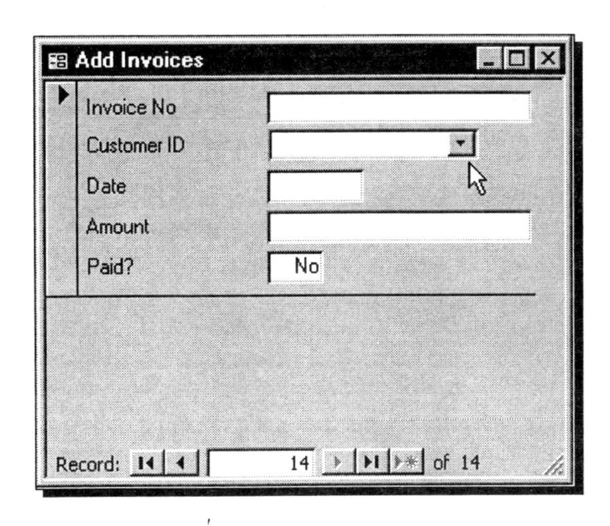

From now on, whenever you want to add a new invoice to the Invoices table, use the Add Invoices form from the Database window, then click the New Record button on either the Toolbar or the Add Invoices form itself to display an empty form. Next, type in the relevant information in the appropriate data boxes on the form, but when you come to fill in the Customer ID field, click instead the down arrow against its data box to display the drop-down menu shown here. Select one of the existing customers on the list, and click the Next Record button at the bottom of the Add Invoices form.

Try the above procedure with the following details:

```
AD9714   WEST     28/10/97     £140
```

then verify that indeed the information has been recorded by double-clicking the Invoices table on the Database window.

Using the Report Wizard

We will use the skills gained in manipulating Forms in Design View to produce an acceptable report created by the Report Wizard. To produce a report of the Unpaid Invoices query, do the following:

- Click the Reports tab on the Database window and then press the **Next** button.
- In the New Report dialogue box, select the **Report Wizard** option, and choose the 'Unpaid Invoices' as the query where the object's data will come from, and press **OK**.
- Select all the fields (except for the Paid? field) which are to appear on your report and click the **Next** button.
- Select the InvoiceID field as the sort field, and accept all subsequent default settings. Call the report 'Unpaid Invoices Report'. The report is created for you as follows:

Unpaid Invoices Report

Invoice No	*Order ID*	*Amount*	*Name*	*Contact*	*Phone*
AD9701	97085VOR	£120.84	VORTEX Co. Ltd	Brian Storm	01776-223344
AD9703	97099BAR	£99.32	BARROWS Associ	Mandy Brown	01554-664422
AD9704	97002STO	£55.98	STONEAGE Ltd	Mike Irons	01765-234567
AD9705	97006PAR	£180.22	PARKWAY Gravel	James Stone	01534-987654
AD9706	97010WES	£68.52	WESTWOOD Ltd	Mary Slim	01234-667755
AD9707	97018GLO	£111.56	GLOWORM Ltd	Peter Summers	01432-746523
AD9709	97029WOR	£35.87	WORMGLAZE Ltd	Richard Glazer	01123-654321
AD9710	97039EAL	£58.95	EALING Engines D	Trevor Miles	01336-010107
AD9711	97045HIR	£290.00	HIRE Service Equi	Nicole Webb	01875-558822
AD9712	97051EUR	£150.00	EUROBASE Co. Lt	Sarah Star	01736-098765
AD9713	97097AVO	£135.00	AVON Constructio	John Waters	01657-113355
AD9713	97064AVO	£135.00	AVON Constructio	John Waters	01657-113355

Obviously this report is not quite acceptable. The problem is mainly the fact that all text fields are left justified within their columns, while numerical fields are right justified.

What we need to do is display it in Design View so that we can change the position of the numeric fields. To do this, double-click the Unpaid Invoices Report in the Database window to display it on screen, then click the Design View icon on the Toolbar which displays the Report as follows:

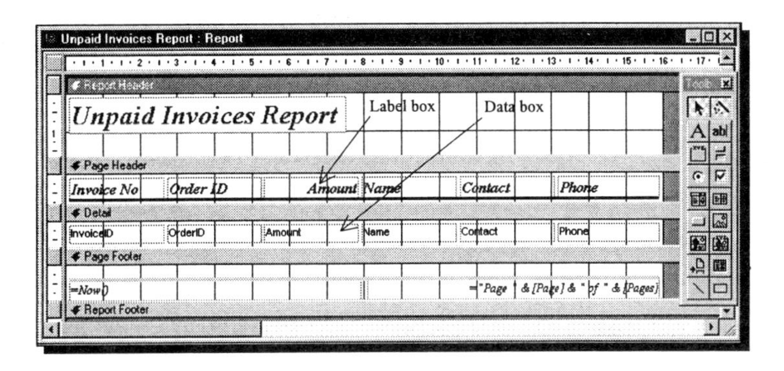

Use the mouse to move the Amount data box to the left, and then right justify the text in the Amount label and data boxes and make them smaller, as shown below.

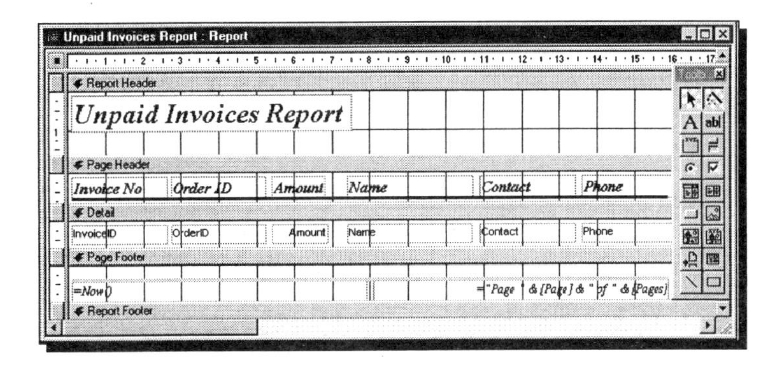

The corresponding report is now as follows:

Unpaid Invoices Report

Invoice No	*Order ID*	*Amount*	*Name*	*Contact*	*Phone*
AD9701	97085VOR	£120.84	VORTEX Co. Ltd	Brian Storm	01776-223344
AD9703	97099BAR	£99.32	BARROWS Associate	Mandy Brown	01554-664422
AD9704	97002STO	£55.98	STONEAGE Ltd	Mike Irons	01765-234567
AD9705	97006PAR	£180.22	PARKWAY Gravel	James Stone	01534-987654
AD9706	97010WES	£68.52	WESTWOOD Ltd	Mary Slim	01234-667755
AD9707	97018GLO	£111.56	GLOWORM Ltd	Peter Summers	01432-746523
AD9709	97029WOR	£35.87	WORMGLAZE Ltd	Richard Glazer	01123-654321
AD9710	97039EAL	£58.95	EALING Engines Desi	Trevor Miles	01336-010107
AD9711	97045HIR	£290.00	HIRE Service Equipm	Nicole Webb	01875-558822
AD9712	97051EUR	£150.00	EUROBASE Co. Ltd	Sarah Star	01736-098765
AD9713	97097AVO	£135.00	AVON Construction	John Waters	01657-113355
AD9713	97064AVO	£135.00	AVON Construction	John Waters	01657-113355

This layout is obviously far more acceptable than that of the original report created by the Report Wizard.

8. MASKING AND FILTERING DATA

In this chapter we discuss two aspects of working with data; masking and filtering. The first is useful for restricting data input into an Access field, such as a postcode or a telephone number, to a given data mask so as to eliminate input errors. The second is invaluable if you are thinking of importing data into Access either from a flat-file database or spreadsheet, or exporting data from Access into another Windows package, such as Microsoft Word or Excel.

The Input Mask Property

You can use the Input Mask property to make data entry easier and control the values you enter in a text box. For example, you could create an input mask for a Post Code field that shows you exactly how to enter a new postcode.

To see an input mask, open the **Adept 1** database, select the Customers table, press the **Design** button, and select the Post Code field. The input mask appears in the Field Properties box, shown below.

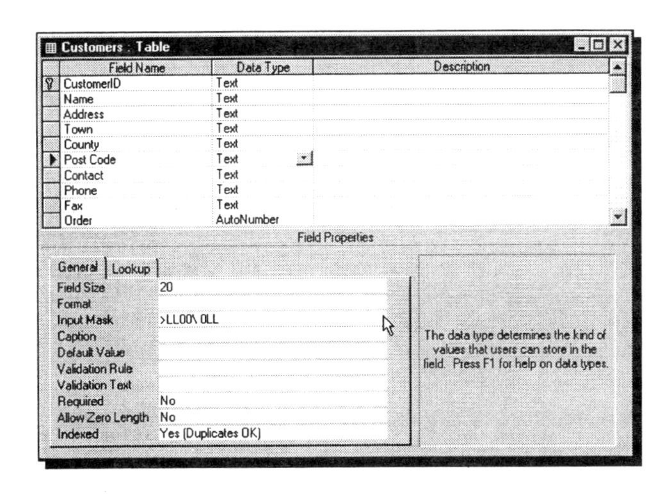

The Input Mask property can contain up to three sections separated by semicolons (;). Within each section a certain number of characters are allowed. These characters and their description are listed below.

Character	***Description***
0	Signifies a digit (0 to 9); entry required. The plus (+) and minus (-) signs are not allowed.
9	Signifies a digit or space; entry not required. The plus and minus signs are not allowed.
#	Signifies a digit or space; entry not required, spaces are displayed as blanks while in Edit mode, but blanks are removed when data is saved. The plus and minus signs are allowed.
L	Signifies a letter (A to Z); entry required.
?	Signifies a letter (A to Z); entry optional.
A	Signifies a letter or digit; entry required.
a	Signifies a letter or digit; entry optional.
&	Signifies any character or a space; entry required.
C	Signifies any character or a space; entry optional.
. , : ; - /	Signifies a decimal placeholder and thousand, date, and time separators. (The actual character used depends on the settings in the Regional Settings section of the Windows Control Panel).
<	Causes all characters to be converted to lowercase.
>	Causes all characters to be converted to uppercase.

!	Causes the input mask to display from right to left, rather than from left to right, when characters on the left side of the input mask are optional. Characters typed into the mask always fill it from left to right. You can include the exclamation point anywhere in the input mask.
\	Causes the character that follows to be displayed as the literal character (for example, \A is displayed as just A).

Thus, we can interpret the postcode shown in our earlier screen dump as follows:

>	Convert all characters entered to upper case.
L	Letter (A-Z) expected; entry required.
L	Letter (A-Z) expected; entry required.
0	Digit (0-9) expected; entry required.
0	Digit (0-9) expected; entry required.
\	Cause character following backslash (in this case a space) to appear as such
0	Digit (0-9) expected; entry required.
L	Letter (A-Z) expected; entry required.
L	Letter (A-Z) expected; entry required.

However, this postcode two letters followed by two numbers, then a space followed by one number, then two letters, will not be adequate for all the variations of postcode encountered in the UK.

For example, some codes have only one number following the first two letters, like CB1 2PU, others particularly in London have only one leading letter, like N1 0RD, while if you write to the BBC you will need the W1A 1AA code.

Thus, a postcode mask suitable for most eventualities in the UK could be:

>LAa&\ 0LL

To experiment with input masks, place the insertion pointer in the Post Code field of the Customers table. This causes a dotted button to appear at the extreme right of the field which, when clicked, activates the Input Mask Wizard, as shown below.

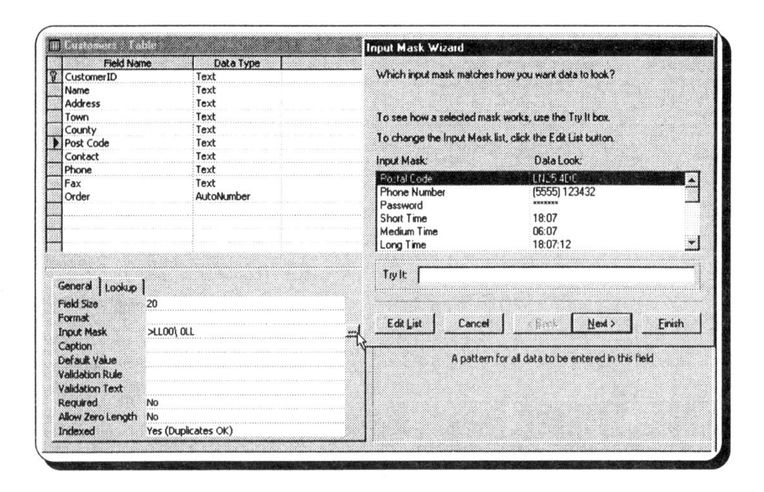

Select the Post Code from the Input Mask list, and press **Next** to display the second dialogue box in which you can edit the default Input Mask. You can also type the variations of the postcode in the Try It box.

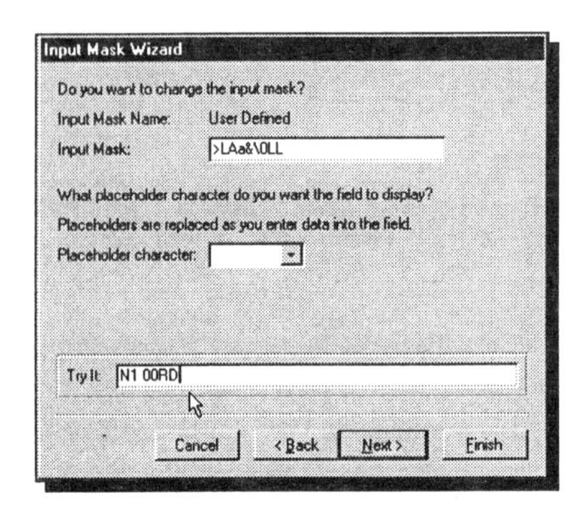

Always place the insertion pointer at the extreme left of the Try It box, and provide one space between the two sections of the postcode (two if the first section has only 2 characters. Can you think of a better input mask?

Note: If you want to create a password-entry control, use the Password input mask to set the Input Mask property to the word 'Password'. This displays an asterisk (*) on the screen for every typed character.

Only characters that you type directly in a control or combo box are affected by the input mask. Microsoft Access ignores any input masks when you import data, or run an action query.

If you define an input mask and also set the Format property for the same field, the Format property takes precedence when the data is displayed. The data in the underlying table itself is not changed, but the Format property affects the way it is displayed.

The three sections of an input mask and their description are listed below.

Section	***Description***
First	Specifies the input mask itself, for example, >LL00\ 0LL or (0000) 000000.
Second	Specifies whether Microsoft Access stores the literal display characters in the table when you enter data. If you use 0 for this section, all literal display characters (for example, the parentheses in a phone number input mask) are stored with the value; if you enter 1 or leave this section blank, only characters typed into the control are stored.
Third	Specifies the character that Microsoft Access displays for the space where you should type a character in the input mask. For this section, you can use any character; to display an empty string, use a space enclosed in quotation marks (" ").

The Input Mask Wizard will set the property for you.

Importing or Linking Data

Microsoft Access has an extensive help topic on importing and linking data created in other programs. Below we present the most important parts of this information so as to make it easy for you to follow.

Access can import or link table data from other Access databases (versions 1.x, 2.0, 7.0/97, and 97), as well as data from other programs, such as Excel, dBASE, FoxPro, or Paradox. You can also import or link (read-only) HTML tables and lists, which can reside on your local PC, a network, or an Internet server.

Importing data creates a copy of the information in a new table in your current Access database; the source table or file is not altered. Linking data allows you to read and update data in the external data source without importing; the external data source's format is not altered so that you can continue to use the file with the program that created it originally, and you can also add, delete, or edit such data using Access.

In general, you import or link information depending on the imposed situation, as follows:

Imposed Situation	*Method to Adopt*
Inserted data needs to be updated in Access as changes are made to the data in the source file, or Source file will always be available and you want to minimise the size of the Access data file.	Link
Inserted information might need to be updated but source file might not be always accessible, or Access data file needs to be edited without having these changes reflected in the source file.	Import

If you have data in any of the following programs or formats, you can either import or link such files.

Data source	***Version or Format***
Excel spreadsheets	2, 3, 4, 5, 7/95, & 97
Lotus 1-2-3 spreadsheets	.wks, .wk1, .wk3, & .wk4
dBASE	III, III+, IV, & 5
FoxPro	2.x, & 3.0 (import only)
Paradox	3.x, 4.x, & 5.0
Delimited text files	Most files with values separated by commas, tabs, or other characters; must be in MS-DOS or Windows ANSI text format
Fixed-width text files	Most files with values arranged so that each field has a certain width; must be in MS-DOS or Windows ANSI text format
HTML	1.0 (if a list), 2.0, 3.x (if a table or list)

If you have a program which can export, convert, or save its data in one of these formats, you can import that data as well.

Access uses different icons to represent linked tables and tables that are stored in the current database, as shown here. The icon that represents a linked table remains in the Database window along with tables in the current database, so you can open the table whenever you want.

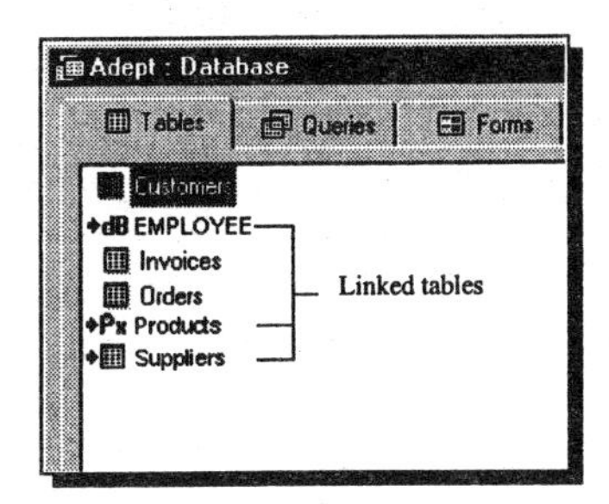

Microsoft Access displays a different icon for tables from each type of source database. If you delete the icon for a linked table, you delete the link to the table, but not the external table itself.

When importing data, you cannot append it to existing tables (except when importing spreadsheet or text files). However, once you have imported a table, you can use an append query to add its data to another table.

You can also import database objects other than tables, such as forms or reports, from another Access database. When importing such objects from another Access database, you can choose to import all, or just a subset of those objects, in a single operation.

When you link or embed an object, such as a ClipArt image or an image you've scanned and saved, in a Microsoft Access form or report, the object is displayed in an object frame. To illustrate this point, start Access, select the Forms tab, and open Form1, which we created in Chapter 3. Then do the following:

- Switch to Design View, then use the **Insert, Object** menu command which displays the Insert Object dialogue box.
- Select the source application from the **Object Type** list (we have selected the Microsoft Clip Gallery - you need a CD-ROM), and press **OK**.

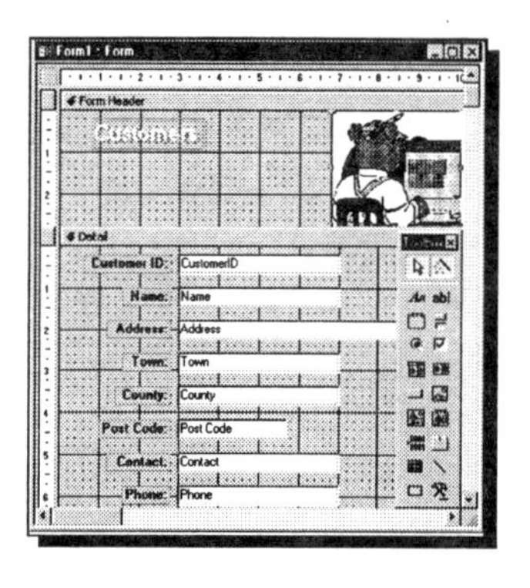

- Select the object and press **Insert**. This inserts the object into an unbound frame.

If the object you are embedding is from an Access table, use a bound object frame.

Converting Data to Microsoft Access

If you have been using Microsoft Excel, another spreadsheet, or a flat-file database to keep an invoicing list, you will soon run out of disc space, as such lists include repeated data, such as the address information on invoices issued to the same firm.

Converting a list from Excel to Access is extremely easy; simply start Excel, open the workbook that contains your list, then use the **Data, Convert to MS Access** command (if the command is not available, use the **Tools, Add-Ins** command to add the Microsoft AccessLinks Add-In program). From that point on, an Access wizard takes over and steps you through the process of conversion, which will be discussed shortly.

Converting a list from another spreadsheet or a flat-file database, whose format cannot be read by Access, requires you to use the original package to save the list in a format Access can import. To illustrate the point, we will step through the conversion process, using data that was originally created in a flat-file database, as follows:

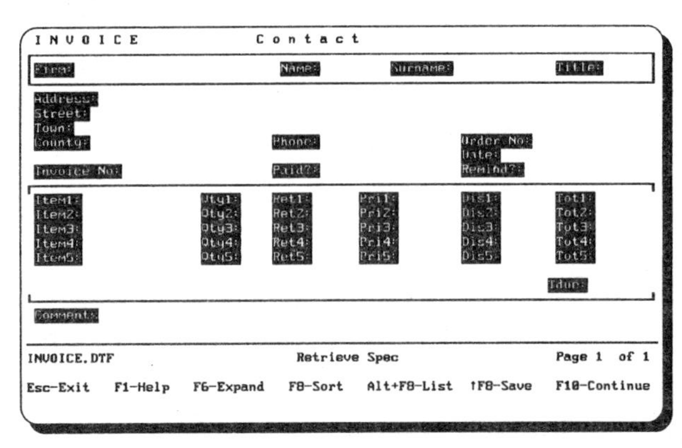

Your database is bound to be different. In what follows, it would be beneficial to you if you could use your own flat-file database data while following our example.

First, we used the package's export facility to convert and save the data into dBASE IV format. Our package displayed the screen below. Yours, of course, might display a different screen.

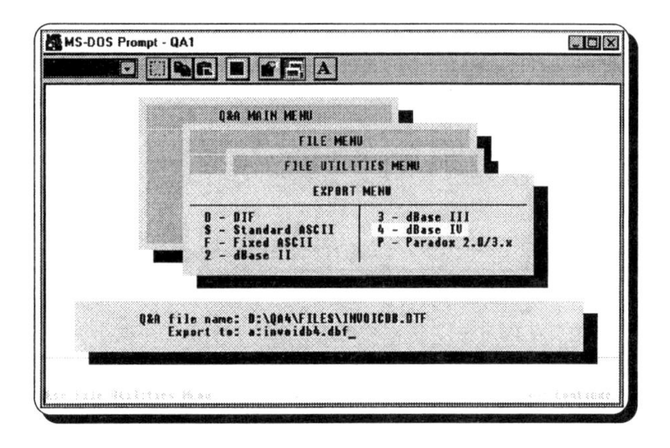

We saved the exported dBASE file in the A: drive, under the filename **Invoidb4.dbf** (we choose here the 8.3 character naming convention demanded by the package). The three character file extension **.dbf** is essential so that Access can recognise such a file as a dBASE type.

Next, start Access, and select to Create a New Database Using a **Blank Database**, as shown below.

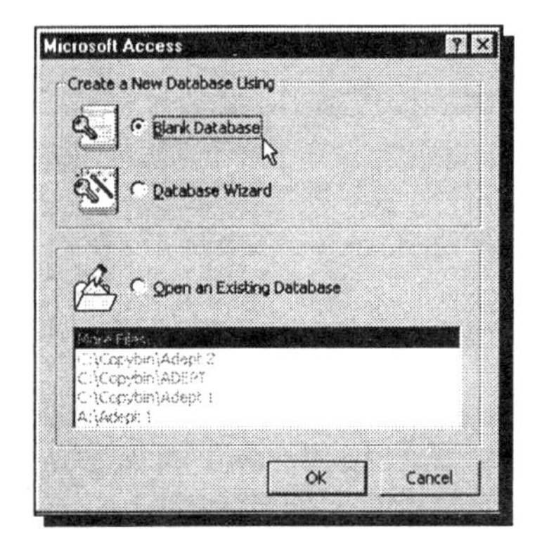

If Access is already running, click the New Database button on the Toolbar, then click the General tab and accept the blank database design. Pressing **OK**, displays the File New Database dialogue box, shown on the next page.

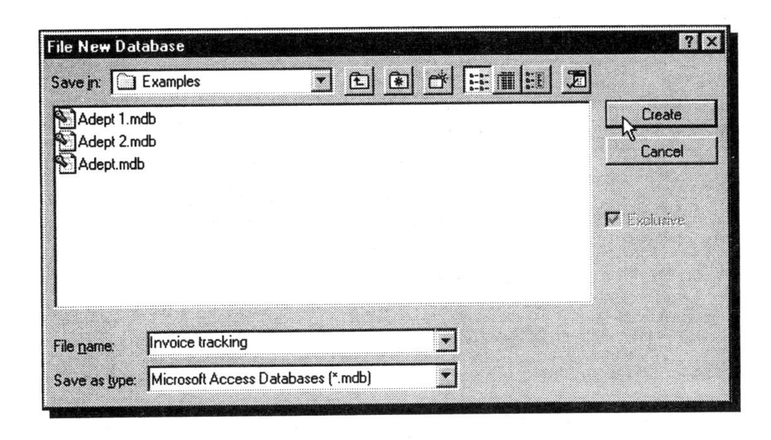

In the **File name** box type the name 'Invoice tracking', and in the **Save in** box specify the folder in which you would like to save your database (we chose the Access\Examples folder) and press the **Create** button.

When the new database window appears, use the **File, Get External Data, Import** command. In the displayed Import window, select **dBASE IV** in the **Files of type** box and instruct Access to **Look in** the drive and folder you have saved the **invoidb4.dbf** file, as shown below.

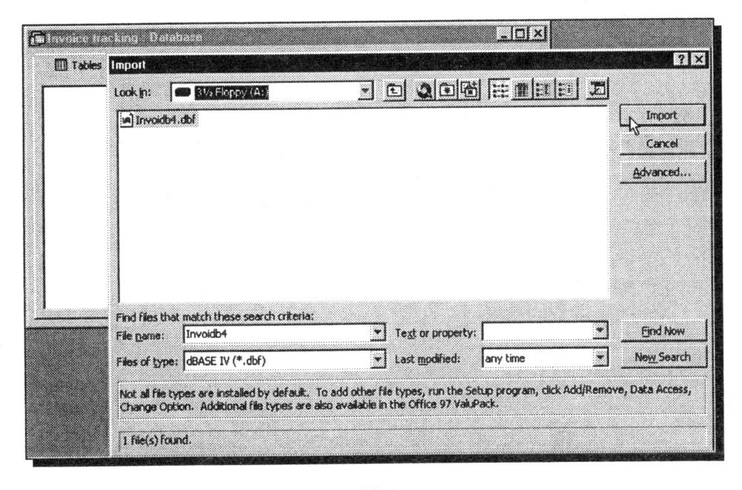

Pressing the **Import** button, automatically imports your data into the **Invoice tracking** file. When this is done successfully, Access displays the following box:

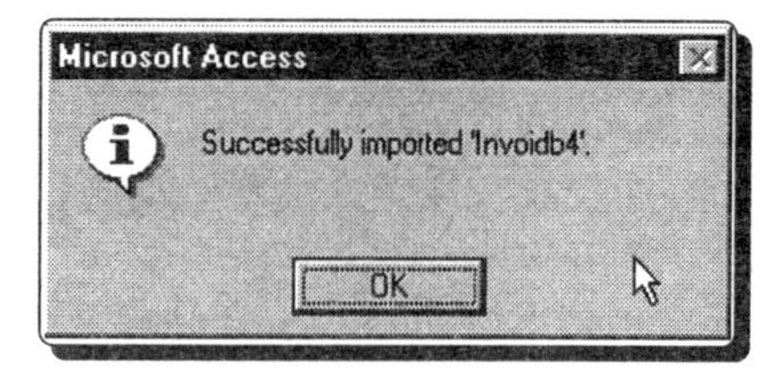

You can now open the newly converted database to examine it, change it, etc. In our case, opening the **Invoidb4** database displayed the following screen:

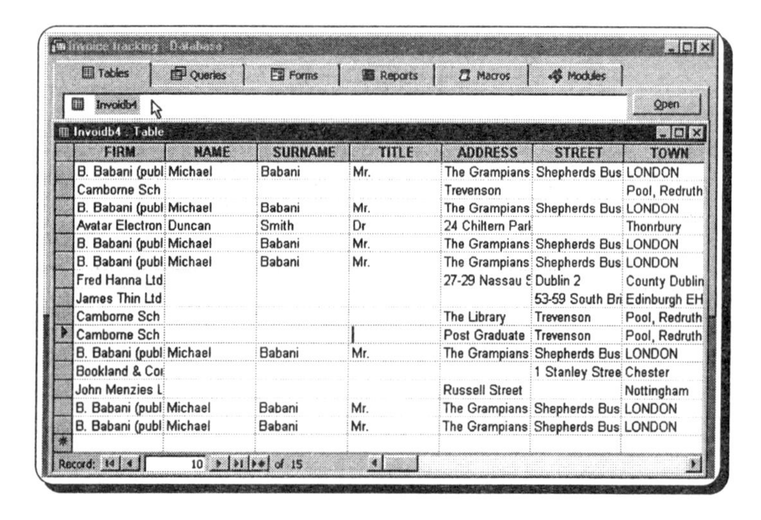

FIRM	NAME	SURNAME	TITLE	ADDRESS	STREET	TOWN
B. Babani (publ	Michael	Babani	Mr.	The Grampians	Shepherds Bus	LONDON
Camborne Sch				Trevenson		Pool, Redruth
B. Babani (publ	Michael	Babani	Mr.	The Grampians	Shepherds Bus	LONDON
Avatar Electron	Duncan	Smith	Dr	24 Chiltern Parl		Thonrbury
B. Babani (publ	Michael	Babani	Mr.	The Grampians	Shepherds Bus	LONDON
B. Babani (publ	Michael	Babani	Mr.	The Grampians	Shepherds Bus	LONDON
Fred Hanna Ltd				27-29 Nassau S	Dublin 2	County Dublin
James Thin Ltd					53-59 South Bri	Edinburgh EH
Camborne Sch				The Library	Trevenson	Pool, Redruth
Camborne Sch				Post Graduate	Trevenson	Pool, Redruth
B. Babani (publ	Michael	Babani	Mr.	The Grampians	Shepherds Bus	LONDON
Bookland & Coı					1 Stanley Stree	Chester
John Menzies L				Russell Street		Nottingham
B. Babani (publ	Michael	Babani	Mr.	The Grampians	Shepherds Bus	LONDON
B. Babani (publ	Michael	Babani	Mr.	The Grampians	Shepherds Bus	LONDON

What you need to do now is to check your data, first for duplicate information, then look at the possibility of splitting the table so that each piece of information is only stored once.

The Table Analyzer Wizard:

Before attempting to analyse a single table imported database, have the database open, and the table closed but selected. Next, use the **Tools, Analyze, Table** command which starts the Table Analyzer Wizard. The Wizard displays several dialogue boxes, some giving you advice, others expecting your input, as follows:

1. Informs you that duplicate information wastes space and leads to errors.
2. Informs you that to solve the problem the original table should be split to create new tables where each piece of information is stored only once.
3. Lists the tables within the database for you to choose one.
4. Asks you whether you want the Wizard to decide what to do or you to decide. In this dialogue box select the option **No, I want to decide**.
5. Asks you to specify what fields contain repeated information. In our example database, the first nine fields (Firm through to Phone) hold information on our customer's name and address which makes them ideal for selection. Select such fields and drag them on the working area of the Wizard's window. Table2 is immediately formed and you are asked to name Table1. We called Table1 'Invoices' and Table2 'Customers', as shown overleaf.
6. In the next dialogue box, the Table Analyzer Wizard presents you with records that it thinks might be similar to others, but for slight differences. For example, you might have abbreviated a firm's name differently, or placed address elements at different fields. It is at this point that you have the chance to correct the original.

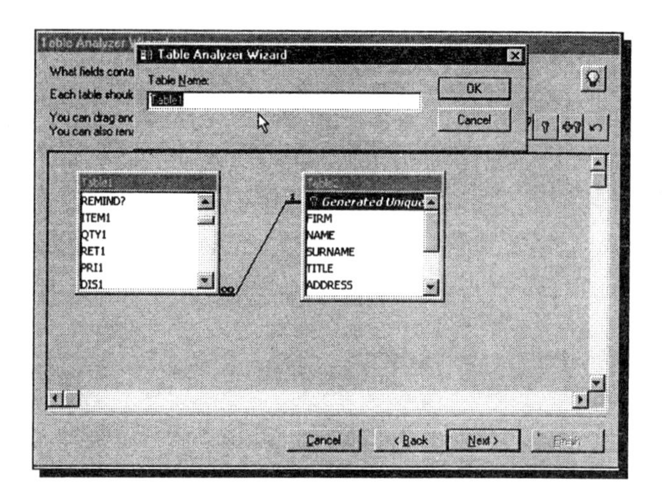

In the sixth dialogue box, select each disputed record in turn and click the down arrow button in the **Correct** column of the window, as shown below. This reveals a list of records that the Wizard thinks are similar to the selected one. You can either associate the selected record with one on the displayed list by highlighting it and clicking, or you can select the 'Leave as it is' option, if the record is different from those in the list.

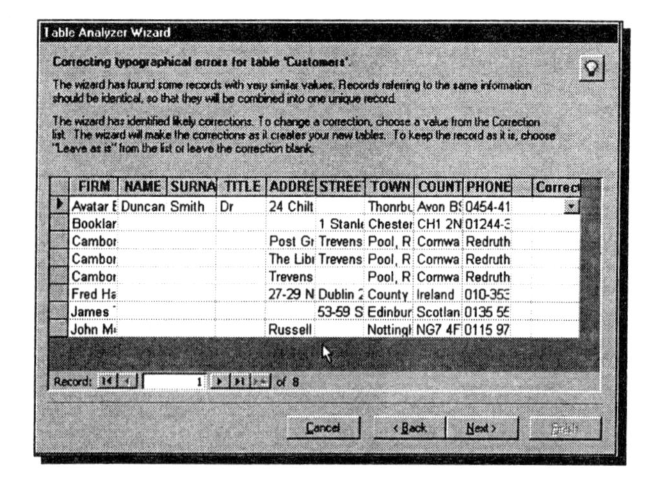

Finally, the Table Analyzer Wizard displays its last dialogue box. Make sure you select the **Yes, create the query** option, as shown below.

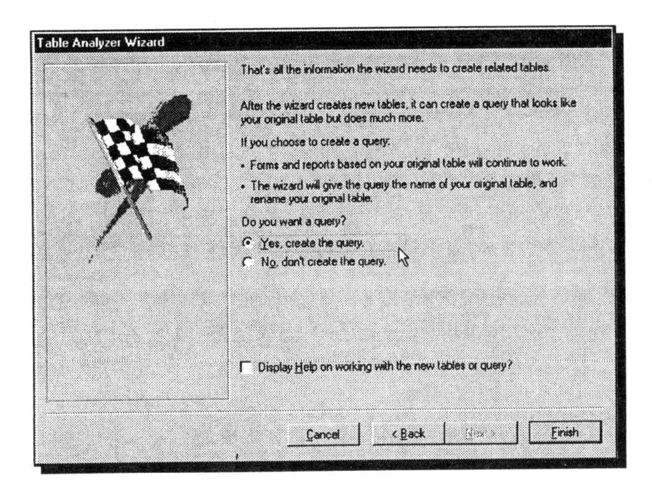

This option builds a query that looks like your original imported data file (see below), but also includes extra capabilities.

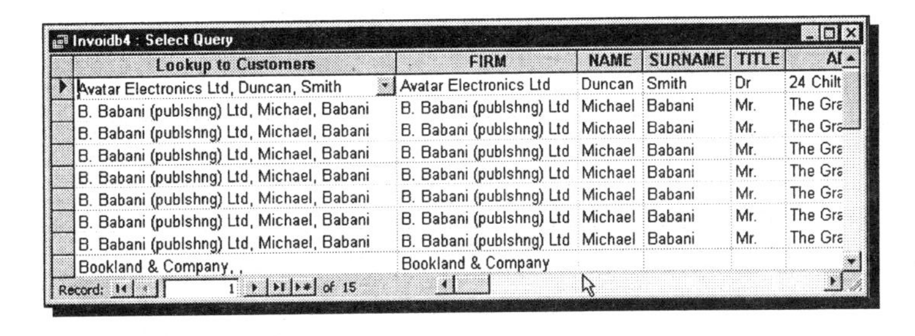

Lookup to Customers	FIRM	NAME	SURNAME	TITLE	AI
Avatar Electronics Ltd, Duncan, Smith	Avatar Electronics Ltd	Duncan	Smith	Dr	24 Chilt
B. Babani (publshng) Ltd, Michael, Babani	B. Babani (publshng) Ltd	Michael	Babani	Mr.	The Gra
B. Babani (publshng) Ltd, Michael, Babani	B. Babani (publshng) Ltd	Michael	Babani	Mr.	The Gra
B. Babani (publshng) Ltd, Michael, Babani	B. Babani (publshng) Ltd	Michael	Babani	Mr.	The Gra
B. Babani (publshng) Ltd, Michael, Babani	B. Babani (publshng) Ltd	Michael	Babani	Mr.	The Gra
B. Babani (publshng) Ltd, Michael, Babani	B. Babani (publshng) Ltd	Michael	Babani	Mr.	The Gra
B. Babani (publshng) Ltd, Michael, Babani	B. Babani (publshng) Ltd	Michael	Babani	Mr.	The Gra
B. Babani (publshng) Ltd, Michael, Babani	B. Babani (publshng) Ltd	Michael	Babani	Mr.	The Gra
Bookland & Company, ,	Bookland & Company				

Record: 1 of 15

For example, changing a repeating entry in one place, updates every affected record and when you enter a new firm's name, in a new record, Access assigns it a new, unique, ID automatically.

Rebuilding Formulae to Calculate Values:

When you export your data, formulae in the original database or spreadsheet are lost. Such formulae are best rebuilt within a database form, as follows:

- In the Database window, click the Form tab and then the **New** button to open the New Form dialogue box.
- In the New Form dialogue box, select the table you want to work with (in our example Invoices), and double-click the **Form Wizard** option, shown here, to display a data entry form for Invoices, as shown below.

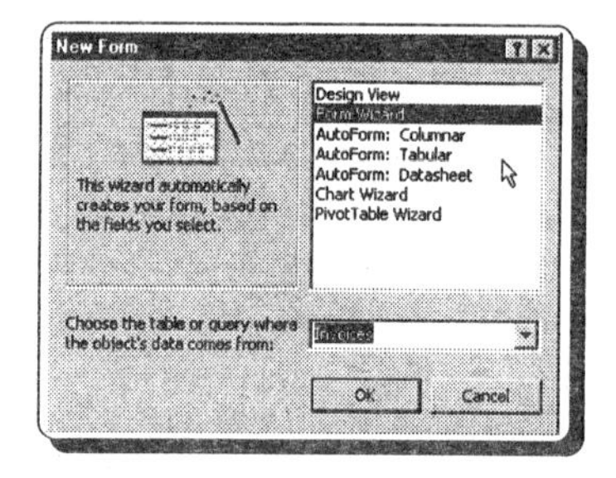

- Rearrange the various fields in the form to your liking. We rearranged ours as shown below. As you can see, we have only imported enough fields to deal with two categories of items, Item1 and Item2. The original database had five categories of items.

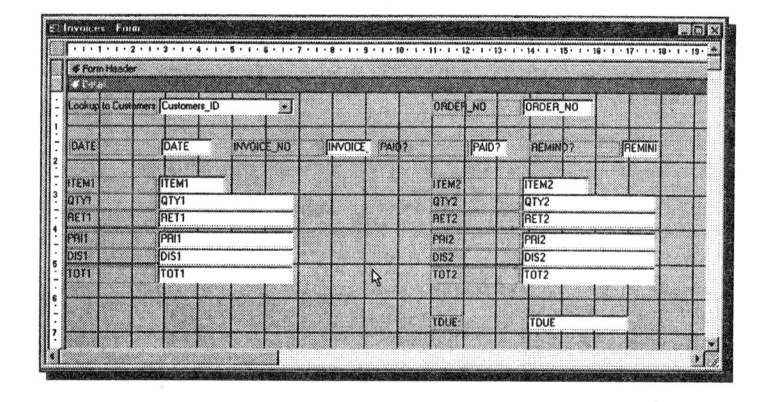

- In our example, formulae were inserted in the listed fields below, by double-clicking the data part of each field in our form in Design View and replacing what was displayed there with our formula. The abbreviation of the field names used stand for: PRI=Price; QTY=Quantity; RET=Retail Price/Item; TOT=Total Price; DIS=Discount; TDUE=Total Due.

Field	***Formula used***
PRI1	=[QTY1]*[RET1]
TOT1	=[PRI1]*(1-[DIS1]/100)
PRI2	=[QTY2]*[RET2]
TOT2	=[PRI2]*(1-[DIS2]/100)
TDUE	=[TOT1]+[TOT2]

You can further format the data values of these fields to currency as follows: While in Design View, point and left-click on the data part of a given field to select it. Then right-click this field, to reveal the shortcut menu shown here. Select the **Properties** option and left-click to display the properties of the selected Text Box.

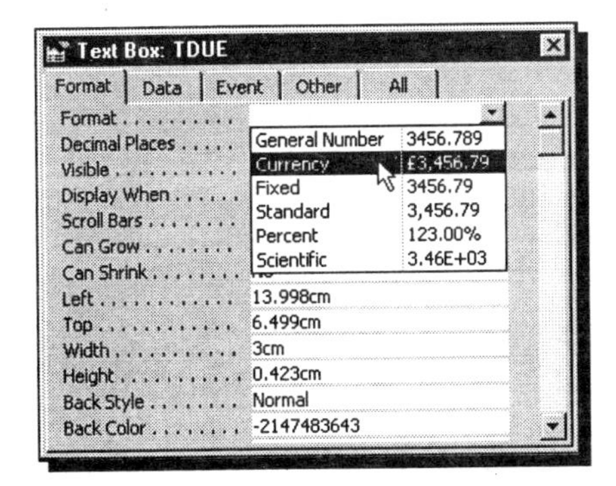

Finally, click the Format tab of this dialogue box, click against the Format entry and select 'Currency' from the displayed list to format the data in the selected field.

* * * * *

Access 97 for Windows 95 is capable of a lot more than what we were able to cover in the space allocated to this short book. However, we hope we have covered enough features of the program to make you want to explore Microsoft Access more fully in you own time.

* * * * *

INDEX

W

NOTES

NOTES

COMPANION DISCS TO BOOKS

COMPANION DISCS are available for most books written by the same author(s) and published by BERNARD BABANI (publishing) LTD, as listed at the front of this book (except for those marked with an asterisk). These books contain many pages of file/program listings. There is no reason why you should spend hours typing them into your computer, unless you wish to do so, or need the practice.

COMPANION DISCS come in 3½" format with all example listings.

ORDERING INSTRUCTIONS

To obtain your copy of a companion disc, fill in the order form below or a copy of it, enclose a cheque (payable to **P.R.M. Oliver**) or a postal order, and send it to the address below. Make sure you fill in your name and address and specify the book number and title in your order.

Book No.	Book Name	Unit Price	Total Price
BP		£3.50	
BP		£3.50	
BP		£3.50	
Name		Sub-total	£............
Address:		P & P (@ 45p/disc)	£............
		Total Due	£............
Send to: P.R.M. Oliver, CSM, Pool, Redruth, Cornwall, TR15 3SE			

PLEASE NOTE

The author(s) are fully responsible for providing this Companion Disc service. The publishers of this book accept no responsibility for the supply, quality, or magnetic contents of the disc, or in respect of any damage, or injury that might be suffered or caused by its use.

rubbish that is served up as art by the lunatics we have in charge of our galleries.'

It was a statement which demanded Eleanor's recapitulation. She said equably, 'I'm too sensible to get myself worked up about it, at any rate.'

'This is a nice soufflé,' I said anxiously.

Eleanor looked at me in amusement.

My father said, 'Very nice,' and refused a second helping. Eleanor suggested we had coffee in the drawing-room. While we waited for her to make the coffee my father sat with his hands clasped, occasionally cracking the knuckles and then staring at them in surprise. It occurred to me that he was as disturbed as we were by his behaviour but unable to do anything about it. He looked drawn and ill. I said, in a miserable attempt at solidarity, 'I must say I thought the bricks were pretty silly.'

After Eleanor had handed round the coffee cups, he said, in the tone of one who has no intention of letting go of a grievance, 'It's good of you to come down here, Eleanor. You must find it dull when you have such a stimulating life in London.'

'I don't have a stimulating life in London.' She was immensely calm and looked like a strong, squat goddess sitting there on our sofa.

'But you are so well-informed about art and drama and music.' He looked at her with disfavour.

'You are the one with the knowledge, Stewart. I've always enjoyed listening to you; you are so sensitive and discerning. Do you remember taking Lillian and me to the National Gallery and I said I didn't like Van Dyck? You stood me in front of a Van Dyck and said, "Look at the painting of that hand, the texture of the ruff, the vein in the forehead . . ." ' She was unexpectedly gentle as she offered him this picture of himself as he had been in days not so far off, before my mother died.

It was a gift he was unable to accept. He said in the

same bitter, complaining voice, 'Where would you see anyone painting like that now?'

'Six months ago you would have given me the answer to that!'

'I've tried to keep up with things, I've told myself that we're going through a period of change and that something worthwhile will emerge.' He looked at the rim of his cup, wincing as though he had toothache. 'I can't delude myself any longer.'

I got up and left them. I went into the kitchen and did the washing-up. As I came into the hall, meaning to return to the drawing-room, I heard Eleanor saying quite pleasantly, ' . . . since you ask me, I think that for the present you'd be much better being miserable on your own, Stewart.'

I wondered what it was that he had asked her. I halted near the door, eavesdropping shamelessly. My father said, 'Well, if that's the way you feel . . . It's been very kind of you to give us so much of your time.'

'I'll come again later in the summer, if I may.'

'As you please.'

There was a long silence which Eleanor did not break. I was beginning to have a grudging admiration for Eleanor. Becoming involved with another person is dangerous work with a high risk of injury; if the involvement led to marriage, she would have to learn to live with my father, and this sort of learning is a never-ending process. How could she contemplate it? The thought of the emotional energy which would have to be expended, apart from anything else, made me feel so exhausted that I decided to go to bed.

Eleanor left after lunch on Sunday. At half-past three Mrs. Libnitz arrived. I did not have time to wonder what had occasioned this visit because she said immediately I opened the front door, 'Iris telephoned me to come. She saw you last evening but you went away before she had a chance to ask how you were.' She stepped into the hall and looked round with interest, but made no comment. She had dressed formally for the visit in a grey suit and a black pill-box hat with a veil and she carried gloves.

'Did you walk?' I asked, thinking how odd she must have looked coming along the lane.

She shrugged. 'It is not far.' She had rooms in the village. Iris had taken advantage of this on previous occasions to get her to deliver messages to local clients. It was the first time, however, that she had been to my home. In fact, she was the first person from the clinic to come to my home. I took her into the drawing-room. She sat on the edge of the sofa. 'I do not stay long,' she assured me.

We sat and looked at each other. This was a situation governed by different rules to our clinic meetings. It was apparent that, in so far as visiting was concerned, Mrs. Libnitz observed the rules of the country of her origin. She looked at me expectantly, waiting for me to open the conversation. I did not want my private world invaded and, although I did not think Mrs. Libnitz planned an invasion, I decided it was important to keep her in her place.

'How are things at the clinic?' I asked, as though I had been away for months instead of days.

She looked surprised, perhaps one was not permitted to talk shop in the drawing-room. But she had lived a long time among barbarians and was prepared to make small accommodations. 'Friday!' She showed the whites of her eyes. 'Friday was terrible. Douglas has the children for the week-end. When they arrive I cannot find him so I put them in the playroom. What else should I do with them? I can't help that they talk to the clients' children and tell them their daddy lives with another man.'

'Was Douglas upset?'

'It is Iris who makes the fuss. She takes the clients and

their children up to Di: then she come down and asks why Douglas's children are in the playroom; the children cry; then Douglas comes and stands there looking . . . you know how he looks.'

I could visualise his standing there with that look he so often had of being immobilised at a time when action of some kind was needed, like one of those on whom the gods have cast a spell.

'Poor Douglas,' I said. 'I hope he knows what he's doing.'

'He's doing nothing. Don't be sorry for him. He knows all about doing nothing, that one.'

Conversation did not flow with Mrs. Libnitz; all her statements were so conclusive.

'It was nice of Iris to worry about me,' I said tentatively.

'She does not worry about your health, she worries about her typing. She is crazy about this hypnotising and she is writing it all down. She means to make a television script of it. So you stay away and have a good rest.'

'I hope she has told Dr. Laver. He's the hypnotist, after all.'

'Why worry? She will write it down, and alter it, and tear it up and start again, and in the end she won't know the end from the beginning.'

'That's only when she's doing several things at once; when she really concentrates, she's formidable. I saw that series she did on local TV and it was good.'

'Formidable? That one!' Mrs. Libnitz could never accept the common verdict; of a beauty, it would be 'pah, nothing, nothing at all, in fact, I find her ugly.' So Iris, who was generally regarded as being gifted, was to Mrs. Libnitz an incompetent. Had Mrs. Libnitz been on the sidelines she would in no time have reduced Bjorn Borg to an all-time loser. I saw now why it was that Iris hated Mrs. Libnitz.

'How about Di?' I asked.

Mrs. Libnitz softened. Di was a favourite; she and Mrs. Libnitz were the only smokers in the office and this shared vice seemed to draw them together.

'She has another man—"a super bloke". You know the way it is with her? He has a boat on the canal and the children love him and they are all going on holiday on the canal. You know what she says to me? "At least my kids have a man around; I think that's important, don't you?" She never learns from experience, that one; but if all your experience is bad . . .' Mrs. Libnitz shrugged her shoulders. 'Who shall blame her?'

I looked surreptitiously at the clock on the mantelshelf, wondering if it was too soon to offer tea. I decided to ask about Dr. Laver and then offer tea.

'Now you are away he comes down to me for coffee. He plays with the switchboard and how he talks! He tells me I know more about the clients than anyone else, so he comes to consult me. He thinks to flatter me, but it is true; of course I know more than anyone else. How can I help it? I have ears and eyes. He says while the clients are waiting I will be noticing things about them which the professional never sees. "They will use a different language with you, too." He tells me as if I don't know already. He says the professional has too much knowledge, it cuts him off from the reality of people. "Whether she is real or not, I don't know," I say to him, "but you have just cut that caller off from Iris." He says that people in his profession view life from behind a glass screen, "we are sheltered, protected and immune." And I am trying to work the switchboard and make coffee! He does not have to tell me all this; I give him the coffee without it.'

'It was a forfeit— confession in return for coffee.'

'Forfeit?'

'Just a silly joke.'

'He is mad, that one!'

And this one, Ruth Saunders, what is she? I did not want to be told, so I said that I would make tea. My father joined us and engaged Mrs. Libnitz in the kind of conversation she had obviously expected. They talked about the death of Tito, whom Mrs. Libnitz had not liked, and what effect it would have on the policy of non-alignment.

'At first they thought Tito was a code name and then they thought perhaps it was a woman. Did you know that?' I did not speak the words, they just ran through my head.

Where Mrs. Libnitz was sitting, I saw my cousin Hilda. She had been attending an independent girls' boarding school for two years and it had changed her. She had become muted and considered in her speech. I had looked forward to being with her again and was disappointed by this talk of Tito.

'Don't you want to come upstairs and get on with our families?' I asked.

'No, Ruth.' She spoke earnestly, as though she was giving up a vice. 'I couldn't, not any more.'

'But why not?'

'I don't think it's right, all this imagining.'

'But it's so dull, talking about Tito.'

'I could lend you this book by Fitzroy Maclean, if you like. It's very instructive.'

'Any book you got out of a school library would be dull; it wouldn't be in it otherwise. I think imagining is much better.'

She looked at me anxiously as though something about my behaviour reminded her of things she was trying to correct in her life.

My father said, 'I think perhaps Mrs. Libnitz would like another cup of tea, Ruth.'

It was no use arguing, I thought as I poured tea. Hilda had changed. The school had made her into a different person.

'What are you going to do about your exams., Ruth, when you get older?' she asked reprovingly. 'If you keep on with this imagining it will interfere with your studies.'

'I don't care about exams.'

'You will never achieve anything without passing exams.'

'I don't want to achieve anything.'

'My teacher would say you are a member of the counterculture.'

'I'm not a member of anything.'

Mrs. Libnitz finished her cucumber sandwich, made some disparaging remarks about Fitzroy Maclean, and took leave of us.

As he cleared away the tea things, my father said, 'I enjoyed her. A very fierce little lady.'

On Monday I went to the doctor. He gave me a more thorough examination than I had expected and said he would give me a certificate to cover the rest of the week and then he would want to see me again. The day passed slowly. My father was late home. A change had come over him. He was very subdued and he still looked drawn and ill; but the bitterness seemed to have left him and there were no more outbursts of self-pity. There was also an indefinable change in his attitude to me. It was as though, very reluctantly and for what reason I could not guess, he had moved a little further from me.

The next day when he had gone to work I lay in bed listening to the noises in the house. I remembered how loving my mother had been when I had childish ailments and I wished that I could hear her coming up the stairs, carrying a tray with some preparation she had devised to tempt me. She would sit on the end of my bed, delighted to have me home with her. 'Don't go back to school this week, lovey. A stay at home will do you good.' We would go to the pictures in Weston Market, feeling agreeably wicked, and she would imitate Miss Petrie, saying, 'If you are well enough to go to the pictures, you are well enough to attend school.' Oh Mother, Mother, why aren't you here now? But it was not her footsteps on the stairs that I could hear, it was someone up above me.

She is older now and no longer has dolls. At this moment, she is climbing the attic stairs. On the attic landing there is a ladder. She hooks it into place and climbs up to the trap door. She has ceased to be Ruth Saunders. Another family lives up in the loft. There are thirteen children, six boys and seven girls. The boys are Kit and Philip and Anthony and Patrick and John and Michael. The girls run to more fanciful names, mostly of French origin, Rosalind, Jacqueline, Stephanie, Antoinette, Coralie, Marguerite and Imogen: not a plain Jane among them. She is Imogen and Kit is her favourite brother. He is in the army and looks very handsome in his officer's uniform. Philip is training to be a doctor; Anthony, Patrick and John are still at school. Anthony wants to train horses and Patrick and John are too young to know what they want from one day to another. The girls are chiefly notable for the colour of their hair which ranges from ash blonde to jet, taking in corn, amber, copper, auburn and chestnut on the way. A London friend of Mother's is a hairdresser and provides swathes of real hair which the girl adjusts to suit the various personalities of her sisters. Imogen (jet) keeps a diary. She is writing it up there now, sitting on the floor, resting the exercise book on an old trunk. She is wearing a school straw hat with two jet pigtails hanging down the sides of her face.

'It is Mummy's birthday today, so of course we are all together. Kit has got leave and Philip has taken time off from college. At breakfast Daddy said, 'It is such a lovely day. Would you all like to go for a picnic on our boat? That's if that is what Mummy would like, because it is her birthday.' We all looked at Mummy and she frowned and shrugged her shoulders, just like Antoinette does when she has to do her music practice when she'd rather be out playing in the garden. We must have looked so disappointed because she burst out laughing and said, 'Darlings, there is nothing I would like more!' and we realised she had been teasing us. The girls helped get the food together while the boys went ahead with Daddy to our boat which is moored at Hunters Quay. We had crusty French bread and cheese and hard-boiled eggs, and a whole chicken, and lettuce and tomatoes and nuts and apples, and several bottles of barley water.

'When we got down to the boat, Anthony was so excited he pushed it out while Daddy was standing astride with one foot on the bank and the other on the side of the boat, which is a FORBIDDEN position! Daddy fell in the river. We tried not to laugh because he was cross at first, but Mummy said, 'That will teach you, my lad, not to do things you tell your children not to do,' and then he laughed and we all laughed. We had a lovely day and Patrick got very burnt across the shoulders. In the evening we came home and we all sat in the garden talking and sometimes singing. When it was nearly dark we did our speciality, which is *The Humming Chorus* from *Madame Butterfly*.

'Mummy and Daddy came to say goodnight to Stephanie and me when we were in our beds, and she said it was the happiest birthday she had ever had. We could hear her talking to Daddy and laughing with him for ages in their room.'

I could see every word of it as clearly as if I was writing it now. As I read it, I began to cry. It was the second time I had cried recently. This was disturbing, because I was the kind of person who doesn't cry. 'There is nothing virtuous about it,' I used to joke. 'I must have missed out on the equipment.' The equipment was certainly impaired by lack of use. The tears did not gush out easily, bringing immediate relief; every muscle and sinew in my body must have been clenched tight: what else could explain the terrible struggle which was taking place? She had stood by the window, with her hands clenched at her sides, saying, 'I will NOT cry!' I could see her now, small, resolute and uncomplaining; such a brave little girl. When, or how often, this had happened, I could not remember; quite often, perhaps, because practice had made well-nigh perfect. Only a betrayal of the worst sort could breach such a defence. The adult Ruth Saunders turned and savaged that brave little girl. No use saying, 'I will NOT cry!' when the will is no longer there; I wanted to cry, I meant to cry, I fought to cry; and the crying was uncontrolled, immature, appalling. I despised myself; I would never feel the same about myself again. But I cried with my whole body, retching, jerking, thrashing about like a demented creature. Punter, who usually came forward to offer sympathy at the first sign of distress, slunk out of the room.

By the evening my body ached as though it had been beaten and I was so hoarse I could hardly speak. I told my father that I had a virus; I said I had been to the doctor and that he had given me something for it. All my standards were slipping; I told the lie without the slightest compunction.

I did not sleep much that night. I sat propped up on the pillows, staring out of the window, listening to the night sounds. There was hardly any breeze, but the temperature had dropped and the air was cool against my face. I was able to examine my grief dispassionately. For whom had I been crying? For Imogen and Mummy and Daddy? They were all right, they lived in a world of perpetual understanding, enjoying every day more than the last and getting better looking all the time. Mummy had had flaxen hair plaited on top of her head; the plaits were thick because she had masses of hair. Occasionally she let her hair down and it streamed around her shoulders and she looked as young as her children. Her face was fresh and rosy like a good apple and her intelligent eyes were grey-blue and full of kindness and wisdom.

Lillian Jacobs had had golden hair; it was strong and thick and when she was young it was so long she could sit on it. She had a skin like a peach and big, appealing grey-blue eyes which were not intelligent or noticeably full of wisdom. I had not wanted another mother; I had only wanted to make a few alterations in the one I had. I lay back, pondering this fact which I had extricated from my grief, not knowing quite what to do with it. Some time around dawn I fell asleep and dreamt of my mother. She was sitting in a deck-chair in the garden, wearing a beautiful filmy dress. Someone was calling to her, someone out of sight, on the far side of the garden wall. I said to her, 'Aren't you going?' Then I saw that she was tied to the chair. I undid the ropes and said, 'There! You're free!' But she only looked at me sadly and stayed where she was.

When my father had gone to work, I went down to the kitchen, made my breakfast and carried the tray up to my room. Punter was sitting on the landing. He shifted his tail warily when I spoke to him, but he would not come into the bedroom with me. I had lost his trust.

I sat in bed, wondering about this new, untrustworthy person. Was she safe to be let out? She might do anything, behave oddly in a train, get into trouble in the street.

I took the tray down to the kitchen and left it there without washing the crockery. I went back to bed, but I was no longer comfortable. My nerves were on edge. I would have to get up. But what should I do, where should I go? I crouched cross-legged on the bed, trying to think. The clock downstairs in the hall chimed ten. As the last chime died away there was a knock on the front door. Too late for the postman, too early for Mrs. James. I was in no state to receive callers. Punter thudded clumsily down the stairs, barking; the caller knocked again and Punter barked again. Then it was quiet. I wondered what to do, where to go.

A shower of pebbles hit the window. I went to the window and looked down. Dr. Laver stood on the gravel path, his upturned face, framed in a ginger frill of hair and beard, looking grotesquely as though it was borne on the platter of his shoulders; he appeared to have little else in the way of a body. It occurred to me that he was a figment of my imagination, an unlikely creature I had conjured up to suit some purpose of my own. He said crossly, 'I knocked on the door and I also rang the bell. Surely you heard?'

'I'm ill. I couldn't come down.'

'We must talk about this illness of yours.' He took hold of the ivy and hoisted himself up a few feet, staring at me intently as though he was a climber and I represented the particular place at which he must today pitch camp. Although it was already very hot he was still wearing the striped suit and pink shirt.

'I'm exhausted and sick,' I protested. 'What I need is rest.'

'You're angry.'

'That is your answer to everything, isn't it? Anger, aggression; don't you ever ask yourself why your vocabulary is so aggressive?'

'Exhausted, sick, in need of rest . . . What an anaemic vision you have of yourself.' He found footholds and hauled himself up higher; his head and shoulders were now just above the level of the ground floor window. He appeared to be unaware either of the ridiculousness or of the danger of his enterprise. I was his present goal and since he saw no other way of reaching me, he was treading ivy.

I said, 'I have been to the doctor and he says I am in need of rest.'

'Your life has been wasted up to now and you are angry about it. So you should be.' He hauled himself up a few more feet. His face was now a little below the level of the window sill.

'You can't come into my bedroom.'

'Of course I must come into your bedroom. How can I talk to you like this? It's very uncomfortable.'

'I didn't ask you to come. You'll have to climb down.'

'I never climb down. And anyway, I have a bad head for heights.' He hooked one arm over the sill and trod more ivy. The ivy wasn't so thick here and his foot slipped. I grabbed his arm. 'You'll have to *pull*! Participate, for God's sake, woman!' I pulled and he strained. A great heave brought his head and shoulders over the sill. Little bits of cement and an old birds' nest were dislodged and spattered down on to the gravel path. This gave him an attack of vertigo. 'I'm finished,' he groaned, still at an angle where it would be easier to fall outwards than inwards. I leant over him and grasped the seat of his trousers. There followed a few moments when it seemed that even if he came in I must go out, then we were both in a heap on the floor. We lay there, panting and breathless, while Punter barked outside the door. Dr. Laver had got himself entangled in my nightdress. 'It's all right, Punter,' I called, while Dr. Laver was freeing us both of the nightdress. 'Quiet now, good dog.' Dr. Laver tossed the nightdress over the back of a chair and I got into bed.

He stood at the end of the bed. 'You must trust me if I am to help you.' He looked at me severely with those penetrating eyes. Now that I came to think of it, his range of expression was very limited.

'You're not real,' I told him. 'When you came into the office I said "Dr. Laver, I presume?" I conjured you up.'

'Nonsense. I summoned you, the real Ruth Saunders.'

'I don't believe you are a psychiatrist at all.'

'In fact, I am a psychiatrist.' He sounded as though he found this surprising.

'There's something wrong with you, though.'

'There is even more wrong with you. But I can put that right.'

The way in which he drove straight at what he wanted, dismissing anything that did not fit into his design as irrelevant, irritated me. I said, 'I feel at a disadvantage and I'm sure that's not therapeutic. Perhaps you should undress?'

'If you feel it will help.' He began to take off his clothes, looking uneasy at thus discarding his persona and unsure what he would find underneath.

'Wherever did you get that suit and shirt?' I asked.

'I stole them. I steal all my clothes; it's so much less expensive.'

He took a hanger from the wardrobe and arranged his jacket on it and hung it behind the door, dusting it lightly with his hands. Then he unbuttoned his shirt and folded it fussily before putting it on the dressing-table stool. He reminded me of old men in launderettes folding their washing with obsessive care because they have nothing else to do and nowhere much to go when they have finished; so they fold and smooth and brood on '*hours, days, months, which are the rags of time*'. But at least when eventually they leave they take their washing with them. When he turned towards the bed his clothes were lying in an anonymous heap like articles found abandoned on the sea shore when the swimmer fails to return. He was in bed before I noticed him; there was no sexual anticipation, only a sense of loss and a smell of deprivation.

No sooner was he at my side, however, than my perception shifted and I had the dizzying sensation that the room was going slightly out of focus. My little fantasy no longer seemed under control. I had the queazy feeling that I had made a mistake which I might not be able to rectify. We sat with our backs against the bed-rest, not touching or looking at each other. In the long wardrobe mirror I could see us sitting side by side, rather prim, and I thought, 'I can't believe that this is really happening. If I will hard enough I shall wake up.'

But our eyes met in the mirror and I felt his eyes drawing me towards an understanding. He said, 'You are at a crisis, Ruth, and you are calling on me to help you. Isn't that so?'

I hated the unclean smell of him and I wondered why I had not noticed it before; the smell was repugnant, yet fascinating.

He said, 'All the time that Iris was talking of the apple tree, I was conscious of a depth of pain that was not in Iris.'

I looked at the heap of clothes on the dressing-table stool and at my nightdress thrown over the back of the chair. A much greater distance than a few carpeted feet seemed to separate me from them.

He said, 'You must understand the past if you are to make anything of the present.'

Is it possible to tiptoe along the corridors of the past, to open doors which have been forbidden, to find that which has been concealed? I looked at Dr. Laver in the mirror and his eyes told me that he had the keys of time and place, that there was nowhere, past and present, where he could not be. A tremor ran through me. I looked at my nightdress again and at his clothes. The thought of the effort which would be necessary to haul myself from his side daunted me; and worse than that was the thought of dressing, going downstairs and talking to Mrs. James when she came, and later to my father when he came, and later still going to the doctor, getting a certificate, eventually going back to work, with nothing to show for it but the smell in my nostrils.

I looked in the mirror again and now I saw another room and the people in the bed were not Ruth Saunders and Dr. Laver. I closed my eyes. My skin was cold and slimy. I had seen my mother and father, side by side in bed, unanimated, like characters in a play who have taken up their position before curtain rise. I did not dare to look in the mirror again because that would be to ring up the curtain. I knew so little of my parents' life together, snatches here and there, half-seen, half-understood, nothing more. What could it benefit me to poke and pry, to violate their past? The voice answered, 'You must understand the past if you are to make anything of the present and to understand the past you must enter into it.'

I was on the landing. Had I been to the lavatory? It was hard to tell, the whole house smelt like lavatories in a subway. The walls of the corridor ran with damp and the floor was slimy. I moved forward, my hands over my ears because I did not want to hear voices through clenched teeth, laughter springing from sources I could not fathom. Was it night, or was it afternoon, an afternoon when my father was at work and I should have been at school . . . ? The voice said, 'You are still trying to keep control, you must let the images float free.' I stood in the reeking tunnel; then, like a criminal, I moved stealthily towards the room. Each step I took gave me an increasing feeling of loss and deprivation; I had not known, until I struggled here, that there was so much to lose. The voice said, 'You are struggling. Let yourself be carried.' But I could not go on, there was sickness in the pit of my stomach and my limbs were boneless; I stood, terrified of going forward or backward, and while I was thus petrified, the front door bell rang.

Dr. Laver said, 'Pay no attention.'

But the sound was sweet as a church bell to this nearly-lost soul. I opened my eyes and saw my own room reflected in the mirror and Dr. Laver sitting beside me in the bed. 'What am I doing?' I thought. 'I must be out of my mind.' The door bell rang again and dear Punter barked.

'It may be something important,' I said.

'Nothing is more important than this.'

'It might even be the doctor called to see how I am.' I jumped out of bed. The realisation of what I had done came over me; I had let him into my home, into my mind. How could I have been so foolish? His clothes were on the stool. I picked them up and threw them out of the window. He sat bolt upright, staring as though he could not believe me capable of such idiocy.

'Life has moved on since the days of the Aldwych farces, Ruth.'

'If you want them, you'll have to go after them.'

'I've told you I never climb down.'

The front door opened and Punter squeaked joyfully. Mrs. James said, 'I expect she's dozed off. Lucky I came along.'

I hissed at Dr. Laver, 'Get out! Get out! You must!' There were footsteps on the stairs. Suddenly, he was alarmed; he looked furtive and hunted, a new range of expression. He went to the window and peered down. There was a knock on the bedroom door. Mrs. James said, 'Can I come in, Ruth?'

'No.' I went to the door and spoke through the crack. 'What is it?'

'There's a friend of yours here to see you.' Her voice was coy. 'A gentleman.'

I opened the door an inch or two. Mrs. James was standing there with Douglas behind her. I said, 'Give me two minutes.'

I turned back to the room. It was empty. I rubbed myself down with a flannel and put on my nightdress.

Douglas said, when I let him in, 'I didn't realise you were still in bed or I wouldn't have bothered you.' He was embarrassed and would not look at me. I was glad about that. He drew up a chair and took my hand. 'How hot you are! Have you got a fever?'

'I may have had a touch of delirium.'

A sharp cry of pain beyond the window indicated that I was not back to normal yet.

9

MY father said at supper, 'I met Mrs. James at the station. She tells me you have had another visitor.'

I said, 'Yes.' I did not know how many visitors I had had in reality. I wondered if this was a common feature of my complaint, but I couldn't think of anyone I could ask.

'Your office is very concerned about you.' He sounded proud in an absent-minded way. 'They must miss you.' He nodded to himself; he had always known I would turn out well.

Douglas had indeed come to tell me that he was concerned about me. He had sat, pale and sweating in the heat, his horn-rimmed glasses making his face look more solemn than ever and also, perhaps because of their size, fragile, as though the small nose had not been fashioned to bear their weight. It was difficult for him, whatever it was he was trying to say to me; his face had what Di called its constipated look. He was saying '. . . quiet and modest, but rather deep . . . a thinker. . . .' He was talking about me. How every odd! When he said 'a thinker' he gave me a brief, slightly disapproving glance, as though I was a secret drinker.

'The office is so chaotic now. You kept it sane, Ruth. We should have been more grateful to you.'

I bit my lip, fighting the desire to laugh at the idea of my being the guardian of sanity. The laughter wasn't a very real threat, it petered out almost at once, leaving black despair. No doubt he had come to ask me to go back to the office. To divert him, I asked, 'How did things go with the children at the week-end?'

'It was awful,' he answered, diverted. 'They didn't get on well with Eddie. I took them on the Nature Trail to get them out of the house, but he insisted on coming, too, I can't think why; he hates the country and he sulked the whole time.' He clenched his hands on his knees, staring down at the knuckles while he talked. 'I couldn't cope with Charlotte and the children. I expected it would be easier for all of us now, that we might even enjoy each other once there were no ties. I've not been ungenerous; I'm paying over the odds on maintenance, and I've bought the children a pony. But you don't get rid of ties, you just keep the old and get entangled in new ones.' He took off his glasses, perhaps meaning to polish them and then forgetting. His eyes were like the eyes of a blind man. 'That time when I was stuck in the window, I had a vision of the life I would like to lead.'

'What happened?'

'Nothing. That was what was so extraordinarily pleasant. I saw myself lying in a punt; it was very peaceful and I was drifting past meadows with willows trailing in the water; all the spring flowers were out and I could smell hyacinths. It was a very still day, nothing moved, only the punt carried me on. I didn't see all that then, of course; I've extended the experience since. At night, when I am trying to sleep, I put myself in the punt.' He sat there, holding his glasses, drifting out of reach.

'It sounds like "*The Lady of Shalott*",' I said, to bring him back.

'Do you think she was autistic? I'm sure I would have been if autism had been fashionable when I was a child.' He breathed on his glasses and polished them meticulously. 'My trouble is that I was born into a world where everything has been found to be bad for us, all our pleasures and most of what we eat and drink, to say nothing of the air we breathe. What's left? With my temperament, I might have been a contemplative. But it's centuries too late for that. There is nothing to contemplate.' He put on his glasses, indicating that he had himself well in hand now.

'I didn't come to tell you about myself. But this talk of escape into contemplation serves as an introduction. I was disturbed to hear you talk about that teashop you want to run. It struck an echo in my mind. The teashop is your form of escape. No doubt you would say it is a harmless daydream. But our daydreams are significant.'

'I'm not going to run a teashop, I haven't the capital any more than you have a poleless punt.'

'But there are things you have got, Ruth. You have energy and will power and a good brain. Up to now, you haven't had motivation. But with the death of your mother, a new life will start for you whether you like it or not. And you can make something of that new life, because you are a more positive person than I. Go to university, Ruth. It's not too late.'

'I am never going to university! I made a vow, a long time ago, that I was going to be the great non-achiever of all time and I'm not going back on it.' If this wretched discussion served no other purpose, it clarified the university issue: this was the only childhood battle I had fought; I had constructed something, staked out a territory, made a place that was entirely mine. I intended to defend it.

He did not take me seriously. Here he was, lazy, indecisive, draining his limited emotional resources on my behalf, in fact, making a sacrifice. It was important to him that the sacrifice should be accepted and to underline this, he sacrificed some more. 'I've needled you in the past, Ruth. You seemed so secure, so rounded, and it angered me. Your serenity seemed to be a comment on my failure as a person. I came to think of it as something aggressive and I resisted it with aggression. I think I may have hurt you. In fact, I tried to hurt you in order to prove that underneath that calm exterior you were no less inadequate and confused than I.' He was sweating. This was very difficult for him. So why did he have to do it, since neither of us wanted it? 'During the days that you have been away I have realised how much we all depend on you. From what I have gathered of your home life, your mother depended on you, too. You *must* get away, Ruth; otherwise you will become the kind of person who needs to be used by other people, who colludes in her own exploitation. That pattern is all too easily established and very difficult to break.'

'I'll think about it,' I said because I did not want him to go any further. He was still getting at me, even if his motives were more respectable.

'I hope I haven't hurt you?'

'I'm sure you're right about a lot of things. You're very perceptive. You should have been a woman.'

Not a muscle of his face moved; yet it was like watching a car windscreen when it is hit by a chance stone and the original hole is gradually concealed by the total fragmentation of the glass.

'I'm sorry,' I said. 'I'm sorry, I'm sorry! Or perhaps I'm not, perhaps I meant to get my own back. How can I tell? It's your fault. You and Iris are always analysing motives until in the end nothing is what it seems, nothing adds up.'

My father said, 'I wonder if Mrs. James would do it.'

I stared across the table at him. 'Do what?'

'Our laundry.' We looked at each other, our minds not yet meeting. He said awkwardly, 'I've done a bit of it myself, but . . .'

'I'd forgotten all about the laundry. Why didn't you remind me?'

'You weren't well, so. . . .'

I thought of him creeping down the stairs with his shirt and pants while I was lying in bed, worn down by my misery. 'It must have been awful for you,' I said, feeling very ashamed. The little things matter so much; he must have felt unloved and neglected.

'I didn't mind,' he said, 'only I don't seem to get the stains out. Do you use a special powder?'

'Leave it to me. It will do me good to have something to do. I shall enjoy it, really I shall.'

He kissed me and told me how good I was, and I told him how good he was and then he made an excuse to go out of the room because neither of us could handle this much emotion.

While I was doing the washing the telephone rang. It was the vicar about the flower festival. My father had promised to act as a steward, and he came into the kitchen to ask me if I minded him going to a meeting to discuss the arrangements. 'There's no need for me to go if you would rather not be alone.' Hitherto when he had made this kind of remark he had been hoping I would provide him with an excuse for remaining in the house; but I could tell that this time he wanted to go out.

I said that I did not mind being alone, but when he had gone I found that I did mind very much. I could not bear the thought that at any moment the telephone might ring and Dr. Laver would be on the other end of the line.

At night I lay listening to the noises in the garden and once I got up to look out of the window because I was sure that someone was prowling about beneath my window. I got up early. I was afraid the telephone would ring, but also dreaded the thought of the morning wasting away with no pebbles thrown against my window. When my father had gone I decided to visit Miss Maud.

I hoped she would be in, though how I intended to explain my call, I had no idea. I seemed to have got beyond the stage of explanations. Perhaps that was why I was going to see Miss Maud. She had got beyond that stage, too. Miss Maud had stayed at home with her father after her mother died. Miss Maud and I had a lot in common.

It was a sunny day. It had been sunny for a long time now, a world of light and abrupt shadow. Was this summer something of a record? I didn't seem to have read about it; but then lately the papers hadn't been delivered because there was a newspaper strike, or because our papers weren't getting through to us. Now that I wasn't going to the office it was difficult to remember which day it was. Time stood still. It had been hot like this when old Mr. Leveridge had taken me out into the garden to pick mulberries; the garden had been beautiful. Nowadays it would be open to the public at week-ends in aid of the local charity, but then it had had all the charm of a private place which few strangers had seen. The old man had treated me with grave courtesy; it had been hard to believe that he was cruel to his family.

I could see the Mill House in the distance. As I approached it I was surprised at how tall the weeds had grown. It was that time of summer when vegetation is at its most straggly; but even so, the vitality of the Mill House vegetation was surely phenomenal. It was not only the weeds which had grown; as I drew nearer I saw that the privet hedge which surrounded what had once been the croquet lawn was an impenetrable wall. It had grown so high that it was impossible to see whether anyone was in the garden, let alone the house. I wondered if Miss Maud had been taken ill and continued towards the house with apprehension.

The laurels had grown high over the stone wall at the front of the house. A branch, heavy and ponderous, impeded my way as I opened the gate; there was something unpleasant about the shiny, speckled leaves. There seemed to me to be no purpose in a laurel, except to keep the outside world at bay; this one had certainly performed that task. I was surprised when I had fought free of the laurel to see that the front garden had been tidied up. The earth had been turned and several rose bushes had been rescued from the weeds which had once choked them. On an impulse, I walked round the side of the house, past mounds of cut grass and uprooted weeds, and garden implements ranging from a trowel with a broken handle to a rusty scythe and a quite presentable motor mower. I looked towards the croquet lawn and received a shock. The privet hedge seemed even untidier from this angle, but in comparison the lawn was smooth and orderly and had the look of a place with a secret life. There was a deck chair on the lawn and Miss Maud was sitting in it, elegant in a long Liberty print dress. There was something eerie about the scene; it was not so much a sensation of stepping into the past as of having intruded into a little enclosure outside time where I had no right to be. I had an urge to go away before Miss Maud saw me. But it was too late. She looked across at me and laid the book she was reading face down on the grass. It was almost as though if she had not actually expected me, she was prepared for me. I walked towards her. The grass was not as smooth as it looked, and it scratched my feet. I wished I had not come.

There was something unusual about Miss Maud's hair. Perhaps it was just that she had washed it and this had made it fly about in the breeze forming a spidery halo round her face. Her skin was too heavily powdered for me to tell whether she had washed it as well. Her cheekbones were lightly touched with lavender and her lips looked as if they were stained with bilberries. Miss Maud usually applied make-up with slapdash bravado, but the effect on this occasion, although startling, had a premeditated quality which I found rather disturbing.

'What do you want?' She was looking at me with hostility as though I, too, had changed.

I was aware that I was a trespasser and said awkwardly, 'I was just passing.'

'I don't think we are on visiting terms.'

'I'm sorry.'

'And, in any case, people don't pass this house. It is not on the way to anywhere.'

'I was walking across the fields. I thought . . . ' I remembered Dr. Laver and said, 'I came for eggs.'

I had, it seemed, said the worst possible thing. 'You came here to spy on me, did you?' She got out of the deck chair with some difficulty. 'Really, one has no privacy from your kind of person.'

This conversation made no sense. I could not think of anything to say and was a little frightened. Now she was looking at me as though my body was an affront to her. The summer breeze stirred in my dress and made me conscious of my body, too. I found that I was thinking of Dr. Laver and, afraid that the thoughts must show in my face, I turned my head away.

She said, 'You don't look like your mother; but I suppose bad blood will out. Are you a whore, too?'

'My mother!' I wanted to be angry, but this turn of the conversation was so bewildering that my voice came out in a startled yelp.

'I've seen her walking back from the shops across the fields, wearing high-heeled shoes; making out she was surprised when she met him. I used to laugh when I saw them walking together, a bull of a man and an overblown woman, holding hands! But it was nothing to me. Good luck to them, I used to think. At least she knew her place; she never came flaunting herself in here, asking for eggs.'

I said, 'I'll go,' but I could not bring myself to turn away while her eyes were on me.

'Now you've come, you can at least let me decide when you are to leave.' She turned towards the house and indicated that I was to follow her. 'I think there are things you ought to know.'

She led me through the french windows. We stepped from sunlight into shadow and I felt goose pimples on my arms. The room smelt of incense and moth balls. There was a joss stick burning in a jar on the mantelshelf. I looked for an explanation of the moth balls and saw, glimmering in the subdued light, a crêpe-de-Chine shawl draped over the piano; its tasselled fringes moved slightly as we walked by. Potted plants had been placed about the room; one large one had dark leaves which gleamed as though they had been oiled. There was a decanter on a side table with exquisite Venetian glasses on a Florentine tray, and a packet of Turkish cigarettes.

The hall smelt of carbolic and was full of furniture, cane chairs, chess tables, a tall cake stand with a Benares bowl on top of it, a long mirror, a brass bedrest and a mattress. Miss Maud threaded her way past these obstacles and I followed. We went up the stairs. Sheets and blankets were draped over the balustrade on the landing. Windows were open and doors creaked and banged all along the corridor. There were pillows airing on the window seat and a white cat was curled up on one of them. Miss Maud opened wide the door of the first bedroom. It was a handsome room with a big sash window; there was a bottle beneath the window containing ammonia and a pink flower in the Chinese carpet bore witness to its application. The walnut chest of drawers was open and its contents were spread about the room, on the floor, the mantelshelf, and the window sill.

'I have been turning out,' Miss Maud said. Before I could comment, she went on, 'My lovers were all very devoted.' She took one of several bundles of letters down from the mantelshelf and handed it to me. I could see her fingerprints in the dust; I could also see that the top letter began, 'My darling Maud.'

'Poor Gerald!' Miss Maud said. 'He would have been very dull to live with; but he wrote amusing letters. He married his second choice, eventually. She'd been hanging over him like a ripe fruit for quite a time. Elspeth, she was called. It's a name one should outgrow, don't you think?'

'Did you reply to the letters?' I asked for want of something to say.

'Of course I replied! One should always encourage lovers. It is such tremendous fun leading a man on.' She looked at me in the sharp, malicious way that had characterised this exchange. 'None of my lovers has ever cared for another woman.'

'Didn't you ever want to marry?'

'Marry! Oh, my dear, what a vulgar little creature you are!' She snatched the bundle of letters from me and threw it down on the bed. 'Really, it's quite intolerable to be insulted in this way! I can't think why I ever bothered with you.'

She must be quite mad, I thought; and yet I sensed a purpose in her madness which I was unable to understand. I tried to think of something harmless to say. 'You've got your house looking very nice now, Miss Maud.'

'Nice?' She raised her eyebrows at the word. 'It is beautiful. A world on its own. The only way to be free is to create a world of one's own. The present world, after all, is scarcely one in which any sane person would want to live, so it is no place for those of us who don't give a fig for sanity.'

It seemed best not to reply, but silence availed me little.

'I suppose you think you know all about sanity and madness because you work in that place.'

'It's all very confusing,' I replied truthfully.

'That's not what you tap out on your typewriter, is it? Your psychologists and social workers like to pretend they know everything about everyone; but I know the truth about *them*. They are very timid. They have to label everything to make it safe, that's why they use all this jargon. It makes them feel they are in command. But it's all an illusion. I see the world more clearly; because I have a much better brain than any of them, and I'm not afraid of where it will lead me.' Her eyes were so bright and penetrating that it was difficult not to believe her. 'People are dying of tedium, rotting away quietly in their sitting-rooms—or lounges, as they would have it. When I was young we had customs and conventions, but they were just ways of avoiding tiresomeness, like unexpected callers and guests who don't know when to leave; they didn't inhibit us. Provided people didn't make a damn nuisance of themselves in public no one was illbred enough to enquire what they did in private. My father drank and he got the parlour maid with child; my dear mother, who was the gentlest of souls, turned the silly creature out of the house and she drowned herself in the village pond. But none of our neighbours thought it was any concern of theirs. My brother and my sister were lovers. My father would probably have killed them had he known. I don't think our neighbours would have cared much for it, either; but they wouldn't have interfered. Nowadays, people don't have private lives, they just sit in front of television congratulating themselves that, since they don't do anything, nothing can ever happen to them. "Where did it get him?" they ask, looking at a man who has lost an empire.' She was silent for a moment, and then she said, 'I have written to the Shah and told him that if he would like to stay here he would be welcome.'

'Do you think he will come?' I asked, nervously trying to keep my eyes from the big double bed with its lace coverlet and faded silk cushions.

'I hope so. He would be safe; no one would ever know that he was here.'

The white cat strolled into the room and rubbed up against my legs. Miss Maud went to the window. 'There would be no reason for him to leave, no one whom he had to consider, no duty he had to perform. There is all that one needs here. One is free to live as one likes.' She gazed with contempt at that other world of consideration and duty now almost hidden by the high hedges and straggling weeds. 'Your mother should have gone off with her farmer. They could have taken a farmhouse somewhere; it would have been easy for them, farmers are so self-sufficient.'

'I don't think one comes by working farms all that easily.' I tried to inject a note of practicality into the discussion, as much for my sake as for hers.

She said, 'The poor-spirited can always invent a few difficulties.'

'And there was me. She had to think about me.'

'You?' Miss Maud turned; her eyes glinted as she looked at me. 'Yes, I can see that you have probably been grossly indulged.' She was looking at my body again. I had a quite overwhelming sense of Dr. Laver; the smell of him was there in the room. 'But because your mother made sacrifices for you, you must not assume that other people will deny themselves on your account.'

I felt guilty about neglecting my father and so I assumed that she was talking about him, that she was telling me that he wanted to marry Eleanor. I wondered how she knew about Eleanor. There was little hope of finding out because she was talking about her life with the Shah again.

'The important thing is to order the day. The nights will present no difficulty; we shall tell stories and play charades. But during the day the imagination must be held in check, otherwise the magic will be lost. So we shall breakfast at ten, and have a few hours in the garden before the sun gets too hot. There will be a light lunch at noon, followed by an afternoon's work. I am proposing to write my autobiography and I daresay he will do the same; we might even combine on a project, I can think of several subjects which would be suitable. At four, we shall have tea, followed, I am afraid, by housework and gardening. He can have his choice as to which he does, but I am hoping he will choose the housework. Sherry at six, and music, flute or violin, while we watch the light fading. Dinner at eight. And then the night is ours.' She looked at her watch. 'A quarter to noon. I am afraid I must ask you to leave now as I have to prepare lunch. I am trying out the programme for the day as it may need a few adjustments here and there. I don't seem to have allowed much time for cooking.'

I went quickly before she thought of anything else that she wanted to tell me. The catch was down on the front door and I had difficulty opening it. My hands were shaking and I was sweating. It was a relief when it opened and I stepped into the noonday sunlight.

As I walked home across the fields I thought of Miss Maud and the Shah living in that house which he must never leave. A world on its own. It was crazy; but people did that sort of thing. I had read in the papers of men who had remained hidden ever since the war because no one had told them we were at peace. When I went to bed I thought of Miss Maud and the Shah, telling stories and playing charades.

The next day I went back to work.

10

UNTIL now I had ordered my life in compartments. When I was a child it had been Sunday school and home; then it was school and church and home: then it was office and tennis club and church and home. It had worked well, giving changes of pace and mood, light and shade, and it had given an agreeable degree of elusiveness to my conception of myself. Now everything had changed. I seemed to be moving along a tunnel aware of people in adjacent spaces but unable to communicate with them. The spaces were like small rehearsal rooms in which I caught glimpses of scenes from plays I did not recognise. The players conveyed a sense of purpose but the scenes were too many and too fragmented for them to have any meaning for me.

March House presented me with a new set of scenes but apart from that matters did not improve. Mrs. Libnitz greeted me from the reception-room. When I last saw her she had been talking to my father about Tito. Now she was saying, 'It's a good job we don't have neighbours.' I could hear distant shouts and screams. Mrs. Libnitz told me that Dr. Laver was seeing two of Douglas's clients and their children were playing in the garden. I went into the garden to observe the scene.

At first I did not recognise Iris. She had her hair clawed fiercely back from her forehead and secured by a bow at the nape of her neck; her face looked rather shockingly bold and hard. She and Douglas were standing on the path discussing role playing and family alignments while a sturdy four-year-old was dragging her brother and elder sister around in a cart. It was easy to see who was going to be the hewer of wood and drawer of water in this family. Di, who had been sitting on the garden seat, suddenly stubbed out a cigarette and advanced on the children. She said to the older girl, 'Now, come along, princess; it's time your kid sister had a ride.'

The child thus addressed, who bore a remarkable resemblance to the young Shirley Temple, burst into tears. Di lifted her out of the cart and deposited her screaming on the grass. The little boy, shaken by this show of authority, scrambled out of the cart and trundled his younger sister round the garden. Iris asked Douglas, 'What did you do when your kids behaved like this?'

'It was usually past their bedtime when I got home.'

My mind recorded all this, but it had no more reality than a scene from a play.

Di came across to me and said that she had missed me. 'No one around here has any sense of humour.' I tried to think of something humorous to say. Behind us, the french windows opened. Dr. Laver came out and bellowed, 'Stop that noise at once or I'll slice off your ears.' He returned to the house and an eerie silence descended. After a few moments' contemplation little Shirley Temple junior got to her feet and helped her brother to pull the cart round the garden. Iris caught sight of me and held her arms wide. Douglas acknowledged my presence with more restraint. We talked while we watched the children. I was so far into myself that I found it hard to respond. My mind had lost its sharpness and my vision its clarity, everything seemed dull and smudged.

After about ten minutes the parents came out through the french windows followed by Dr. Laver; the mother gazed at her first born and said loudly, 'She's never like that at home.' The child immediately let go her hold on the cart shaft; her face turned mottled purple and she began to scream, 'Nasty man . . .' pointing a chubby finger at Dr. Laver. Her mother gathered her up, but she was not to be comforted and threw herself about so much that she had to be put on the ground where she lay banging her head on the gravel path. Dr. Laver retreated through the french windows. Iris said to the parents, 'Perhaps we could go to my room for a talk? It's quieter there.'

Di said, 'If that was my child I'd belt her.'

Douglas said, 'No one is looking.'

The fabric of civilisation was breaking up. I turned and went into the house. I had never realised how large the garden was; I was out of breath when I reached my room. There was an untidy pile of work on my desk and I leafed through it without taking much note of it. The thoughts that troubled me at home still engaged my mind and seemed as relevant here. I must get out, I thought; but I could no longer think where was out. I thought about Miss Maud and the Shah. When Iris came in, having finished talking to the clients, I said:

'I went to see Miss Maud yesterday. She's spring cleaning her house and she says she is expecting the Shah to come and stay with her.'

'What Shah?' she asked, echoing an uneasy idea at the back of my mind.

'The Shah of Iran. Who else could she mean?'

'That would be enormous fun, wouldn't it ? I wonder what they would make of each other.'

'I'm serious.'

'I doubt that Miss Maud was. She's well in control of her fantasies, although she may like to give a different impression when it suits her.'

'But why should she be spring cleaning?'

'Yes, I must admit I find that a trifle sinister. But I

shouldn't worry about it. There is usually a method in Miss Maud's madness.'

Iris was at her most confident. There did not seem to be anything more I could say about Miss Maud and the Shah. I looked at the pile of papers beside my typewriter; it seemed unimaginable that I should ever shift them. Iris extracted something from the pile. 'I'm afraid there is a lot of typing there. The most important thing is this draft of a TV script. I've told Dr. Laver that he must put his reports on tape, so you won't have to take dictation from him.'

I suspected she was trying to keep me from Dr. Laver and this gave me a feeling of guilt as though I had not washed and the smell of my condition had betrayed me. I found it difficult to answer without showing my concern; it wasn't so much the words, as finding the right pitch for my voice.

'I would prefer dictation.' My voice sounded staccato and unnatural. 'I don't like doing audio work; it gives me a funny feeling in the head.' I emphasised this with a nervous giggle.

'It's just a matter of getting used to it.' She looked at me with those big, colourless eyes which seemed always to study another person's face in order to read their mind and take an opposite view. 'And quite apart from the question of dictation, I think it may be rather a strain for you to do Dr. Laver's work. For one thing, he is a very strong personality; for another, his methods are rather unorthodox. It is stimulating for people like Douglas and myself, but I think it would not be right to involve you too much.'

'I am the clinic secretary,' I said on a rising note. 'I have to be involved.' I had unfinished business with Dr. Laver. He had taken me into the past and without his aid I could not haul myself back into the present; I would remain trapped in that reeking tunnel. The thought appalled and excited me.

Iris laid the TV script on my typewriter and said something about it being wrong to place burdens on people not qualified to bear them.

I was about to protest when Dr. Laver came into the room. 'Is that your handbag in the hall?' he asked Iris.

She looked round vaguely and said, 'Yes, I expect so.'

'Then I have to tell you that abominable child has been sick in it.'

The door banged behind Iris and we heard her running down the corridor, opening the playroom door, and then it was quiet. The walls were thick and we could hope for a few minutes' peace. We breathed. It seemed a great luxury just to breathe. When Dr. Laver spoke it was like an echo of something I had already said. 'I've got to get out of this place.' I looked at him and saw that his need was as desperate as my own. 'I'm going to London for the week-end. Come with me.'

I knew that there were objections if only I could assemble them.

'You can go home at lunch-time and pack a case, if that's what is worrying you.' He stood beside me, agitatedly scratching his behind. 'I'll meet you on platform two at Weston Market at four-thirty.'

I managed to put a couple of words together. 'It's impossible.'

'Are you really intending to go through life saying that it is impossible to catch a four-thirty train to London?'

I tried to put more words together. There was the sound of voices in the corridor. I said, 'The five-thirty is a better train; it only stops at Cambridge.'

I went home to lunch and put a few things in a zip-bag; then I wrote a note to my father saying that I had had an unexpected invitation to spend the week-end with my cousin Hilda. Hilda was a nurse and my father was always saying what a 'sterling character' she was: I hoped her character would vouch for mine. As I moved about the house I was barely aware of what I was doing; the present had no reality, it was moving away from me.

The afternoon passed quietly and I did not see Dr. Laver. When I went up to his room with post to sign at half-past four it was empty. I told Iris that I would like to leave early because I was going to spend the week-end with my cousin. She made no objection and fortunately it did not occur to her to offer me a lift to the station. I caught the ten past five bus.

Dr. Laver was waiting for me when I arrived at Weston Market station. He was standing with his back to me studying a timetable on the wall. It was then that I had a moment of panic. As a result of my mother's illness it was a long time since I had ventured beyond Weston Market. I felt in no condition to enlarge the boundaries of my world and if Dr. Laver had not spotted me at that moment I would have turned back.

'Have you got your ticket?' he demanded.

'No, I. . . .'

'Well, hurry up! We're going to miss the train otherwise.'

'I thought you would have got it.'

'I'm a bit short of money until we get to London.' He took my zip bag. 'I'll get seats while you get the ticket.'

I was short of money myself, not having planned this week-end. It was an unpromising start. I had to wait in a queue and by the time I got on to the platform the whistle had gone; Dr. Laver was looking out of one of the windows. He waved as I ran along the platform. The train was already moving as he hauled me into the carriage. I could only assume that had I been a minute later he would have gone without me.

We sat side by side. The carriage was crowded and very hot. Dr. Laver seemed particularly affected. As the little town fled away behind us he flopped back in his seat, panting. There were four students sitting opposite us; they talked loudly in a manner which suggested that they were infinitely superior to the other hundred or so people on the train. Occasionally they spared us an amused glance, obviously thinking us dull beyond belief. Their conversation was liberally punctuated with four-letter words which, judging by the effect they seemed to anticipate, they must have found rather shocking. Poor things, I thought, with nothing to excite them but this intellectual slumming! Whereas I . . . whatever was I doing?

The train was going fast now, jerking over points, finding no rhythm. Images flashed by, a signal-box, shunting yard, hoardings, a row of grimy cottages, a crane with open jaws swinging predatory above a scrap heap, warehouses with a canal insinuated between them; bits and pieces of life broken up by the relentless passage of the train leaving who knew what chaos and confusion in its wake. I felt disorientated, as though the crane had snapped me up in its jaws and there was no telling where it would deposit me. I closed my eyes, sick and dizzy. But now I was more conscious of the train itself, of the brutal thrust of it carrying me forward recklessly. I must get out and have a quiet think about this; I must get out at once! It was too late; with a banshee wail the engine plunged into a tunnel. There was a roaring in my ears and a smell that must be brimstone. I gripped the edge of the seat with both hands. The sense of being projected forward at great speed was worse and the enclosing walls of the tunnel emphasised the danger of the enterprise. I decided that this madness must be brought to a halt and looked for the communication cord. It was above my head and seemed rather high, obviously firmness of purpose was required, a quick snatch would not do. While I was debating this the train came out of the tunnel and, leaping forward into the sunlight, found a rhythm and went purring down the track.

I looked out of the window again. Now there were fields and trees, a level greenness with here and there a hunched down house, and across the quiet, still scene hurtled this extraordinary phenomenon, a horizontal tube in which people sat, talked, read papers and moved swaying down the central aisle, went to the lavatory, ordered coffee; a totally alien life briefly superimposed on the pastoral scene. We passed through a small station where people waited, but not for us. I tried to catch the name but it fled past me. Now that I had tried to identify something, it seemed that it was the train that was still while everything else was in motion. Fields raced towards us, a man on a tractor was suddenly on a level with my window and then retreated into the past. How strange that I had not realised before what a surrealist experience train travel is. I looked at my companions. When I first got into the train they had seemed a long way away, at the far end of my own private tunnel; but now I found to my surprise that they were at normal range. The train had settled to a steady rhythm; it was saying 'Why am I here? Why am I here? Why am I here?' There were fields on one side, a river on the other, a level crossing; more fields, the river winding away from us now; here-and-there houses, then houses arranged in planned relation one to the other, a huge roundabout, streets leading towards a solid mass of buildings, a maze of railway lines. Another train went by, masking the view, and then we were running into Cambridge station. No one got into or out of the compartment. The train started, rattled over points, slowed for a signal, surged forward and found its rhythm again, 'Why am I here? Why am I here? Why am I here?' Fields, another river, children at a level crossing waving. I waved back. Beside me, Dr. Laver said, 'I never thought we'd make it.'

I was not sure what it was that we had 'made'. I still felt

disorientated and prone to fly apart at any minute, but the desire to pull the communication cord had gone. I concentrated on the business of holding myself in one piece. As the train gobbled up the miles it seemed to be saying, 'Here am I, here am I, here am I,' and this produced an uneasy, but not entirely unpleasant, sensation in my stomach. This feeling had nothing to do with Dr. Laver who was sitting beside me; it was an apprehensive anticipation which I usually only experienced when I was travelling to meet someone whom I did not know well enough to take for granted.

Fields were now giving way to the repetitive pattern of houses and small parades of shops which marks the sprawling suburbs of London. Dr. Laver said, 'Thank God', with such evident relief that one might have thought us to be riding in a stagecoach with a pack of Redskins on our trail instead of a British Rail diesel. He put his arm round my waist and explored my thigh. I said, 'Not now,' and he said, 'I must, I must . . .' and went on moving his hand in a twitchy way which I found irritating rather than erotic. For a moment, I felt about him as I had felt recently about my father; he was clinging to me because everything else was slipping away from him.

'Where are we staying?' I asked.

'Pimlico, Soho, Holborn . . .'

'But where?'

'I don't like making plans.'

'But I have to know where I am spending the night.'

He took my hand and said persuasively, 'It will be all right when the time comes, I promise you. It's barely seven. How can we possibly tell what we shall be doing at midnight?' His hand in mine was sweating and I realised he was in a panic at the very idea of committing himself so far ahead.

I said, without believing it would happen, 'All right; I

suppose if the worst comes to the worst we can sit on the Embankment or go to an all-night movie.' He put his arm round my shoulders and hugged me. The students had stopped talking, they were looking at us and I saw that this behaviour in people who were no longer young had embarrassed them. The train slowed down. We had arrived at Liverpool Street Station. It was beyond belief.

There were a lot of people on the platform waiting to board the train on its outward journey. As soon as we alighted we were pushed and jostled. One well-dressed man collided heavily with us, and then drew back with a startled exclamation. The swirl of passengers carried us away from him to the ticket barrier. As soon as we were past the barrier, Dr. Laver said, 'You go and wait for me up there.' He pointed to a restaurant which stood out like the prow of a ship high above the concourse where people waited for friends or studied the Departure board.

'Is anything the matter?' I asked.

'I've got bellyache . . . be all right in a minute or two.' He turned and made for the gents in a considerable hurry.

I climbed slowly up the stairs which led to the restaurant. There were only a few people inside and when I had paid the price of a cup of coffee and a cake I understood why. But as this was the only high living I seemed likely to have this week-end I determined to enjoy myself and took a seat by the window. The restaurant had a sober chocolate decor, and was furnished with high-backed cane chairs and marble-topped tables. There were healthy-looking aspidistras in big brass tubs. It was restful and pleasing and offered a good view of the station with its great arched fans of glass supported on slender pillars. Beyond the platform I could see the blue sky paling into grey and the tower of a church rising elegantly between buildings like concrete packing cases. A man at the next table said to his companion, 'I don't even know whether I'm on the short list. . . .' I sipped the coffee which was good.

There was an announcement for the 'off-shore party booked at the rear of the Yarmouth train.' A porter, hands behind his back, walked down number eleven platform which at present lacked a train; he moved leisurely as he might have done in a little country town. There was music over the tannoy now, unobtrusive, big-band style. A girl at another table said, 'My grandparents used to have chairs like this,' with respect for the very distant past. A train came in on number eleven platform, doors opened, people got out; not as many people as there had been on our train, but it was later now. In fact, it was ten to eight. I wondered idly what I would do if Dr. Laver had not come out of the gents by eight o'clock. I supposed I could call a policeman. I had another coffee and a rum baba.

In the event, I did not call a policeman because I had never sufficiently believed in Dr. Laver to warrant making a fuss about his non-appearance.

As I walked down the stairs from the restaurant the voice on the tannoy was announcing that the train for Cambridge would leave platform twelve in three minutes, calling at Harlow Town, Bishop's Stortford, Newport, Audley End . . . If I hurried I could catch it; it was the sensible thing to do. There were only a few people about on the platform now and the taxi drivers were no longer doing brisk business. I took pity on one of them and told him to drive me to the Strand.

My cousin Hilda was one of the diminishing number of natives who had a house in the West End. It had been bequeathed to her by an aunt. She was constantly propositioned by estate agents acting for wealthy Arabs, but so far she had held out; I had never been able to understand why, since with the amount of money they were prepared to pay she could have bought herself a sizable country mansion. Hilda, a rigid Calvinist, merely stated that she disliked profiteering: she could afford to dislike it, for the aunt had left her well-endowed and not only did she have the London house but a cottage in Norfolk. The London house was in a cul-de-sac in the area at the back of St. Martin's Lane; there was a Chinese restaurant on one side of it and the offices of a film company on the other. Hilda was not in when I arrived. I had an idea that she now had a rather exalted position at the hospital and no longer did night duty; if I was right, she would probably return before ten o'clock because she kept sober hours.

So, here am I, standing on the corner of St. Martin's Lane on a still summer evening, light, mellowed by dust and petrol fumes, slanting across the traffic-littered street, shadows of plane trees dappling the grimy pavements of Charing Cross Road; people hurrying to and from Trafalgar Square, like so many quavers and crochets, their apparently haphazard activity contained by the rising tide now flowing leisurely in from the suburbs.

I began to walk towards Trafalgar Square where I could see the fountains playing. People passed close by me, occasionally eyes rested on my face, but I was of no interest, an incidental woman. After a time, I began to savour this anonymity; and as I walked I looked more frequently for confirmation of it from those around me. My father had said that he would be late home this evening so probably he had not yet seen my note; Dr. Laver, if he thought about me at all, would imagine I was on the train back to Cambridge. I was particularly glad to have eluded Dr. Laver who always gave the impression of knowing things about me that I did not know myself. It was a great relief to think that at this moment no one in the whole world knew that Ruth Saunders was now walking past the National Gallery, heading towards Haymarket. I could not recall a time when I had so completely slipped free of the web of love and concern. I had not realised until now how used I had become to being noticed, how, lately, I had come to suspect that everyone had designs on my independence. Here, in this indifferent crowd, the idea seemed a monstrous conceit; not even monstrous, that was too pretentious, just a conceit. A bearded man waved to a shorn girl and they came together in front of me, joining hands and blocking my way as though I was invisible. I extricated myself and collided with a man who was in too much of a hurry to hail a taxi to heed my apology. As I walked I felt increasingly light and unburdened and, standing on the corner of Haymarket, I enjoyed a moment of indecision, surprised to find myself free of that inner prompting which usually told me so unfailingly which way I was to go at every turn. I drifted with a group of Italians to the traffic island and then crossed to the far side of Haymarket, but did not walk up it because my feet went on towards Lower Regent Street.

But it had been a mistake to take note of that moment of indecision. She was back with me again, that exacting prefect who monitored my behaviour. My mother, she reminded me, had liked Lower Regent Street. We had done this walk several times. I had hated it, feeling hot and sticky, longing for the time when the train would take us back to the country which was fresh and wholesome and better in every way, spiritually, morally, physically, than this ugly, sprawling city. What an ungracious, complaining companion I had been, refusing to be appeased by promises of ice-cream or a new pair of sandals. This priggish child threatened my new-found anonymity. I turned into Piccadilly and when I came to St. James's Church I went inside hoping that in return for an act of atonement I might be able to leave her there, at least for the week-end. The office of Compline was about to be said. I was faintly irritated at having to share my devotions at this moment, but I accepted the copy of the service and allowed myself to be shown into a pew. The minister said, '*May the Lord Almighty grant us a quiet night and a perfect end*.' He spoke soberly and unemphatically and continued in the same manner to speak of the devil going about as a roaring lion. I did not open the copy of the service, but phrases came to my ears from time to time. '*Thou hast set me at liberty when I was in trouble* . . .' '*Bow down thine ear to me; make haste to deliver me* . . .' I felt I should make some offering of my troubles, enumerate a few of the afflictions from which I was in need of deliverance. But the service was so spare, so lucid, that it did not allow for the relating of the phantasmagorical experiences which had recently disturbed me; and the more I tried to reduce them to orderly proportions, stripped of emotion and imagination, the less there seemed to be to relate. '*Thou shalt not be afraid for any terror by night: nor for the arrow that flieth by day; for the pestilence that walketh in darkness; nor for the sickness that destroyeth in the noon-day* . . .' These great phrases sat so lightly on the mind that they seemed more of a rebuke than a reassurance, a reminder that it is neither necessary nor profitable to enlarge on affliction, that in the matter of suffering, as in everything else, a degree of modesty is required. As the service went on, I had increasingly the feeling that here, too, I was, if not exactly anonymous, then of no peculiar interest. I tried to forget about myself, to think of my mother and make an act of atonement. But nothing came of it. I had nothing to offer, everything seemed to have dropped away from me, even the sense of loss which had been with me for so long seemed to have gone. Nothing was required of me, no busyness of mind or spirit. I did not feel exactly rejected, but there was a coolness in the air. The calm voice spoke not of dramatic confrontation, a lurid journey into the past, but simply of '*time for the amendment of life*'. I put down my copy of the service and was one of the first out of the church after the Blessing had been said.

The sun had set but the light was still good and I sat on the seat in the courtyard, probing this absence of loss as one probes a tooth to see if it can be made to ache again. I watched the people walking along Piccadilly and thought of my mother; a passionate, insecure woman married to a shy, deeply wounded man. She had said to the farmer, 'I couldn't leave Ruth.' Would she have made her life with him had it not been for me? Or had she been glad of the fetters that prevented her from taking so challenging a step? Nothing came of these thoughts, except the knowledge that the tragedy, if tragedy there was, was my mother's and I had no business with it. I realised then, not with sadness, but a dryness that was beyond sadness, that almost without knowing it was happening, I had said my farewell to my mother and must now let her rest in peace.

It was beginning to be chilly. I got up and walked into Piccadilly. It was too soon to return to Hilda's house and I must find some way to pass the time. By now I was rather hungry, so instead of turning into Green Park I went in search of food, but all the restaurants were expensive. There seemed to be nowhere for the person on the way to an evening class to stop for a snack, for office friends to meet for a brief exchange of gossip on their way home, for the solitary one-roomers to have a meal if not in conversation with, at least within sight of, other human beings. Soon, if it had not already happened, London would be given over to the big spenders. Eventually I found a small Italian restaurant where I had a highly-priced pizza with a scrape of vegetables, cheese and anchovy on a cardboard base.

It was ten o'clock when I turned into the cul-de-sac

and there was a lighted window on the first floor of Hilda's house. I knocked on the door, but there was no reply. The house held its breath. I knocked again, louder, and there was still no reply. It had not occurred to me that anyone as imposing and resolute as Hilda would not open her door in the evening, but this was obviously the case. I beat a tattoo on the door and then stepped back from the house, hoping that curiosity would impel Hilda to peer out of the window. It did. I waved and gesticulated. She moved away from the window and after what seemed a long time the curtains on the ground floor twitched slightly. I pushed back the flap of the letter-box and shouted, 'Hilda, it's me, Ruth! Your cousin, Ruth!' Again, a long time seemed to elapse, then the door was opened fractionally and one eye peered out. There was the sound of a chain being unfastened. Hilda said, 'Come inside' and backed into the hall, one hand holding a dressing-gown between her heavy breasts.

'This is awful of me,' I said, stepping inside with some trepidation. But once the door was safely closed and the chain replaced Hilda let go her hold of the dressing-gown and embraced me boisterously. 'What a gorgeous surprise!' There was no doubting her delight, but it seemed to me that I was doubly welcome because my arrival had initially occasioned her alarm.

'I get so fussed,' she said as she carried my zip-bag into the sitting-room. 'I can't think what I'm going to be like when I'm menopausal.' It was only when we were drinking Ovaltine that she recollected her usual role and said, 'What is this all about? I hope you haven't done anything silly?' Her voice reminded me of a time when she was nine and I was five and had eaten too much ice-cream.

'I felt I had to get away.'

'It's not another Reuben?'

'Nothing like that.'

'Of course, you've had a lot of unhappiness with your

dear mother's death; and I expect you are finding it a strain looking after your poor papa.'

'You know all about that,' I answered. She had lovingly nursed her own parents through their respective terminal illnesses.

'You mustn't feel trapped because you have to look after your papa, Ruth. It will be much worse when he's gone and you are on your own.' She looked at me, hesitating, with troubles to tell; then seemed to take a grip on herself. 'It's late and we can talk tomorrow. I shall be on duty all day, but I could meet you for lunch.'

She took me upstairs to one of the spare rooms and I helped her to make up the bed. It was a tall house, though narrow, and there must have been at least four spare rooms.

'Do you let any of the rooms?' I asked, remembering that she had planned to do this.

She shook her head and thumped a pillow. 'You will find it very noisy after your peaceful home,' she warned.

'I expect you get used to it.'

'No. It was lucky for you that I was on duty this Saturday. When I have a free week-end I go down to the cottage, can't get there fast enough.'

She fussed over me, bringing a tray with an electric kettle so that I could make myself tea if I could not sleep. For some time I lay awake. The house seemed rather sad with all those unused rooms; I thought how I would have enjoyed hearing other residents coming in, filling kettles in the kitchen, exchanging the news of their day over a drink in one of the bedrooms above. Just as I was dozing a fight broke out in the road. Hilda called out, 'Don't get alarmed. It happens every night.' Someone broke up the fight and it was comparatively quiet until two o'clock. From then until four o'clock they seemed to be smashing plates in the Chinese restaurant next door. After that I slept and did not wake until half-past nine. There was a note from Hilda saying that she had not wanted to disturb me and had left breakfast things out in the kitchen; I was to meet her for lunch at the hospital and she gave instructions as to where I would find her.

I had a pleasant morning window-shopping in Regent Street and wandering down side-streets into beautiful, expensive squares. There were a lot of tourists and young people who probably did not belong in any particular country but were constantly on the move and who sat on the steps of the terraced houses throwing banana skins and paper bags on to the pavements, the world their dustbin.

In spite of Hilda's instructions I got lost at the hospital and ended up in out-patients which had a parochial atmosphere I had not expected in a big London teaching hospital. It was apparent that to the people of Soho this was their local surgery; there were butchers with cut fingers, Italians talking like old friends to the woman with the tea trolley, a gloriously apparelled Nigerian in transit accompanied by his wife and what seemed to be his entire family trailing feudally behind him. One of the girls at the reception desk was vainly trying to convince a small Chinese man that there was no need for him to see the doctor again. 'You've been discharged.' The Chinese nodded his head and talked quietly and urgently. After a time the girl retired for consultation with the other receptionists; there were hisses of '*You* tell him . . .' 'I can't, he never understands . . .' 'Send him to Casualty . . .' 'They sent him here.' Eventually, a pony-tailed lass was thrust forward. She advanced to the counter, thrust out a dramatic hand, and intoned, 'Go away! No come back many moons.' The Chinese turned away, puzzled, and held a whispered conference with several compatriots who were sitting on the benches. I went to the reception desk and asked for Sister McIver.

Hilda had decided that we should go out to lunch and

we went to an Italian restaurant in Soho. Hilda explained that she was not doing her full duties at present and so could afford to take a long lunch hour. 'In fact, I'm going in for an op. next week. Nothing serious, a bit of trouble with the waterworks.' It sounded rather elderly and Hilda indeed looked more than her age, her skin was a bad colour and there were pouches beneath her eyes; but it was apparent that she did not want to talk about it and for a few minutes we chatted in a desultory way about life in London. Then I said, idly flying my kite, 'I would like to open a teashop. Then if it was successful, I'd buy another and then another. All reasonably priced. I'd change the eating habits of London.'

'You'd never make a success of it.' Hilda took me up vehemently as though the project was already on the drawing-board. 'You don't care enough about money. It's only the people who are primarily concerned with money who can bring about change on that scale.'

'Just a daydream.'

'London isn't a place for daydreaming. It's a depressed society.'

Hilda's face was hot and her eyes were angry; for some reason she was very much on the defensive. While she set about demolishing my pretensions I looked over her shoulder into the street. The sun was still shining brightly; people were walking by, dark people, yellow people, pink people, people from trim houses in the suburbs and rootless people, old, young, hairy and kempt. At a stall across the road a woman was pulling the leaves of pineapples before making her choice.

'She is the one I would ask the way,' I said, expecting Hilda to follow my train of thought.

She did not even follow my gaze, she said, 'But you don't need to ask the way when you're with me.'

'I meant that she has the look of belonging, not being a tourist . . .'

'How can you possibly tell.'

The waiter came and took our order.

'She's here to buy vegetables and fruit,' I said when he had gone. 'She's not sight-seeing . . .'

Hilda went on talking about the depressed society and its effect on the individual. The woman had left the stall and was walking past a restaurant on the far side of the road. I judged her to be young, but not a girl; there was something elusive about her and it was difficult to guess at her age at this distance, she might even be in her mid-thirties.

Hilda said, 'In a depressed society the most the individual can manage is a small personal adjustment. It would be a great mistake to imagine . . .'

'It's not the end of the world to make a mistake or take a wrong turning . . .'

I found myself looking to the woman for confirmation, but a couple of men coming out of the restaurant masked her from my view; then I fancied I had a glimpse of her further down the street. I could not keep her in focus long enough to have a clear picture of her. The waiter came with whitebait. When he had gone I looked out of the window again, eager to see what the woman was doing now, but she had been swallowed up in the crowd and I had to supply the answer myself.

'. . . very risky,' Hilda was on to the violent society now, 'what with muggings in the subways and fights on late-night buses.'

I saw her continuing her walk: a woman in a big city where the beautiful and the squalid interact and safety can never be taken for granted. I saw her shopping in winter evening streets, lamps lighting pavements gleaming in a drizzle of rain, the frantic homeward bound travellers jostling those who would be staying behind when night fell and the streets gradually emptied. I saw her shopping, knowing what she wanted and at what price, looking into the faces of shopkeepers and passers-by without a need to placate or to challenge, meeting them on a level, one person to another, unafraid of where each new encounter would lead her: an incautious, venturesome person, not seeking alliances to safeguard herself against bad times.

Now, for a moment, I did not see her so much as sense her. She breathed and I felt the breath stir my body. My body felt different, the pulse of blood was unfamiliar; or was it that I had never listened to my blood before?

'. . . in Bayswater and the only person to come to her help was a Negro. It upset her dreadfully because she's very colour conscious.' Hilda pushed her plate to one side. 'You haven't been listening to anything I have said. You've been dreaming again.'

I knew that I had not been dreaming, but I did not want the woman to be investigated by Hilda, so I said, 'Some parts of London are lovely, you must admit. The parks . . .'

'There's a mosque in Regent's Park now, did you know?'

'My father was talking about it last week.' I thought about home and my father in dismay. 'Perhaps I could give him a ring tonight?'

'Yes, of course; whenever you like.'

I looked out of the window again, feeling unsettled. I wondered what Dr. Laver was doing; for all I knew he might have died in the gents at Liverpool Street station.

Hilda said, 'You have a bad effect on me, Ruth.' I looked at her guiltily, but she was gazing down at the veal escallop which the waiter had just placed in front of her.

I telephoned my father that evening and he said that he was all right but that Punter was missing me. I told him to tell Punter that I would arrive at Weston Market on the four-ten train the next day.

Hilda prepared a light supper and after we had eaten

we went for a walk in St. James's Park. It was cool for the first time during the day. There were people sitting in deck chairs and lying on the grass; it was quiet, the peace undisturbed by the noisy thoroughfares which surrounded the park. We crossed the bridge over the lake, pausing to look towards Buckingham Palace and in the other direction at the turrets of the Admiralty mirrored in the still water.

'London *can* be beautiful,' I said.

'But it's only skin deep.' Hilda looked nor' west of Buckingham Palace. 'There are some squalid areas around Victoria.'

We crossed The Mall and walked slowly through Green Park past Clarence House and the Ritz. She said, 'It's the same wherever you go, there's a lot of nastiness back of all the posh terraces and squares.' In the twilight we walked down Piccadilly and men eyed us speculatively. There were gangs of youths in the area between Piccadilly Circus and Leicester Square, rootless and unstable as autumn leaves which may swirl up at the first breath of wind; their activities were watched by quieter people lingering in doorways or lounging against walls. I thought of that woman I had half-recognised and I knew that she had thrown away the chance of a quiet life; she had decided to pay the penalty which might be violence in a dark street or the less spectacular fate of those who are left alone because they do not fit easily into the conventional pattern.

That night, when Hilda brought Ovaltine to me in bed, I said, wanting reassurance, 'But you do like living in London, don't you, Hilda, in spite of everything?'

She sat on the end of my bed, wrapped in her old woolly dressing-gown, looking cold in spite of the warm air. 'I hate it. I'm at the Middlesex all day and then I come back here; and I try not to notice what goes on in between.'

'Why don't you take people in, Hilda? You've got the upper floor empty and spare bedrooms on this floor. I remember you had another bathroom put in and a shower because you planned to let off rooms. You could take four or five people. It would be splendid, even better than running a teashop. There must be such a need for rooms.'

She turned her head away. 'I ought to, of course; it troubles my conscience having a house this size to myself. But it would be a big risk to let rooms. You never know who might turn up; there are some very nasty stories.'

I realised she was lonely and afraid and I put my hand in hers.

'Hilda, don't let things get you down. Just think how lucky you are to be doing the one job you always wanted to do.' She looked at our clasped hands, her face unhappy. 'You are a very rare person,' I told her. She looked at me then, surprised. 'You are the person you would like to be. I think most of us are two people, the person we are, and the person we would like to be, and we have to make sure they don't get too far apart.'

'And if they do?' She did not quarrel with this, which surprised me as she was not usually responsive to my flights of fancy.

'We have to let go of the person we are and make a leap towards the other person before they get right away.'

She bent forward and kissed me. 'Try and get some sleep before they start banging about next door. I'll give you some cotton wool to put in your ears.'

The next morning Hilda went to her chapel and I went to St. Martin-in-the-Fields. After lunch Hilda insisted on coming to Liverpool Street station to see me off. We arrived early. The Cambridge train had just come in and we had to wait at the barrier while the passengers alighted. I looked round for Dr. Laver but I did not see him. One of the last of the arriving passengers was the man who had bumped into us on this very platform on Friday evening. I probably would not have noticed him had he not nodded to Hilda as he passed by. 'Who is that man?' I asked.

'Dr. Cumner Asche. He's one of our consultants.' She walked past the barrier carrying my zip-bag and saw me safely into a carriage. 'I hope things will be all right, Ruth—for both of us.'

The whistle went and the train began to move. I waved until I could not see Hilda any more. The train rattled briskly past the tall, grimy buildings of Inner London. We were at Harlow in no time at all. I watched the houses and parades of shops falling away and the fields running towards me, welcoming me back to that country world which I had always regarded as fresh and wholesome and safe until Dr. Laver showed me otherwise.

11

THERE was a man with a dog waiting under the clock at Weston Market station. That was how I saw them, standing there in the evening sunlight; figures in a composition. Beyond were a row of white-washed houses and shops, some ancient, the upper storeys overhanging the street; an old man rode down the street on a bicycle, the evening breeze in his wispy hair. I observed the scene in the detached way that one studies photographs not of one's own period.

Punter saw me and leapt about, tugging on his lead. The man and I took steps towards each other. He looked at me as though I had become distanced from him; although there was no reproach in his gaze there was sadness. He let Punter leap up between us but he did not tell me how much Punter had missed me.

'How was Hilda?' he asked as he took my zip bag from me.

'A bit under the weather; she has to have a minor op. this week. She sent her best wishes to you.'

We got into the car. Punter, in the back seat, refused to settle down and kept thrusting his nose between us.

'Was the weather good here?' I asked. 'It was lovely in London; none of that awful haze.'

'We've had quite a wind. The woman in the post office assures me it is all to do with the hydrogen bomb.'

When we reached the house I asked, 'Did you have a proper lunch?'

'Yes, Punter and I finished the joint between us. I shan't want much supper.'

The house was in order, the kitchen tidy, the sink clean. If he had had difficulty in managing, he had not left evidence of it for me to find. After supper we settled down to listen to the radio adaptation of Anthony Powell's *Dance to the Music of Time*.

'I don't think the chap who's playing Peter Templar has struck the right note yet, do you?' he asked me.

'It's not how I imagined him,' I agreed. 'I think Stringham may be good, don't you?'

I went to bed when the programme ended. My bedroom seemed quieter than usual. I went to the window and looked out. The wind had dropped and it was a bright, still night. Tomorrow I would cycle to the office and the man who was my father, Stewart Saunders, would take the train to London. What a long daily journey it was for him; what did he do in the train, did he have travelling companions or did he sit alone, wrapped in his own thoughts? What were his thoughts? I did not know what had gone on in his mind over the last few weeks, what battles he had been fighting, what effect my sudden departure this week-end might have had on the outcome. For some reason, at what cost I could not guess, he had adjusted his view of me. Whether this was a sacrifice to give me freedom, or a change he found necessary for his own sake, again, I did not know. Perhaps I exaggerated my importance? Perhaps my actions had not been so significant as I imagined. In his desolation after my mother's death, he might have tried to construct a new life in which an imaginary daughter played a part; in time, the imaginary world had palled and he had found he could not sustain it. Perhaps that was how it was. But whatever the answer, he had decided to let go his hold on me as I must let go my hold on him. It was as it should be, but I had not yet reached a stage where I could be sanguine about it. I felt lonely and hollow inside.

The next morning I woke early. The temperature had dropped during the night and it was pleasantly cool. I decided to walk to the office and set out early. Although the day was as yet cloudless I could smell damp borne on the wind from the Fens. The visibility was good and many miles beyond the Mill House the tower of Ely Cathedral was just visible. The fields seemed at this moment to stretch uninterrupted between me and the cathedral, and in the clear morning light I could make out quite easily the dark line of shadow, with lighter lines on either side of it, which marked the course of an old river which had been silted up in times before the Romans came. These and other features of the landscape had been pointed out to me many times when I was at school, but it was only now that it struck me as a thing to marvel at that every day I was treading history. I recalled that votive deposits from the Bronze Age had been found in Grunty Fen, not so many miles from here.

I arrived at the office only to find the front door locked. I had not brought my key with me, so I sat on the grass verge to wait the arrival of Mrs. Libnitz. I had not thought until now what I would do if Dr. Laver showed up at the office. Surprisingly, I had not thought about Dr. Laver since I made my escape from him in London. It was inconceivable, of course, that he should return. But just supposing the inconceivable happened, my course of action was quite straightforward: I should walk out immediately. I was very angry. I sat and contemplated my anger. It did not quite satisfy me and I was trying to devise ways of stimulating it when the postman arrived and handed me our letters. There were only three; two were for Douglas and one was for Iris. The letter addressed to Iris had the crest of the Foundation on the back of the envelope; the envelope itself was crumpled and bore signs of having got very wet at some time.

'It looks as if that letter's been in the pond,' the post-man said.

'Does that really happen to our letters?'

'We had one fellow who used to throw the mail bags away when he got tired. Town chap, he was. Said the farm dogs went for him.'

When he had gone I opened the envelope. The letter, dated three months previously, stated that Dr. Laver would not now be coming to our clinic as he was ill; it was hoped that the clinic would continue to function until such time as another psychiatrist had been appointed. I looked at the date on the letter again; the third of March, three days before Dr. Laver had, in fact, arrived at the clinic.

A few minutes later Mrs. Libnitz arrived. She was annoyed to find me waiting and explained irritably that the bus had been late. 'Why didn't you knock at Douglas's flat?'

'I had forgotten he lived here. And anyway, I wasn't in a hurry.' I hesitated on the porch, not wanting to go into the house. 'It's going to rain. I can smell it coming up from the Fens.'

'I don't smell anything. I smoke too much.' She banged open the hatch in the reception room and flipped a key on the switchboard.

I went reluctantly to my room, holding the letters in my hand, not prepared to think about Dr. Laver. Iris had left a pile of paper tied up in a file on the side of my desk. She normally kept her papers in good order but this file was filled with scraps of paper on which only a few words were scribbled, as though she was organising an intellectual paper chase. I studied one scrap which read '. . . revealed that I was, in fact, intensely envious of my adored Podge.' While I was looking at it the door opened and Iris came in.

'I meant to get here before you,' she said, taking the

file from me. 'I was going to put my notes in order. You may have a little difficulty deciphering them as it is.'

'But *what* are they?'

'Notes for a series of TV programmes.' She was intensely excited and zoomed erratically about the room.

'A series?'

'Yes, isn't it splendid? I shall be doing the introductory programmes with a psychiatrist, possibly Dr. Laver, although there is a very interesting young man whom I met at a party in Cambridge . . .' She had been shuffling the papers while she spoke and now she looked down at them frowning. 'Oh dear, now where did this come in?' She closed her eyes. 'Mmmh . . . ah, yes! The prize-giving where I came second to Cecily Brandt and tore up my certificate and put it down the lavatory.' She did some more shuffling and dropped several pages on the floor. 'It is absolutely fascinating.' She squatted, laying the scraps of paper out on the rug like pieces of a jig-saw puzzle. As I looked down at her form, which seemed to be gathered into a tight knot from which hands darted back and forth like feelers, I was amazed at the ferocity of her activity; almost, I expected to hear an angry buzzing. 'Fascinating! The unrealised part of oneself that escapes analysis is here revealed unequivocally . . . Oh, bugger!' She looked first at one scrap, then at another, while another was held in a poised hand, the head moving busily from side to side all the while. This feverish squandering of energy distressed me, but I could not think how to quiet her. All our exchanges at the clinic were in close-up, we interacted eyeball to eyeball, the exterior world was of no more relevance than a blurred map without date or compass point. What would she say were I to speculate about Celtic chalk figures on the Gogmagog Hills to the south of us or the importance of the preservation of Wicken Fen to the east? 'Yes, I recall now,' she said. 'That goes in *here*, when I got lost at the Ideal Home Exhibition and I told everyone that I was Iris Fowler and it didn't help at all. My first crisis of identity! Oh dear, there must be one piece missing; it doesn't make sense without it.'

The sycamore beyond the window had the wind in it, I could hear the dry rustle of the foliage; there were bands of purplish cloud above the tree. Iris said sharply, 'Close that window! The wind will blow these papers everywhere.'

'Does it matter?' I welcomed the intervention of the wind.

'Matter?' She sprang to her feet and ran to the window, slamming it shut, a swirl of movement which further disarranged the papers on the floor. She looked at me, her eyes snapping open and shut angrily. 'You are thinking of just a few pieces of paper, aren't you, a silly game? But it's much more than that. I always felt it was so unfair that men had made all the great voyages of discovery. Women have been liberated far too late to share in that. But *this*, this is the last unexplored territory. Doesn't it excite you? The last kingdom to be conquered, the most intractable, the most deeply defended . . .'

'You sound like Dr. Laver.'

'Don't be misled. I'm not under Dr. Laver's influence and I don't intend to go too far with this myself; but it is a technique which I can see will be very useful in helping people who are sick.'

'You're not accepting the challenge of the last undiscovered territory, then?'

'What a sharp little tongue you have, Ruth. I'm certainly accepting the challenge. All I am saying is that if one is to pursue it effectively a certain objectivity will be necessary and that can best be achieved by research which doesn't involve self-participation at a level where one loses objectivity . . . or something like that. I haven't thought it through yet.' She moved another piece of paper and seemed satisfied with the result. 'Dr. Laver has been helpful, of course; up to a point, he is insightful. But he is not indispensable.'

I said, 'That's good, then,' and handed her the letter from the Foundation. She sat on the edge of the table and read it through; then she folded it and gazed at the jig-saw arrangement on the floor as though wondering where the letter might be fitted into it. She had the look I had seen when she read a report on a new case which she thought had exciting possibilities, a certain jubilation which she could never quite restrain although she was aware that it was unprofessional. She handed the letter to me. 'Interesting, Ruth, don't you think? *Very* interesting.'

'What does it mean?'

'I don't think I'm going to ask that.' She gave me a shrewd, intelligent look, already making calculations about something that was beyond my understanding of the situation.

'But won't you have to take it up with the Foundation?' I said. '*They* will ask questions.'

'The Foundation is in a lot of trouble as it is. I'm sure they would not want us to involve them in any more publicity.'

'So what will you do?'

'When Douglas and Di come in, we will have a talk about it. You had better join us.'

I did not want to join them. I wanted to take them all and place them some distance away, preferably out in the garden; I had the sensation that I could no longer focus on them at close quarters. When Iris had collected her papers and gone to her room, I opened the window and stood looking out, waiting for the rain to come. It was badly needed, there were bare patches in the lawn and the flowers drooped. The waves of agitation settled slowly after Iris's departure.

There was a lot of work to be done but I had great difficulty in organising myself and by the time that Iris telephoned to ask me to come to her room, I had typed only two letters.

Douglas and Di had read the letter when I arrived. Douglas was unimpressed. He said that as the letter had gone astray there must be other letters which had also gone astray which would have explained the whole thing if only they had reached us. His face was set in lines of stubborn resistance and it was obvious that he had no intention of accepting any other hypothesis; he had enough problems and was not prepared to contemplate any addition to them. Di, who had been gazing at her arms which glowed mahogany in the dim light, looked up and said, 'The Foundation must know he's here. Someone has to pay his salary; he's not doing this for love.'

Iris looked at her in surprise. 'I hadn't thought of that.'

'How do you imagine he's living, for Christ's sake!'

None of us knew, and while we were speculating, Mrs. Libnitz came to tell us that Dr. Laver had telephoned to say that he had 'flu and would not be able to come to the clinic until the middle of next week.

'Where was he telephoning from?' Iris asked.

'How would I know? I did not ask.'

'I wish you would put these calls through to me or Ruth.'

'He said he does not want to talk to either of you,' Mrs. Libnitz said with satisfaction and withdrew.

'I think this may be the last we shall see of Dr. Laver.' Iris darted a triumphant look at Douglas. 'But should he return in a few days, I shall have had time to finalise certain arrangements. I think we may able to work this out quite satisfactorily. Don't worry.'

'I don't see any need to worry,' Douglas replied. 'There is a lot of 'flu about.'

Di, who had walked across to the window, exclaimed, 'It's raining! I left the top of Kenny's car down; he'll be wild.' This was obviously more important to her than anything that had happened in the clinic.

It rained all the afternoon, soft, quiet, undramatic rain, but very persevering, one could smell the earth yielding to it. The birds made the most of it. The crackle and vibrancy in the air had gone by the time I left the office. Di, who had spent the afternoon sponging down Kenny's car, offered me a lift, but I refused and set out to walk through the sodden lanes. The dust had been damped down and there was a smell I seemed not to have noticed for a long time, a smell of living, growing things all around me. I remembered how, half my life ago, I had splashed through this lane chanting, '*Little trotty wagtail, you nimble all about, and in the dimpling water pudge you waddle in and out . . .*' The clouds were breaking up now and as I walked the rain gradually ceased. It was cool and the fields did not steam when the sun came out; everything was clear and translucent. When I reached home I changed into slacks and started weeding the flower borders.

On Thursday evening, Eleanor telephoned. Stewart spoke to her. When he came into the kitchen where I was doing the ironing, he said, 'Eleanor is coming for the week-end.' He offered no comment. So, I was to be informed of Eleanor's visit but not consulted! I pressed the iron down hard and burnt the collar of my blouse. Stewart, who had been watching me, said, 'Oh, darling, not that pretty blouse! Let me buy you another one.'

'It's all right. I've had it a long time.' But I felt tears in my eyes as I put it aside.

Stewart was out watering the lawn on Friday evening when Eleanor arrived. I heard them talking in the garden. Punter came trotting in proudly carrying her handbag. 'You're quite a favourite,' I told her when she followed some minutes later. Stewart put her suitcase down in the hall and said he would take it upstairs when he had finished in the garden. I took Eleanor into the drawing-room and poured her a gin and tonic. She watched to make sure I was not too heavy-handed with the tonic.

'It's good to get away from London,' she said. 'The heat is dreadful now.'

'I was up there last week-end.'

'You should have stayed with me.' She sipped her drink appreciatively. 'In fact, if you ever wanted it while I'm away, you'd be welcome to use the flat.'

'I wouldn't have anything so valuable to offer in exchange,' I said.

She frowned into her gin and tonic; for a moment it seemed she would not follow this up, but then she thought better of it. 'Are we talking about the property value of a flat in South Kensington, or the quality of life?' She gave me a straight, but not unpleasant look.

'A mixture of both, I suppose,' I temporised. 'It's a beautiful flat and it's your own, you've furnished it and you run it your way.'

'I leave my flat at eight-thirty every morning and I return after six,' she said drily. 'I don't furnish my office or run it my way. The business world is very competitive. Competition is healthy for business, but not for people over forty. I'm tired of competing, Ruth.'

'Your flat seems so much a part of your personality,' I protested. 'You wouldn't ever think of giving it up, surely? You chose the furniture so carefully; I remember Mother telling me how you went round all the junk shops searching for the treasures one could still find in those days. And you did it all *yourself*, Eleanor. You're so self-sufficient.'

'When I took on the flat I had to be self-sufficient.' She was quite unmoved by my eloquence. 'If I ever give it up I shall have to take stock and decide what goes with me and what it is necessary to leave behind. Some of the furniture wouldn't be suitable anywhere but in a London flat.'

If she had reached the stock-taking stage there were items I thought should be brought to her notice.

'My mother always missed London so much,' I said. 'She found life in the country very dull.'

'Life anywhere is dull if you don't get the measure of it,' Eleanor answered. 'Your mother was mistress of a comfortable house which is not so sizable that it can't be run efficiently and without fuss.'

'But village life is awful if you're not sociable.'

Eleanor, who was not sociable, was equal to this. 'Being useful is much more important in village life than being sociable. As soon as the ladies of the various voluntary organizations set eyes on a newcomer they ask themselves one question: could we be sure that any task she undertook would be carried out effectively? If the answer is "yes" the newcomer will be able to play her part in village life.'

'I don't think Mother looked at it that way,' I said. 'She wanted . . .'

'That was your mother's trouble; she always decided what she wanted without considering what was available to her.'

I could think of nothing further to say. Eleanor was sipping her second gin and tonic and reading *Country Life* when Stewart joined us. 'What would you like to do tomorrow?' he asked her. 'You haven't seen much of the country round here. I could take you for a drive.'

'It's rather hot, isn't it? I would settle for sitting in the garden if we could go out in the evening.'

'I'll see if I can book a table at The Lamb and Flag.' He looked hopefully at me. I said that I was going to Finals Day at Weston Market Tennis Club and did not know when I would be back. Eleanor turned over the pages of *Country Life*. Stewart, looking rather dismayed, went into the hall to telephone. 'The Lamb and Flag are fully booked,' he said when he returned. 'But I've managed to get us a table at Markby's; it's an old country house turned restaurant, and I've heard that it's good.' Markby's was supposed to be very expensive, but I did not think it was this that had shaken him.

Eleanor said, 'It sounds interesting.' Her calm reaction was calculated not to increase his perturbation. She gave him a brief smile and went on turning the pages of *Country Life*. Stewart rubbed his hands together and looked round the room in search of activity. Punter, misunderstanding, picked himself up from the hearth-rug, wagging his tail.

'Yes!' Stewart acknowledged the signal with relief. 'You shall have your exercise, my hound.' He and Punter departed in a flurry of nervous excitement. Eleanor put down the copy of *Country Life* and sat back in her chair; she did not move her head but her eyes looked about the room. I was reminded as I looked at her of how I had sat on the bed in a foreign hotel, glad to have arrived, wondering what the place would hold for me during the time I would spend in it. I sensed in Eleanor that blend of travel weariness and anticipation held in check by a reserve which is akin to fear that one experiences in the first moments of being alone in an alien place. She looked into the mirror and her eyes met mine.

'I didn't know you still belonged to a tennis club,' she said.

'I don't, but some of my friends do.'

She nodded her head, accepting that I did not intend to say any more. I think she was satisfied that I would not be actively hostile, and this was the most that she would expect of me.

I went to the Finals Day in the afternoon and sat watching an indifferent men's doubles with Peggy, my predecessor as clinic secretary.

'How is your father taking things now?' she asked as the server's ball thudded into the bottom of the net for the umpteenth time.

'At present he is sitting in the garden with my aunt Eleanor,' I said. 'I think she intends to marry him.'

'No, really? That's something I couldn't do. I'd have to be the first.' Peggy's eyes rested complacently on her brawny husband who was knocking up on a far court preparatory to playing in the mixed doubles final. 'How old is your aunt?'

'Late forties, I suppose.'

'And never been married?' Her voice was sharp with disapproval, as though Eleanor was stealing a march on those who had laboured all day in the vineyard. 'I suppose it's better than living alone, but she won't find marriage easy.'

'I think she'll make something of it.' I spoke in defence of Eleanor, but I meant it. I was beginning to perceive that Eleanor's life with my father might be hampered and restricted, but that Eleanor herself would not necessarily be diminished by this. I did not know how this trick was worked, but I had a feeling Eleanor was going to bring it off. The thought made me feel humble and hollow at the same time.

I returned late that evening. Stewart and Eleanor had only been in the house for a few minutes; they seemed in good spirits in a quiet, more relaxed way. Stewart told me that Markby's was good and proceeded to describe the good features in detail as though they were a credit to himself. As he spoke I could see his confidence returning; this outing with Eleanor was the first enterprise of consequence he had undertaken since my mother died and it had been a success. A prospect was opening out before him. Eleanor watched him, smiling and making no attempt to interrupt. I saw to my surprise that this was not entirely forbearance; for one thing, she was sitting far too comfortably for one who is being forbearing. Her face looked comfortable, too. Eleanor intended to be kind to Stewart and was already finding pleasure in it. She would watch life coming back to him, the strain leaving the eyes, the mouth growing less wary, the sense of humour restored; and she would think to herself, 'I did that.' Perhaps in time she would come to see it as the most creative act of her life and because of this she would come to love him.

'They really are going to get married,' I said to myself as I undressed in my bedroom. It was inconceivable, but it was happening. Stewart and Eleanor were attempting to create a relationship which, although limited, would give them a life together which would not be without its rewards. In deference to my mother's memory they would probably not marry this year; but that would not prevent Eleanor from beginning to make herself a place here. My poor mother, how soon she had been usurped! Even as I thought this, I remembered that when I was cleaning out her wardrobe I had thought there would be more room for my own things. Then, I had dismissed the thought of as little significance; but now I understood better what had prompted it. I had realised that now there was room for me to become myself. But it was one thing to make abstract statements, it was quite another to be faced with the practical reality. Soon, whether I liked it or not, I would be alone, and I had never been alone in my life.

As I combed my hair, I thought of the child with the

doll, the young girl aware of her mother and the farmer, the older girl in the attic with the lovely family. I had seen the child and the girls, and now I looked in the mirror at the woman and it seemed to me that they were part of a continuing process, that my whole life was a slow coming into being. I was not sure what this meant, except that there was another person towards whom I was moving even now, and that I was frightened of her.

12

ON the following Monday I had a letter from Hilda. She began by saying that the operation had not been as serious as she had feared it might be. She then went on, 'It has given me time to think, which is something I have been unable to do in recent years. You must have realised when you saw me that I was not happy. In fact, even now I hardly dare think about how unhappy I have been. My talk with you was a great help. You will be surprised when I tell you why. I have decided I cannot go on like this—physically, I think nursing will be too much for me in future. But that is not all. I am not the dedicated nurse you imagine; there has been too much nursing in my life and too little else. So, Ruth, I am leaving London and going to live in my country cottage. Can you guess what I am going to do there? You should be able to because you gave me the idea. I am going to have a teashop! Now, why don't you come and join me, dear? There is nothing I would like more. But I sometimes suspect that you find a little of me goes a long way. And if that is so, I have another idea. Aunty May left me so much and nothing to you because of not approving of your mother, and it has always been on my conscience. Now, Ruth, I would like you to have the lease of the London house. When you were staying with me I could not help but notice how you looked around it, thinking what you would have done with it had it been yours. Think about it, dear. You could give it a try and if it didn't work out you could still come and help me in the teashop. Country life might have mellowed me by then and you would find me easier to get on with! . . .'

I was shaken by this letter. Eleanor and now Hilda; two people I had imagined to be very set in their ways had shown themselves capable of making big changes in their lives. How brave they were and how generous! I read Hilda's letter through again. Was she in rather too much of a hurry? ' . . . physically, I think nursing will be too much for me in future.' This worried me a little, perhaps because it was so unlike the Hilda I knew. Had her operation really been only a minor one? Perhaps she needed me more than she had allowed herself to say. I could imagine without too much difficulty what life would be like looking after a sick Hilda and running a country teashop and I thought it was something I could do. I knew how I would cope with it and what resources I could call upon; whereas the London idea would call for qualities I was not sure that I possessed. The teashop, so practical and possible, made the London idea seem something of a castle in the air. In the matter of change, it was one thing to be bold but a degree of realism was surely necessary as well? Then I heard Dr. Laver, as clearly as if he was behind me, saying that we never break the patterns of the past and that I would 'find another sick relative to look after'.

I spent some time composing a letter to Hilda which sounded concerned and warmly appreciative without committing me to an immediate decision. On the matter of decision, I wrote: 'You say you have been unable to think about yourself in recent years and I have been in much the same case. So I hope you won't think me ungrateful if I ask for a little time to sort myself out. But I *am* grateful, Hilda, and I shan't be proud. Rest assured, I'll put that conscience of yours to rest and accept one of your options.'

I was still thinking of those options when I went to work the next day. We had heard nothing from Dr.

Laver since his telephone call to say that he had 'flu and by now Iris was convinced that we should never see him again. His presence here was now irrelevant and —although discretion had not seemed to be one of his virtues—she assumed that, this being the case, he would not trouble us again.

'But he can't go away and leave his cases in the air,' Douglas said. 'What do you think, Ruth?'

The only excuse I was prepared to accept for Dr. Laver's conduct was that he was dead; but I thought Douglas might think this a rather extreme reaction, so I said, 'I can't see him coming back.'

'We shall manage very well without him,' Iris said. 'It has been a stimulating experience, I would not deny that. But it is not the kind of experience which can, or should, be prolonged. He has served his purpose.'

'But have we served our purpose for him?' Douglas asked.

'I am reminded of a Buddhist parable,' Iris said magisterially. 'A man has to ford a river and he is fortunate in finding a raft. But when the raft has taken him across the river he does not lumber himself with it for the rest of his journey. The raft was for crossing over, not for retention.'

At this moment the door opened and Dr. Laver strode in, followed by Di.

Douglas said, 'I'm not quite clear which of us is the travelling man and which the raft.'

'No papers have been put out for me,' Dr. Laver said.

'Your papers have not been put out for you because we did not expect you to return,' Iris told him coldly.

'Well, as you see, you were mistaken.' He turned to me. 'Who am I seeing this morning?'

'Mrs. Wilmer.' I had some difficulty in speaking because my throat was dry. 'And this afternoon you have Mr. and Mrs. Brodie.'

'What time is Mrs. Wilmer due?'

'Mrs. Wilmer can wait,' Iris said. 'In any case, she will probably be late.' There was an awful vitality about Iris. Her face gleamed in its frame of white hair and her body was more thrustful than ever; it was as though some force within her had turned to evil and she buzzed with it like a wasp. 'We have had a letter from the Foundation. I think you should see it.' She snapped her fingers at me, impatient for her moment of triumph. The letter was on my desk but I did not give it to her. I kept my shaking hands in my lap. Dr. Laver strolled across and looked down at it, hands in pockets, jingling coins. Iris came to the other side of my desk.

'We will not ask the meaning of this,' she said, more magisterial than ever. 'No one here wishes to be ruthless. Nor are we interested in explanations which can only be painful. By a stroke of the greatest good fortune, I am in contact with a young psychiatrist who would be prepared to work in this clinic, as well as taking part in another project which it is not now necessary for me to discuss with you . . .'

'If it is the television nonsense there is certainly no need to discuss it with me.'

'How did you find out about that?' Iris was momentarily disconcerted.

'The cleaner told me. All the time that she is cleaning your room you are scribbling on pieces of paper. Do you know what she says about you? "The poor creature, it must be hard being so clever you are forever tripping over your own brains." But there will be no fear of your doing that on television because I absolutely forbid you to use any material with which I am concerned . . .'

'When this was first mooted it was to have been an extension of a programme . . .'

'You had no business to moot anything which involved me. I have no intention of becoming a fairground freak.'

'Fairground freak! A regrettable attitude to the value of television as an educational medium. However, I . . .'

'Television is essentially a commercial medium . . . '

'HOWEVER I would not quarrel were you to substitute the word "fake".'

I said, 'I don't want all this drama. Would you please go further away. Both of you!'

Iris whirled away, angry to be cheated of the climax for which she had worked so hard. Dr. Laver laughed. It was the first time I had ever heard him laugh and I could not say that he appeared to be amused, although his eyes glittered with pleasure of a kind.

'Fake? You are the fake. This scene which you have set up is a fake. It is not because of this letter that you want me to leave. Do you remember Mrs. Brodie's dream? She is in her house with her mother and her grandmother, and a man is holding them up with a gun. She manages to escape through a skylight, but when she is outside she sees that the house is being watched by policemen and she knows she will not be able to get away without the policemen seeing her, so she goes back into the house. Do you understand what that means?'

'She is afraid of men,' Iris said scornfully.

'She is afraid of freedom. We are all afraid of freedom.'

'And we have all read Erich Fromm.'

'And you, in particular, are afraid.' I had not realised before that he was so grotesque. He was short, but long in the body and he had very broad shoulders. Perhaps to give an impression of height he frequently lifted his shoulders and when, as now, he made an assertion he raised himself on his toes. There was something vulgar and comic about him, but there was, too, more than a hint of malevolence. Iris laughed when he said that she was afraid, but she looked to us to join in, suddenly finding that she needed support.

'Yes, you *are* afraid.' He did not miss this signal for re-assurance. 'You are afraid of what I have started in you. When we begin to examine ourselves the going gets rough. We may find wholeness, or our personality may be shattered into fragments. That is a risk you are not prepared to take. So, as Mrs. Brodie returns to the place where she was a prisoner, you want to return to the clinic as it was before I came, with you in control; and the greatest adventure which you will permit yourself will be to take part in a television programme which you will fill with tepid superficialities.'

Iris said in a high, stretched voice, 'I see no point in prolonging this argument. If you will wind up your affairs at the clinic today, making what explanations you consider appropriate to the clients, I think I can answer for my colleagues when I say that we shall not seek to embarrass you.'

'Embarrass me!' He laughed, baring his teeth. Iris turned her back on him and he gave her a sharp slap across the behind. '*You'll* never embarrass me, duckie!'

'How uncouth,' Iris said disdainfully, her voice trembling a little.

Dr. Laver turned on Douglas. 'And you? How were *you* proposing to embarrass me?' Douglas backed away, knocking over the waste paper basket. 'Well, speak up, one of you. She may say there is no need of explanation, but I certainly intend to have one.'

'Don't look at me,' Di said. 'It's been made pretty clear to me ever since I've been here that the nurse isn't a senior partner in this outfit. Any decisions that have to be taken, Douglas and Iris will take.' She went out of the room, banging the door noisily behind her.

Iris said to Douglas, 'For goodness sake go after her, or she will tell Mrs. Libnitz about this.'

'But I should have no objection to her telling Mrs. Libnitz,' Dr. Laver said. 'I am not sure what it is we are telling, but I see no reason why it should not be widely known, bruited about, blazened abroad, or whatever cliché comes to your mind this morning. In the meantime, I suggest that we should all go away and think about this quietly. You gave me until tomorrow morning; so, I give you until tomorrow morning. We will talk about it then. In the meantime, I should like Mrs. Wilmer's file, please.'

When he had gone, Douglas said to Iris, 'I hope you are satisfied.' He walked hurriedly to the door but had a little trouble with the handle before he could get it to turn.

Iris said, 'If he had bothered to wait for an answer I should have told him that I am perfectly satisfied.' She walked across to the mirror and spoke to the woman in the mirror. 'The Laver creature could hardly have demonstrated more unanswerably that he is not fit to run this clinic, could he? I hope we are going to be able to deal with him in a dignified and compassionate way, but if he does not have the sense to accept our offer when he has had time to reflect on it . . .' She stood, turning her head from one side to the other, looking at the changing planes of the face. 'Not that I *want* to destroy him; I would not want to destroy anyone.' She paused, considering the possibility of destruction. Then something disturbed her, some blemish; she bent forward, peering, but her breath misted the mirror. She rubbed at the glass fretfully and then turned away.

I threaded paper into the typewriter and began to type. Even after she had gone, the atmosphere in the room was oppressive with drama. There had always been a lot of drama at the clinic, and, come to think of it, in my life. All this fermenting and highlighting of incidents was as though life itself was not enough, but some extra ingredient must be injected into it. I did not want any more drama.

I was angry with Dr. Laver for returning apparently safe and well, but not as angry as I should have been. Fear predominated. His disappearance had been a relief; he had departed at an opportune moment allowing me to make an accommodation with life. I had nearly gone too far in probing my problems and might well have made myself into a tiresome neurotic. I did not want to have anything more to do with Dr. Laver because, however fraudulent he might be, I was more than ever convinced that my first impression of him had been right; he was a man who knew too much for his own and other people's good.

I decided that I would finish the typing which I had on hand and then I would go home. I would accept Hilda's offer to help with the teashop and I would not return to the clinic or ever see Dr. Laver again. I typed steadily while my mind worked out what I would say to my father and what arrangements I would have to make with Hilda. Time passed. It must have been early afternoon when a shadow fell across my typewriter and I looked up to find Mr. Brodie standing in front of me looking more than ever like a despotic Roman emperor.

'My G.P. has not received any information from Dr. Laver,' he said. 'In fact, he was quite surprised to learn that my wife was seeing a psychiatrist here.'

'I'm sorry about that,' I said.

Mr. Brodie chewed at his lip thoughtfully, perhaps considering whether I should be thrown to the lions or reserved for a worse fate. 'I sit on a committee with a consultant psychiatrist,' he said eventually. 'I think perhaps I'll ask him what the procedure usually is.'

'It might be simpler to ask Dr. Laver.'

Mr. Brodie raised his eyebrows. 'My dear young lady, do you really think so?'

'Have you told the consultant that your wife is being treated here?'

'As a matter of fact, not. I thought it amusing to see how far things would go. My wife claims to be gaining new insights; but my impression is that she has become even more disturbed. I shall make a point of speaking to the consultant this afternoon when I shall be attending a meeting at which he will be present. He is a very eminent psychiatrist, you may have heard of him: Dr. Cumner Asche.'

I said drily, 'Yes, I have heard of him.'

Mr. Brodie went out of the room chuckling to himself. Some ten minutes later he left the building with his wife and I heard them arguing as they walked towards his car. The buzzer on my telephone sounded querulously and I picked up the receiver automatically as I watched the Brodies. Dr. Laver said, 'Will you come up, please, Ruth.' I put the receiver down without answering and wondered what to do. I decided to leave and I was just about to put the cover on my typewriter when Iris came in. 'Dr. Laver is waiting for you,' she said.

I did not want to explain my actions to Iris, or to anyone else. Douglas was standing outside the reception-room talking to Mrs. Libnitz. I decided to go up the front stairs and down the back stairs. I picked up my handbag and put my jacket over my arm. 'It can be chilly in his room,' I said to Iris, but there was no need of explanation; she was intent on the woman in the mirror. I went lightly up the front stairs and was in sight of the back stairs when I saw that the door of Dr. Laver's room was open and he was standing waiting for me.

'No doubt you feel you are entitled to an explanation,' he said, taking me by the elbow and pushing me into the room.

I shook my arm free. 'You had better save your explanations for the police.'

'The police?' He shut the door and moved away from me towards his desk. It occurred to me that once I had told him about Dr. Cumner Asche he would not spare a thought for me, so I said, 'Do you know a Dr. Cumner Asche?'

'I know of a Dr. Cumner Asche,' he said casually.

'So does Mr. Brodie. He is going to talk to him about you this afternoon.'

Dr. Laver sat down heavily; he looked as though something unpleasant which he had always suspected had been confirmed. 'How all the little pieces of life slot into place, don't they? Who could believe it is a random event!'

'It was Dr. Cumner Asche on the station platform, wasn't it? He recognised you.'

Dr. Laver waved a hand in the direction of the chair on the other side of the desk. 'In the words of Iris and her cohorts, it may be therapeutic for me to "share" this with you. But it will take some time, so you had better sit down.'

'I'm not interested.'

He began to talk as though I had not spoken. 'Every examination he sat Dr. Consummate Ass had to take three times, whereas it was all too easy for me. Psychiatry is very boring now, everyone is so afraid of exerting undue influence that it is all left to the patient; it doesn't require any more skill than putting on a long-playing record. But I had a gift. A great gift. However, even hypnotising people can be boring; most people lead dull lives and their innermost secrets are remarkably trivial; there is no such thing as original sin. In time, I wanted something else. I began to hypnotise myself. The results were fantastic. I was in a world with an extra dimension. So much was explained that it was difficult to get my mind round it. The trouble was that once I could explain one thing, another question was posed, a question that no one else in the world would ever think to ask because they hadn't discovered that dimension, and so it went on, explanation, question, explanation, question, and all the time I was going further and further out . . .' He had been talking faster and faster. Now he stopped; when he continued, he was petulant. 'My mind cracked. No one tried to help me. I was out in space and they were light years away, mouthing at me from their little earth capsule, yapping about "abuse of patients", "fraudulent use of national health resources." You know how petty-minded these bureaucrats are. I was put away somewhere. It seemed best to acquiesce; the alternatives were very unpleasant.' Observing his face as he talked, I saw that the eyes were set too close to the bridge of the nose, and the nose itself was a clumsy, triangular affair like the matchbox noses children make. His exhibitionism was that of the conjuror distracting attention from that which must not be noticed; in his case, his ugliness. He was saying, 'I don't remember much about what happened; that part of my life is blocked, but one day I shall find a way through and then it will all start again and I shall take up where I left off. However . . . One day I saw the sunlight shining in through a window: the sun had not shone for a long time. It drew me out. There was no one about, but there was a baker's van in the yard. I climbed into the back of it. It took me away from that dark place. Then it stopped in a country lane; the driver went behind a hedge to pee and I got out and walked away. I was not sure where I was in time or place; I didn't know what year it was or the actual part of the country I was in. So I hitch-hiked. On the way I came by these clothes; I won't bother you with the details. Eventually, I arrived at Weston Market and went into the information office. I saw a leaflet about "caring agencies" and March House was mentioned. The name lodged in my mind and I came here. I walked into this building and opened a door and you said, "Dr. Laver, I presume." I thought to myself: keep close to her and she'll see you through; the clinic secretary knows all that it is necessary for anyone to know.' He was quiet for a moment, gazing at me.

'There was something between us, Ruth, from the very beginning. You were waiting for me to walk into that room. There was something in you which had to be broken; a composed, unshakable Victorian miss to be shattered.' He enjoyed saying 'broken' and 'shattered'. 'Isn't that right?'

'I think I know myself better now,' I conceded.

' "Know yourself better"!' he mimicked. 'Dear God, she's back again, that prim little puss! You talk as though it was an exercise in self-knowledge which you had passed with B+. Let me tell you that you are only on the edge of knowledge. I can show you a Ruth Saunders you cannot even dream of; because, make no mistake about it, you haven't the stamina, let alone courage, to explore on your own. You are the kind who has never got beyond a No Entry sign. Without my help you have no hope of finding yourself.'

'You make it sound like a treasure hunt, as though I could dig myself up whole.'

'And so you can, if you dig deep enough.'

'Into the past? I've finished with the past.'

' "Finished with the past" she says! We spend our lives struggling towards an illusory future while being carried into the past, like people running up the down escalator. All our life is in the past.'

He was bitter; behind the eccentric façade and the ugliness it masked, there was a rather ordinary man with a grievance which had taken root. I felt a change in myself. What could this man possibly know to make me so afraid of him? I said with a nice show of reasonableness, 'Even if I don't agree with everything you say, I have learnt a lot from you. And one of the things I have learnt is that I know as much as I need to know about the past.'

'How arrogant! A few words of advice and you think

you know it all and can go strutting off on your own.'

'The last thing it has made me is arrogant. I'm beginning to see that too much of Ruth Saunders can be very boring.'

'You are afraid, like Iris! You saw things you didn't like in the past and now you are running away because you don't want to be hurt. Isn't that so, eh? eh?' I had not escaped him after all; something very unpleasant was going to happen. I remained quite still, waiting. 'But you *are* hurt, my dear. Damaged goods, that is you. A flawed personality, if you prefer that kind of language.'

I was surprised at how calm I felt. This was the thing I had most feared and could not have articulated myself. In this building where they were forever diagnosing human failure I had often wondered what labels were attached to me. Now he had found the words for me; he had let them loose in this room where I had first seen the child with the doll, and I must test their power. 'Hurt, yes.' It was such a simple acknowledgement, but it had been hard to make and had taken a long time. Nothing seemed so bad as the admission itself. A little encouraged, I said, 'But I don't see it in terms of loss, of things which have prevented me.'

'Are we to hear how you do see it, or haven't you worked that out yet?'

I looked at him, an ugly bearded man at a desk, a window behind him framing a tree and a patch of sky. 'It was a set of circumstances, my situation. Different from your situation, or Iris's. Not better or worse, but different. My given situation.'

'Is this supposed to mean anything?'

'It means that I have to accept it and get on with my life; just as I would have to accept it if I was short-sighted or diabetic or had one brown eye and one blue eye!'

'Don't deceive yourself, dearie. There are some things which will always be denied you because of your past.' He was bent on destruction, yet I told myself not to resist, to be still and let it happen. He spoke dryly and sombrely, but with a rhythm like a man reciting poetry in which he has a secret pride. 'You were a solitary child; other children learnt the give and take of life as they learnt to read and spell, effortlessly and without pain; they grew naturally into their role of man or woman, knew instinctively how to love and be loved. You botched that. And there isn't any late flowering in these matters, whatever you may read in the hairdressers'. Believe me, you will always have to struggle and make an effort, you will never carry off the major events of life lightly and easily. Marriage is probably not for you, or, if it comes, it will be a poor, late, twilight thing. You will have no children and you have no creative talent; you are not competitive so you will have no success in whatever career you may choose.' He paused; perhaps he was holding a few good things in reserve, but if this was so it did not show in his face. 'You think this is cruel, but it is as well to be aware of one's limitations.'

I did not answer him immediately but waited until the vibration of his words died down and the room was still. In a distant room the telephone rang. Beyond the window there was no movement in the leaves of the sycamore and the birds were silent, but far away across the fields came the sound of a train whistle, mournful as a marsh bird.

I said to Dr. Laver, 'You talk about things which will be denied me because of my past; but won't there be other things which will be given because of my past? I loved my parents and they loved me. All that struggling to love and failing and trying again, the mattering to one another, never indifferent, holding together somehow: that's progress of a kind, something to build on. I love my mother more now than I ever did, and I understand my father better. There's more gain than loss in that.'

His mouth twisted sourly, 'If you want to be romantic.'

'Perhaps you are being romantic, because you talk as though there is an ideal human situation against which we must measure our own. And you speak of flawed personalities, as though there were flawless personalities. I'm not sure that's the way it is.'

He half-closed his eyes and allowed his head to nod forward, telling me how much my foolishness bored him. Another person seemed to slip past my guard. I leant forward and banged on the desk. 'You shall not sit there saying those things and then just switch off!' The blow seemed to have little effect on him, but jarred something loose in me. I wasn't taking things so quietly. 'Single, childless, no marketable talent . . . that's what you said, isn't it?' He did not answer and I went on, 'Well, all right. That's only a recipe for disaster if I compare myself with other people. But I don't have to live Di's life, or Iris's, I have to live my own.'

He said, with his chin sunk on his chest, 'And what is this life which you will live?'

I could not organise my thoughts to make his kind of sense.

'Age thirty plus,' he said to the blotting pad, 'and she is not sure about that little matter of what her life will be.'

'Do you know what will come to you tomorrow, or the next day?'

'Nothing comes, except to the rare ones who have their moment written in the stars. You're not of their number.' He looked sour, a small, sour, destructive man wearing absurd clothes. 'There is only one way for you, Ruth. Turn your back on the here and now, it's not for you. I knew the moment when I saw you that you needed me. What a little ghost you were! But in your eyes I could see a quite different woman, and I knew that I was the person who could release her. Isn't that true?' I did not answer because I was thinking about those absurd clothes. He said, 'Well, there you are, then! You must explore further and I shall show you how to do it.'

I said, 'When I was a child I found it a relief to take off my clothes at night. But that was a small relief. What would be truly wonderful would be to slough off my skin, to feel it wrinkled round my ankles and step right out of it.'

'You're flushed as though you had been drinking. Compose yourself.'

'And then to step out of *my* room, *my* home; to move about the world without that hidden camera ordering, selecting, composing . . . *That's* what I want! I want to get beyond Ruth Saunders.'

'All this passion is misdirected. There is no beyond; nothing at all.' He tapped his forehead. 'It is all in here, we never get beyond self. The only exploration is inwards. We have the secrets of the universe within us. You are mad if you think otherwise.'

'I'll be mad, then, and leave the secrets of the universe to you. Maybe mine won't be such a big adventure . . .' I hesitated, but what did a little more misdirected passion matter? 'It will be paradise.'

There was a long silence, then he said, 'What is to become of me, then? Had you thought about that? No, I don't suppose you had. You just thought of yourself wallowing in bliss.' He looked at me for the first time as another man might have done, assessing me as a person not committed to him. 'You are reckless.' He was surprised as though I had deceived him. 'I see now that there is a reckless streak in you.'

The telephone on his desk rang and I picked up the receiver. Mrs. Libnitz said, 'The police are here for Dr. Laver.' She spoke in a voice from which all emotion had been ironed out, yet I had never heard such fear in anyone's voice.

I said, 'Ask them to wait, will you?'

When I told Dr. Laver he became quite calm and resting his elbows upon the desk, his chin supported on his folded hands, he seemed to reflect upon some unseen equation. Eventually, he looked up at me and said, 'Will you come away with me, Ruth?'

'Never again!'

He persisted gravely, 'You could save me, you know. It could be the most splendid thing you would ever do. As a Christian you have no alternative.'

'I'm going to have my hands full saving myself.'

He looked thoughtful, contemplating another move, and then said, 'Do you realise what you will condemn me to if you refuse?'

The cuff of his pink shirt was missing a button and fell away from his wrist. There was a long scratch just above the wrist. I rememembered him cradling the cat in his arms in Miss Maud's drawing-room. He was looking at me. He rubbed his fingers up and down the long scar, his eyes holding mine. There was reproach and regret in his gaze, but also something which the twist of his mouth now underlined, a deep satisfaction that I had failed him. It was as though it was necessary to him to have this confirmation that there was nothing for him in the world outside his own skull.

He said, 'Ruthless as well as reckless. Well, well . . . Will you at least give me five minutes' grace, keep the police talking . . .'

'Wouldn't it be wiser if you . . . ?'

'We have nothing more to say to each other, have we?'

The police turned out to be one man, a rotund, apple-faced countryman holding his radio against his chest like a shield. Iris was talking to him and Douglas and Di were standing behind her making background noises which were reinforced by the policeman's radio which talked incessantly. The reception hatch was closed and I could not see Mrs. Libnitz.

Iris was saying, 'I think you should understand,

Inspector, that we knew nothing about this, nothing at all, until last week.'

'Last week?' The policeman's radio jerked and peppered us with car registration numbers.

'Yes, well, that may seem surprising, but I can assure you that the postal service is entirely to blame.'

Di edged up to me and whispered, 'Where is he?'

'Gone down the back stairs, I hope.'

'I've got Kenny's car. I'll take him to my place; he can shack down with us.'

I moved forward in the hope of distracting attention from her departure, but there was no need because the door to Douglas's quarters flew open and a man ran out, his body agitated as though his flesh had been scalded. He laid a hand on Douglas's shoulder.

'It's okay, fellah; it's okay.' He turned anguished eyes on Iris. 'Don't say a word, sugar, until your lawyer comes; not one word. I know the way these guys operate and believe me it's the same whichever side of the Atlantic you are, only there's more pretence over here. They'll talk soft to you now, but once they get you down to the jailhouse, it's the same ball-game.'

'If you would allow me . . .' the policeman began.

'No, sir, I would not allow, not any way at all! None of these folks says a word until their lawyer is present.'

'If you will allow me to explain, sir, I am not charging anyone here . . .'

'Who isn't here?' Eddie did an agonised count; he seemed to know us better than we knew him. 'The doc. and the nurse. Well, that's not a crime that I've yet heard.'

The policeman was dumbfounded. I did not think he could be that good an actor. I said, 'Iris, have you parked your car in the farm gateway again?'

In the lull which followed this suggestion the policeman took his chance. 'It's about a Mr. Brodie,' he said.

Iris held up a hand before Eddie could come to Mr. Brodie's defence. 'What about him?'

'He fell in front of a train, ma'am.'

'Oh, my God, is he badly hurt?'

'It was the London express, ma'am.'

'How dreadful! Poor Mrs. Brodie. I must go to her at once.'

'The lady seemed calm, like it was all a dream.'

Di came running in. 'He's gone. I couldn't see him anywhere.' She turned on the policeman. 'What had the poor sod done, anyway? He didn't hypnotise any of the patients; only Iris.' Iris began to explain to her. In a corner of the hall Eddie was addressing Douglas in an angry, throbbing voice, 'Now take it easy, fellah, there isn't anything you have to worry about, I'm here and I'll see you through.' Douglas said, 'I am NOT worried. I don't care what has happened to Dr. Laver or to Mr. Brodie; I don't care about anything AT ALL except being left in peace!'

I went up a few steps and looked down on them. I felt like Alice and I wanted to tell them they were all a pack of cards; but I couldn't do that, so instead I went to my room and typed out my notice.

Later that afternoon we found a note in Dr. Laver's room saying that he had been called away to the bedside of a sick aunt and could not say when he would return; in the meantime, he wanted Iris to know that if she made use of material involving his sessions at the clinic, he would sue her.

At the inquest on Mr. Brodie the coroner recorded a verdict of accidental death, although the village gossip, who had been on the station platform at the time of the disaster, put about a rumour that Mrs. Brodie had pushed Mr. Brodie.

Weeks went by and there was no news of Dr. Laver. Iris eventually wrote to the Foundation. 'I think there is no need now to mention that Dr. Laver passed this way,' she said cheerfully. 'The important thing is to look to the future.' The future was represented by Iris's new-found friend, Dr. Rainer Brown, who used hypnotism in his treatment of patients. Unlike Dr. Laver, Dr. Rainer Brown would welcome participation by his colleagues. 'Once the patient is hypnotised we shall be able to put questions to him, even make a few suggestions, though that is a function which would have to be exercised with extreme caution,' she told Douglas. 'I suppose you might describe it as a variation on joint counselling.'

Douglas was not so sure that this was a correct description of what would take place; but he saw that once again Iris would be in charge and no great demands would be made on him, so he raised no objection. Di decided to go along with it until she and Kenny were married, which, as she was not yet divorced, might be 'quite a little while'.

Mrs. Libnitz said she would not stay at the clinic now that it had become involved with the police. She and I left at the same time, a week before Dr. Rainer Brown took up his appointment.

The last week-end in September I went to stay with my friend Dorothy. She was having an affair with a married man of formidable integrity who was devoted to his wife and six children and crippled mother-in-law. In comparison, my own problems hardly seemed worth mentioning; but just before I left I told her that as my father would probably marry again I would be leaving home. She hugged me and said, 'Once you are in the driving seat, there will be no stopping you, Ruth; you'll end up with that big family you always imagined. I promise you!' I, in turn, prophesied that some totally unforeseen event would occur which would sort out her love affair so that they all lived happily ever after. We parted feeling infinitely better and having resolved very little.

13

ONE late autumn evening Stewart told me that he was to marry Eleanor. We were in the garden; I was raking fallen leaves from the rose beds and he had mown the lawn for the last time this year. I felt a surge of feeling for the house, the garden, and the still, flat landscape beyond the garden wall.

'You may find it hard to understand,' Stewart said. 'But I want you to know it doesn't affect the way I feel about your mother.'

'No, I'm sure it doesn't; I think you are very wise,' I said quickly, wanting it over and done with. I raked the leaves into a heap as I went on, 'It's rather a relief to me because I have given in my notice at the clinic; I am planning to go and live in London, and I wouldn't like you to be alone here.'

'To London?' He was dismayed, and so was I because until this moment I had thought I would join Hilda in her teashop. He said, 'I didn't want to drive you away from your home, darling.'

'You're not driving me away; it's more than time I left home.'

He looked at me, disbelieving and reproachful. 'I had so hoped we could all be happy together here.' He was fighting his old battle again, trying to make everything conform to his purpose. It wasn't so much that he was selfish, but that he was too sensitive to ignore the feelings of others and so his pleasure would always be marred by guilt. I felt sorry for him and for myself. I had wanted him to accept my departure and thereby make it easy for me. In a way, I suppose I wanted him to conform to my purpose.

'Where will you live?' he asked.

I told him about Hilda's offer, which convinced him that in one respect at least this was a practical proposition. 'But I think you should train for a career.' He went on to list the careers which were still open to me. 'Life has much more to offer a woman now.' He had spent years in the civil service doing a job for which he was not suited and now he offered the same prospect to me as though he was making me free of a better kind of life. But I did not want to be strait-jacketed by a profession. I wanted to keep my mind free to run along the wrong lines, like a little local track the railways have forgotten to close down, running away into a territory of its own.

'Think this London business over carefully,' he said. 'Don't do anything hasty.'

I knew then that I would have to go soon. The strain would be intolerable for us both if I stayed. I must get in touch with Hilda and find out when I could move into the London house. The telephone was ringing and Stewart went into the house to answer it.

'I'll put the mower away,' I called after him.

I put the cut grass and the mound of fallen leaves on to the compost heap and then walked slowly round the flower beds picking up a few of the leaves which had escaped the rake. This had been my task as a child, not always then enjoyed. But in future a scattering of autumn leaves, the smell of compost, would fill me with happiness; just as I would recall with a particular thrill the moment when it was discovered that the rain had stopped and we could now go for a walk, although at the time I had been reluctant to go out into the still-dripping lane and had only begun to enjoy myself when we were some distance from the house. Some joys had been immediate, though: the evening primrose shining in the dusk and the night smell of honeysuckle. I faltered, made uncertain as I so often was at the thought of joy, and told myself that I was behaving like Garbo in that old film where she walks round the room saying goodbye to the furniture.

I put the rake and lawn mower in the shed; then, reluctant to return to the house, I walked to the front gate and leant over it. The sky was a darker blue now and the evening star was out. I looked over the fields and saw the distant trees furred by mist and I recalled how several weeks ago Stewart had recounted a piece of information he thought I would find amusing. It seemed that Miss Maud had a man living with her; he did not go out much, but the milkman had had a glimpse of him. 'It's probably that brother of hers,' the woman in the village shop had said. 'He's come home from abroad,' and she had added darkly, 'perhaps he had to.' Nothing had happened subsequently to give rise to speculation and by now interest had died down. Once, the vicar's wife saw the man walking in the lane late one evening; he turned his head away without answering her 'good evening'. There had seemed to be something faintly familiar about him, but she had been unable to place the memory.

The rest of the week-end passed uneasily. Stewart was restrained. I had become an uncertain factor in his life; Eleanor was now more committed to him. I could see him working out his options in a way which would at one time have seemed to me to be chillingly calculated. Eleanor's words about my mother came to me. 'She always decided what she wanted without considering what was available to her.' Perhaps a measure of practicality was no bad thing in dealing with the business of life.

I left home the following week and went to live in Hilda's house in London. Stewart and Eleanor planned to be married early in the spring. It would be barely a year since my mother died and the village church held too many memories for Stewart, so they decided to be married in London. By Christmas, Eleanor had left her job and was spending much of her time redecorating my old home, while I was redecorating the upper floors of the London house. I had some strange moments while I worked in that house. It did not immediately become home to me as I had hoped it would; it felt alien, a place that had belonged to a lot of people over the years in which I would always be a visitor. I cheered myself with the thought that it would only become home to me when it was home to others. I had been in touch with the Principal of a nearby college which ran courses in English for foreigners and had arranged to provide accommodation for four students. It seemed sensible to take lodgers for whom someone else could vouch until such time as I had become wise in my chosen way of life. I got a lot of pleasure imagining how the house would come to life when my extended family moved in and the dream world of the girl in the attic came true.

There were times, however, when I was afraid I had embarked on something which would prove too much for me. The weather was bad, it rained a lot; I found that I was not very good at painting and I hated the preparation, all the rubbing down and scraping and infilling. I had a part-time job in an employment agency and although I enjoyed this I got very tired, getting back to the house at two o'clock in the afternoon and then working on the decorating until late into the night. But there were rare moments which made up for all this. Occasionally, the gloom cleared and the world seemed radiant; I would stop on my way to the kitchen to get more white spirit, and I would look out of the window on the half-landing at that moment when the light changes and the sun comes out after rain. I had the sense of a reality which was usually obscured here where I lived in my half-world.

At such moments I wondered if progress is really the journey from one place to another, or is it that we are always in the same place and the changing intensity of light is our journey? Then the radiance would pass, the glass would be smeared and darken again, and I would find that part of a window frame had rotted away.

By April two of the rooms were ready and my first lodgers were a middle-aged Epyptian man and a Dutch girl. The day after they moved in, Stewart and Eleanor were married.

The wedding was attended by about a dozen people. A fairly subdued affair, I thought, feeling subdued myself. Stewart and Eleanor made their vows with sober understanding of their meaning, and so concentrated was their attention on the words that one could not doubt their steady resolve to fulfil their commitment. I had not been prepared for this, but it was good to know they intended to be mature and responsible. It was when we were out of the church that I was really surprised. They paused briefly in the porch and looked at each other in such an odd way that a shimmering reminder of youth seemed to flit briefly across their faces. They themselves appeared unaware of anything inappropriate and walked slowly down the drive holding hands, as though they were young.

The reception was held at a hotel in Westminster. Eleanor did not move about at the reception, but stood, passive yet indefinably powerful, letting people come to her. This is how she will live in the future, I thought; life will flow to her and she will accept what it brings. How unpredictable people were! I had imagined her being bossy, organising Stewart, and me being called in as occasional peacemaker. Before she and Stewart left she kissed me and assured me that I could come home whenever I chose. 'It will always be your home, Ruth.' She spoke warmly because she felt secure; but neither of us now believed that I would ever make my home there again.

Afterwards I walked through St. James's Park. I was free as I had never expected to be free. So. I was over thirty, unmarried, childless, and with no career prospects, but with a home and rooms to offer. No doubt at times I would be sad and frightened and think I had made a mistake; but it seemed that joy and pain were interwoven, a part of the genetic code of our becoming. I knew something of pain, but the difficult thing was to believe in joy.

A bird was singing, telling of spring, and I felt an ache in my heart as I listened. Why should spring always remind us of time that has run through our fingers? Perhaps the bird was not saying, 'It was, it was, it was.' Suppose it was saying, 'It will be, it will be, it will be'? As I stood on the bridge looking towards the turrets of the Admiralty, I decided to make an act of faith. It was surprising how much resolution was needed to say, 'This is where I am and so it shall be good.' Immediately, I wanted to hold my elbows tight against my sides and hunch my shoulders. But I didn't. As I walked on over the bridge, I spread my arms out and let my coat fall loose so that the sharp spring air made me tremble.